THE THOR CONSPIRACY

Bestsellers by Larry Burkett

Fiction

The Illuminati

Nonfiction

The Coming Economic Earthquake

Debt-Free Living

What Ever Happened to the American Dream?

THE THOR CONSPIRACY

THE SEVENTY-HOUR COUNTDOWN TO DISASTER

LARRY BURKETT

A JANET THOMA BOOK

THOMAS NELSON PUBLISHERS
Nashville • Atlanta • London • Vancouver
Printed in the United States of America

Published in Nashville, Tennessee, by Thomas Nelson, Inc., Publishers, and distributed in Canada by Word Communications, Ltd., Richmond, British Columbia.

Library of Congress Cataloging-in-Publication Data

Burkett, Larry.
    The THOR Conspiracy : the seventy-hour countdown to disaster / Larry Burkett.
        p.   cm.
    "A Janet Thoma Book"
    ISBN 0–8407–7801–5 (hardcover)
    ISBN 0–7852–7200–3 (trade paperback)
    I. Title.
PS3552.U7243T48   1995
813'.54—dc20   94—23593
                                                                CIP

With the exception of *The Illuminati*, the books I've written have been nonfiction, so the readers of my books must make a transition and remember that, as they read, this book is totally fiction, and the only purpose in my writing it is for enjoyment. I have no inside information from the government, and neither am I a prophet of what is to come. Read and enjoy.

Printed in the United States of America.
3 4 5 6 — 01 00 99 98 97 96

*To my grandchildren
and the others of their generation*

CONTENTS

Acknowledgments

I'd like to express my appreciation to my editor, Adeline Griffith, who has worked tirelessly on this book; to Janet Thoma, for working to make this second novel a reality; and to my wife, Judy, for tolerating me during each writing project.

Part One

Discovering the Conspiracy

1

△

The THOR Documents

It had been an unbelievable two weeks for Dale Crawford. *Just two weeks ago I was a mid-level Washington bureaucrat, pushing papers at the EPA. Now I'm probably the most wanted man in the country.*

He was headed for Casper, Wyoming, and an army of FBI and CIO agents—each one committed to his capture or his death—were searching for him. *For what?* he wondered. *Is it really the information I'm carrying with me? No, that's only part of it.* Crawford knew it was about power and control, and his information could threaten that.

How did this happen? he asked himself as he nursed the old Ford over the next hill. The slightest grade made the tired engine rattle. *The country's under the control of fanatics; Americans are living in constant fear of their lives; free speech is banned; and our government is trying to murder me!*

"The whole world's gone crazy," he yelled as the engine coughed a couple of times. *Just what I need—to get stuck out in the middle of nowhere.* The countryside he was traveling through was so bleak he could have stuck his head out the window and yelled to the top of his lungs, and no one would have heard him. It didn't look like there was another human being for a hundred miles in any direction.

You really are a nut case, Dale Crawford, he chided himself for the hundredth time since that fateful day in Washington. *I should be back in D.C., loafing in a nice cool building. Instead, here I am in the heat, in a stolen FBI car, with half the government looking for me.*

Probably there had been hotter summers in the country, but since the phaseout of air-conditioning the heat seemed more intense. Dale felt a dark cloud of anger sweep over him as he thought about what had happened—and why. In spite of the heat and dust, his determination came back.

"Idiots!" he shouted as the dust swirled in front of the car. His eyes were instantly filled with the fine grit common to Wyoming's back roads. "Washington idiots!"

Then he remembered that until very recently he had supported the very policies he now feared—including the one that eliminated car air-conditioning. It hadn't seemed like such a bad idea at the time. The ozone was being depleted, and the use of Freon substitutes was the primary culprit, or so he had believed.

Besides, the environmentalists had argued that eliminating individual air-conditioning from private transportation would "encourage" people to use public transportation more. He hadn't thought much about the effect this would have in places like Wyoming—especially when he was in Washington, riding the air-conditioned subway back and forth to work every day.

Crawford had been one of a whole cadre of lifelong civil servants—at least until two weeks ago. Until then, there had been nothing unique about his life. He had been a part of a system: the Washington bureaucracy. Then, in one day his whole life changed forever.

He thought back to the time when he had first met Andy Moss and his nightmare had started.

▲

Dale Crawford was a supervisor assigned to help the new interns adjust to life at the Environmental Protection Agency (EPA). Andy Moss' arrival was coincidental with the transfer of thousands of military personnel to the ever-growing ranks of the EPA "regulators."

Dale was sitting at his desk in the "bull pen," as the 19,845 employees of the central EPA nefariously referred to the giant building with thousands of desks crammed in side by side.

The "logic" behind the bull-pen concept was that people who sat behind closed doors had something to hide, so all of the office walls in the EPA's massive building were eliminated. The resultant noise was almost deafening at times—especially when news of some new, EPA-initiated raid swept throughout the building.

Under President Rand the EPA had reached cabinet-level status, immediately qualifying the director for equal appropriations with all other departments. As the assignments to the agency grew and America's military influence in the world shrank, the EPA gradually assumed massive proportions, eventually dwarfing all other agencies except the National Health Services.

When the Democrat-controlled Congress came out in favor of President Rand's plan to eliminate all but the essential active military commands and rely on reserve units only, the phasedown happened quickly. There was an angry protest about so many military personnel being dumped on an already depressed economy. To combat the resentment, President Rand had a brilliant idea: He would "temporarily" shift the surplus military personnel over to his environmental program.

The idea was an instant hit with the public, if not with the top brass of the military. With the support of the Armed Services Committee, the president easily sold the idea. It was, after all, a novel way to kill two birds: phase down the military and build up the environmental enforcement group at the same time.

Andy Moss, like thousands of other interns, had just completed college and had been assigned to the EPA's informant division. He originally had been scheduled to serve out his three-year internship in the military, but, just as he was finishing his sensitivity training, the military phaseout began and he was assigned to Crawford's EPA unit instead.

Shortly after Moss joined the EPA, the first use of armed enforcement "regulators" was initiated. It was in Belden, Oregon, site of the riots between the Wildlife Preservation Society and the loggers. Tensions had been building for years as the environmentalists won case after case in the federal courts. But the final straw came when the Supreme Court decided the U.S. Forestry Service could forbid all logging in the national forests.

Overnight, more than one million people were put out of work. Taking a page out of the inner-city riot handbook, used so effectively to force the government to divert funds to inner-city jobs, the loggers and their families started burning everything in sight, including the offices of the EPA and the Wildlife Preservation Society.

When the Society and their EPA friends tried to stop the loggers, the riots got out of control. Before the EPA regulators were called in, more than one hundred environmentalists and government agents either were dead or seriously wounded. To reestablish order, over 100,000 paramilitary troops were ordered into Belden.

Not only were the loggers barred access to the forest, but so was the public at large. The environmentalists had succeeded in shutting down access to most of America's public lands—all in the interest of public safety.

Dale Crawford was the supervisor of one of the technical assistance teams sent to Oregon to evaluate the situation. During the buildup leading to the enforcement action, Dale and Andy had developed a casual friendship. Even though he was a unit supervisor, Dale was barely ten years older than Andy.

They both were excited about actually going out into the field. The EPA briefings were more like pep rallies than government strategy sessions. The "regulator" units were told their mission was to reestablish "order" and to bring the radicals under control. Crawford sensed the sessions were more propaganda meetings than directions on how to conduct an armed riot control action, but he kept it to himself.

Neither man had known what to expect, but certainly it was not what they found when they reached Belden. All of the access roads in and out of Belden were blocked by the EPA's paramilitary personnel, and several squads were engaged in door-to-door searches for the rioters. They saw doors to private homes kicked in and women and children terrorized—all in the name of environmental protection.

But when the inevitable happened and a logger fought back, shooting one of the regulators, all stops were pulled. Tanks and armored personnel carriers were called in and used as battering rams to push over houses. Just living in the logging community was sufficient grounds to have your house gassed and the front door demolished by a 20mm cannon barrel. Only the lack of live ammunition for the tanks prohibited their use on the residents.

Once the killing started, it was like a shark-feeding frenzy. The paramilitary troops went berserk. Before the three-day "riot control" ended, more than three hundred civilians had died. The "terrorists," as the EPA quickly labeled them, were subdued by necessary force, according to EPA Director General Stanton Barnett.

When it was discovered that several of the loggers' family members belonged to a church group headquartered in Wyoming and listed as a cult by the Department of Justice, the link was made instantly in the national media. Once that link was made, the public accepted the premise that the rioters were members of the cult, committed to Earth pillaging. Those who were killed were written off as religious fanatics, willing to die rather than accept authority.

Dale had been shaken by the Belden experience, but his response was totally different than Andy's. As soon as they returned to Washington, Dale simply crawled back into his EPA shell. He had dedicated his life to environmental protection; he could not accept the idea that the EPA might be wrong.

Andy, however, reacted with revulsion over what he had witnessed. He didn't know much about politics or religion; he'd been pretty much uninterested since high school. But he did know what he saw: murder on a mass scale without restraint. During the frenzy he witnessed, it would have been impossible to sort out any terrorists from those who were simply trying to flee or defend themselves.

It shook him thoroughly; he knew the EPA was wrong. There were no trials or juries—only judges: young men and women with automatic weapons turned loose on a town. He still got sick when he thought about mothers with children being cut down as they ran. And now the EPA was being hailed in the media for its forceful and decisive action in preventing further bloodshed.

It had been almost one month to the day since the riots, and Andy was sitting at one of the spare desks going through the motions of doing his job. He and Dale hardly said anything to each other anymore. The one time Andy had tried to discuss the Belden event, Dale just sidestepped by saying, "You just don't see the big picture: Those rioters were tearing the country apart."

"Nonsense!" Andy retorted. "What we saw in Belden was mass murder, not riot control," he added angrily.

"But . . . you don't understand," Dale was still muttering when Andy stormed away.

All EPA personnel associated with the Belden action were required to submit a detailed evaluation of what transpired. Since Andy was a new intern under Dale's authority, he wasn't required to submit a report. Instead, Dale submitted one that followed the straight EPA policy line.

Andy sneaked a look at the report on Dale's desk and felt his blood pressure rise. "That's all lies!" he said angrily, looking directly at Dale. "I'll write my own report!"

"You don't have to," Dale muttered feebly. "You're still an intern."

"I know I don't *have* to," Andy snapped back. "I want to."

Andy bypassed Dale and gave his report directly to the division supervisor, providing what he knew was a fair assessment of what he had seen. Later that day he was startled by the noise of the report being slammed down on his desk.

"What is this?" Janet Glass, the EPA enforcement division supervisor, screamed at Andy, as all other activity around them abruptly ceased. "How dare you imply that EPA regulators violated the rights of that radical scum!"

"But that's what I saw," Andy argued. He was unnerved by the outburst from the supervisor, but he was determined to hold his own.

"I don't care what you *think* you saw," she screamed. "No one else who was there reported any violations! Don't you ever submit a report that is derogatory to this department again, you snotnosed college kid! People risked their lives to reestablish order, and you want to make those fanatics into martyrs?"

Andy tried to interrupt a couple of times, but it was piercingly clear that Janet Glass wanted no explanations, other than the official department line. He shut up and dropped his report into the wastebasket beside the desk, but he had a sinking feeling in his stomach. *America, the land of free speech*, he thought to himself.

He went through the motions of doing his work, but inside Andy knew something had changed. He had been excited about working with the EPA after college, but now he was more than a little disillusioned. *What's happening here?* he wondered as he got out the clipboard every intern was assigned; it signaled their inferior status in the huge government bureaucracy.

Two days later, at about ten o'clock Sunday evening, his home phone rang. "Oh, hi, Jimmy. What's wrong?" He already knew there had to be something wrong, because his brother never called unless he had a problem.

Andy never had been really close to his brother. Jimmy was the oldest and had left home when Andy was only three years old. He had spent twenty years in the Navy, so he had fought in the Persian Gulf war, as well as the last Iranian conflict.

Jimmy was ultrasensitive to the fact that he'd had little formal education and never had advanced beyond the rank of chief petty officer. He also resented the military's forced phasedown to support the government's new social programs. In the process, many military perks had been eliminated. Indirectly he blamed Andy because he had been educated on government loans and now was employed by the Environmental Protection Agency.

The two brothers always got into heated arguments at family gatherings, and the last few times they almost had come to blows. Andy defended the administration to irritate Jimmy more than out of any serious conviction about President Rand and his reinvention of government ideas.

Now he probably agreed with Jimmy that the EPA regulators were "a bunch of tree-hugging thugs." Since the Oregon raid, he had raised them to the level of "tree-hugging murderers."

"Andy," Jimmy gruffed, as was his nature. "Aunt Anna died."

"Oh, no! When did it happen?" Andy had always loved Aunt Anna. She was about the kindest person he'd ever known. He had visited her as often as possible after she'd been moved into the nursing home a couple of years earlier. Even though her health had been failing for several years, it was still sad to think that Anna was gone.

"She died a couple of days ago."

"I'll really miss her," Andy said sadly. Anna was the last of the old generation in Andy's family. Her brother R.S., or Pappy, as he'd been called, had been a family legend. He had countless stories about everything, especially his thirty-year tour with the Navy and ten years at Cape Canaveral with Von Braun and Deitz during the early days of the space program.

"Yeah, I'll miss her too," Jimmy replied. "She was the last of a breed."

"She was that all right," Andy agreed.

"Listen, little brother, I know you and Anna were close. That's why I called to let you know; but there's somethin' else."

His brother's tone made the hair on the back of his neck tingle all of a sudden. *My nerves are shot,* Andy chided himself.

"I can't talk right now," his brother whispered into the phone, "but there's somethin' strange about Anna's death."

"What? What do you mean?" Andy shouted.

"Take it easy," his brother said. "I don't know for sure. I just suspect. Apparently Anna had been sent to some government detention center in Maryland. I've heard rumors about old people being sent to something like intern camps, but most of it is just that—rumor. But there's something else too. You still work for that tree-hugger's police force, don't you?"

In spite of himself, Andy found he was rankled by his brother's sarcasm. He didn't trust the EPA now himself, but he didn't like to be needled. He started to make a caustic remark, but thought better of it.

"Yes, I still work there," Andy replied. "What does that have to do with Anna, and . . . what camps are you talking about?"

"May be nothing. May be everything," his brother began in his normal irritating manner. "I need some help to find out."

"What kind of help?" Andy asked, the tingling feeling increasing. It irritated him that he felt anxious.

"Like I said, Aunt Anna died recently and . . ."

"I know. You said that already," Andy snapped.

Ignoring his comment, Jimmy continued. "The Health Services people sent me all of Anna's stuff. Since I'm the oldest, she had listed me as her nearest of kin. She had a bunch of junk stored in an old chest. When I was looking through it, I discovered a secret compartment and found something real strange."

"What do you mean, strange?" Andy asked as he sat up in bed.

"Do you remember that stuff Anna used to tell us about Pappy being killed by the government and all that? Well, apparently there was some truth to it, and there's still a cover-up going on," Jimmy said.

"Pappy died fifty years ago!" Andy said sarcastically. "Come on. Even a John Bircher like you couldn't believe the government has a fifty-year-old cover-up going on. For what?"

"Maybe you're right. And just maybe Pappy knew something the government still wants kept secret."

"Like what?" Andy asked, rubbing the back of his neck. After what he had seen in Oregon, he could believe almost anything at this point.

"It had something to do with a missile Pappy worked on. You need to look at some of the stuff I found. It's incredible!"

Andy had not actually met Pappy Moss, but stories about him were told at every family reunion. Pappy had been twenty years older than Anna and, according to other family members, when he died he looked to be more her age than his own.

At family reunions, during the fifties, Pappy had kept the whole family entertained with his tales of World Wars I and II and, later, espionage at the Space Center. No one really believed all the stories, but they made great conversation for young and old alike.

Later, when Pappy was killed at the missile testing range in New Mexico, Anna had become obsessed with his death. At the reunions she told everyone who would listen that Pappy had been killed because of some top secret project he was working on. Most of the family assumed the story simply gave Anna a way to cope with the death of her only brother.

"Tell me about the papers," Andy said. He had a sinking feeling inside—a premonition.

"Apparently at least some of those stories Pappy told were true. He was involved with some secret project—something to do with nuclear rockets. I found some official records hidden away in a secret compartment in Anna's old chest. We were emptying it and there they were! I don't think even she knew they were there."

"Are you putting me on?" Andy said, knowing his brother's penchant for complicated pranks. "I'm in no mood for games."

"This is for real. You'll have to see for yourself. I sent a package to you, postal express. You should get it tomorrow."

Anna dead, Andy thought as he mumbled a good-bye and hung up.

The package from Jimmy arrived the next morning. Remarkably, the documents were fifty-year-old originals in nearly perfect condition. Andy spent several hours poring over them. The intent of the material was clear: to expose a government boondoggle of such proportion that it nearly destroyed civilization as we know it. Pappy and a Colonel Wells had gathered some top secret documents that were later hidden away in the false bottom of Anna's Civil War–era chest for safekeeping.

The chest had been passed down through Anna's family for generations. The secret compartment in the chest was common for that era since many families used similar means to hide whatever valuables they owned. Pappy obviously knew about the hidden compartment, even though Anna either hadn't known about it or had forgotten it was there.

Once he started into the files, Andy couldn't stop, so he called in sick. He simply couldn't face the dullness of his job while his mind was racing like it was. He doubted that anyone even cared that he was out. Since his tiff with Janet Glass, the others in his department shunned him—even Dale.

He knew any career plans he had with the EPA were on a downhill slide. The only thing that kept him on the job was typical government inertia. Eventually Glass would find a way to shuffle him off to an even more dead-end department, if there was one to be found.

The records Pappy had pirated told an incredible story surrounding a nuclear test program in the early sixties called "project THOR." The project was based on the theory that the U.S. could protect itself from a Russian nuclear attack by exploding a string of missile-launched hydrogen bombs in the path of the oncoming Russian missiles.

The concept was simple enough: The exploding nuclear weapons would cause the Russian warheads to be vaporized during the reentry phase. The trick obviously depended on early launch detection and exploding enough bombs to saturate the reentry window.

It was the *conclusion* of the initial test data that got Andy's attention: a possibility that high altitude nuclear explosions could initiate a spontaneous reaction in the upper atmosphere. In governmentspeak this meant that the explosion of high altitude nuclear bombs could potentially set the stratosphere on fire.

Reading on, Andy discovered that this sobering analysis did not deter a full-blown test program. Indeed the program ultimately succeeded in launching and detonating a hydrogen bomb carried by a prototype rocket.

In the fifty-odd years since the THOR had been launched, the most incredible hoax of all time had been perpetrated on the world—so incredible that Andy had a difficult time believing it.

2

△

What Is THOR?

The hours seemed to tick away as Andy reviewed all the data, including listening to some old reel-to-reel audiotapes Pappy and Colonel Robert Wells had used to dictate a detailed description of the events. It was clear that Pappy and Wells had shared the same concern: that Washington would initiate a total cover-up of the THOR project, including their own deaths.

Putting the reports down, Andy turned the desk lamp off and sat in the darkness a long time, trying to formulate a plan. *Something has to be done. But what?* For sure he wasn't going to give this incredible information to any Washington bureaucrat. In fact, if what he had heard on the tapes was true, and he was reasonably certain it was, it might not be healthy to even tell anyone in Washington about it—certainly not anyone associated with the environmental movement.

Suddenly the truth struck him: *Somebody in Washington has to know about project THOR—maybe a lot of somebodies. Why has no information on the THOR project ever been released?*

Clearly he was in over his head and he didn't know where to start. Then an alarm went off in his head: *I need to call Jimmy! If Pappy was killed to keep the information buried, it's possible that those who share the secret today won't allow this information to go public.*

It was nearly midnight, but he decided to call his brother anyway. The phone rang seven times before someone answered.

"Yeah. Who is it?" Jimmy grunted into the phone, his mind dull with sleep.

"It's Andy. We need to talk. Wake up!"

"What time is it?" his brother growled. "Call back in the morning."

"No!" Andy demanded. "I need to talk to you now. It's important!"

"Okay, okay," Jimmy groaned as he tried to clear his head. He was more awake now and was able to remember why he had contacted Andy in the first place. If his little brother was calling in the middle of the night, it really had to be important.

"Hang on a minute. I need to splash some water on my face."

In the background Andy heard his sister-in-law complaining. "Jimmy, who is that on the phone at this hour?"

"It's just Andy. Go back to sleep, Harriet."

Less than a minute later he was back on the line. "Okay, little brother, what's up?"

"Listen, Jimmy, I listened to the tapes and read the documents you sent. I have to assume they're real or Pappy wouldn't have gone to all the trouble to hide them. If they are, this thing is big. You've got to promise me that you'll keep this information to yourself. Have you told anyone else?"

"Naw. Just you and Harriet."

"Did Harriet tell anyone?"

"I don't think so, but you know Harriet."

Andy knew Harriet very well. If she hadn't told anyone else it was only because she had lockjaw. But, since she talked constantly about anything and everything, maybe her friends would write this off as another wild story—like the spaceship she saw that turned out to be a weather balloon.

"I think this information cost Pappy his life," Andy told his brother. "I need to do some checking; but still, it may be dangerous to know about that project."

"Hey, I'm glad you called, little brother," Jimmy replied. "Oh yeah, I did check on how Anna died. It was a stroke."

Strokes can be faked, Andy thought darkly. "What did they say at the nursing home?"

"Anna wasn't actually in a nursing home. She and some other old people were sent to that government facility in Maryland. Some friends of mine said their parents were sent to one too—some new cost-saving program, I suppose.

"Anyway, it seems the move rattled Anna and she started ranting about how Pappy had told her that he probably would be killed. The doctors thought it was just the delusions of an old lady until some government guys came down to talk with her; but she was pretty incoherent by then."

"What kind of government men?" Andy asked. The nerves on the back of his neck were tingling. He knew the government wouldn't normally be interested in a demented old lady—unless something she'd said had pressed a hot button.

"Uh, I don't know," Jimmy replied. "But they had CIO badges."

"CIO!" Andy exclaimed. "Jimmy, just do what I ask for once in your life, would you? Keep this under your hat until I do some more checking."

"Okay, little brother. Project THOR is our own little secret."

Andy had a very bad feeling inside about just how secret his brother could or would be. *But at least,* he thought, *I've got the documents.*

Actually, Jimmy already had made inquiries with a friend in Naval Intelligence to see if there was any interest—financially speaking—in the copies he had made of the documents.

I should've kept the originals, he thought as he flicked off the table light. *But I guess copies will have to do.*

Andy was up early the next morning and spent most of the next day in the Library of Congress CD-ROM files, looking for anything he could find related to the original THOR project in the sixties. There was nothing, absolutely nothing. It was as if the THOR project had never existed.

THOR had been totally purged from all government archives. Even the GAO files had no record of past allocations. He did a thorough search of Pappy's personnel records and, although his service record was totally intact, there was no mention of any project called THOR.

He did a cross-check of other personnel who might have worked with Pappy during the late fifties and sixties. *Maybe someone is still alive,* he thought. It was a long shot; but again he hit a dead end. Andy knew he wasn't a sleuth; and someone had done a very thorough job of eradicating project THOR.

Several names appeared on some of the early projects with Pappy, including Wernher Von Braun, Kurt Deitz, Bonner Steinholtz, and other nationally known scientists. But by the early sixties most of these names disappeared. *Died or retired,* Andy concluded. *Pappy had to be in his late sixties by then, but you never would have known it,* Andy thought as he scanned the photo records.

Andy concentrated his personnel search on the one person he knew had worked with Pappy: Colonel Robert Wells. Pappy had worked on at least ten different projects at the space center, and Wells' name came up on most of them.

Too common for just a coincidence, Andy concluded as he called up the record of Colonel Robert Wells. *Hey, maybe I'm getting good at this sleuthing thing,* he thought as he typed in his instructions.

Robert Wells had been a lieutenant colonel in the Army Air Corps during World War II and, later, a colonel in the Ballistic Missile Systems Command. *That's where his path crossed Pappy's,* Andy concluded. Colonel Wells was assigned to the OSS during World War II, the file record revealed. No further data was available.

A complete word check of Colonel Wells' file showed no reference to any THOR project, but he had not expected to find any. However the next inquiry stopped him on the spot. He requested the current status of Colonel Robert Wells.

DECEASED, JULY 7TH, 1963, the screen responded.

Three days after Pappy died at the Alamogordo test range, Andy realized.

DETAILS ON DEATH OF COLONEL ROBERT WELLS, Andy typed into the search program.

ACCIDENT, ALAMOGORDO MISSILE TEST FACILITY, NEW MEXICO, came the reply.

They died from the same "accident"! Andy surmised. *Talk about your basic coincidences.*

NEXT OF KIN, Andy typed into the terminal. The data appeared, and Andy discovered that Colonel Wells had been survived by his wife, Lisa.

A check of Lisa Feldstein Wells' personnel file revealed that she was a physicist, assigned to the Atomic Energy Commission from 1961 until 1963. *She quit right after Wells' death,* he noted. There was no further data available on Lisa Wells since she apparently never worked for the federal government again.

The last entry was the date of Colonel Robert Wells' and Lisa Feldstein's wedding: They had been married less than a year at the time of his death. No other family members were listed in the official file.

Dead end again, Andy thought grimly. *Colonel Wells is my best link to Pappy, so maybe Lisa Wells can be, but I have no idea where to start looking. She would have to be well into her seventies by now, if she's still alive.*

Reading through Colonel Wells' file, Andy noticed that Wells had been born in Wyoming and had been living there when World War II broke out. *Wyoming,* he thought. *Why not? It's as good a place to start as any.*

He left the Library of Congress building and headed over to the Computer Service Center. From there, federal employees could link up with any other public computer system in the world, including the state of Wyoming's public records department.

If Andy had had the right clearances, which he didn't, he could have accessed the CIO's files as well. He suspected that in those files was information on every citizen, living and dead. In fact, he now wondered about his own file. He suspected that something extra had been added since his unpleasant encounter at the office with Janet Glass.

Andy entered the building and showed his ID to the totally disinterested receptionist. She glanced at the card and then immediately went back to reading her magazine. *With forty percent of our population on the public payroll, I guess that's what we get,* Andy thought dryly. Then he remembered that he was drawing a federal paycheck too. He clenched his teeth in an involuntary grimace.

He dropped into the well-worn secretarial chair behind the computer terminal and pushed his ID card through the slot above the keyboard. Instantly the terminal powered up and the familiar flashing icon showed on the screen. Most personal computers had long since been converted to voice-activated commands but not the antiquated relics the government used, so he typed in the codes to access Comserve—the master system that would allow access to the worldwide computer data system.

COMSERVE ON LINE, the screen responded. WHAT SERVICE DO YOU REQUIRE?

Andy typed in, WYOMING BUREAU OF PUBLIC RECORDS.

ONE MOMENT PLEASE, the screen responded. Then another message appeared: DO YOU WISH THIS BILLED TO YOUR DEPARTMENT, MR. MOSS?

Why not? Andy thought with a smirk. *After all, it is government business—after a fashion.* YES, he responded with a stroke of the keys.

THANK YOU, the screen responded. THE STATE OF WYOMING'S BUREAU OF PUBLIC RECORDS FILE IS NOW ON LINE.

It's for sure the government didn't program this system, Andy thought with a chuckle. *It didn't insult me one time, and it actually works.* He settled down in the chair and went right to work.

He typed in ACCESS FILE: WELLS, LISA, and hit the "enter" key.

The screen began to fill with a list of names and personal data on all the Lisa Wellses who had lived in Wyoming since records began being kept in the mid-nineteenth century.

"Oh for . . . !" he said audibly. *Andy, you dummy,* he chided himself, *you called up every Lisa Wells, past and present, in the state of Wyoming.*

He scanned the keyboard for any key that would abort the process, but the well-worn letters were illegible. Irritated with himself and the inefficiency of the government he represented, Andy could do nothing but sit back until the search program ran its course. Twenty minutes later the routine halted on the last, most current, name, giving control of the keyboard back to the operator.

CANCEL SEARCH, Andy typed in.

INVALID INSTRUCTION, the program responded.

STOP, Andy typed in, hoping for the correct instruction.

INVALID INSTRUCTION, the machine again noted.

"Stupid!" he muttered aloud—more at himself than at the machine. He knew he had only one choice: He would have to ask the young woman on duty for help.

Walking over to the desk, Andy said timidly, "Miss, could you help me?" He waited for at least fifteen seconds, but the young woman never looked up from the magazine she was reading.

"Miss!" he said more forcefully this time. Andy wasn't feeling particularly long on patience and wondered how she would react if he just reached over and snatched the magazine out of her hands. *Not very well,* he decided—wisdom being the better part of valor.

So he decided to try the polite approach. "My terminal is hung up. Could you help me?"

"Use help," she replied with some irritation. Then she went back to reading her magazine.

Andy hadn't a clue as to what she meant. *Maybe she has brain damage,* he thought dryly. Although he hated to admit it to her, he said, "I don't understand what you mean."

"It's HELP, you dummy," she said in a piercing tone that caused everyone in the room to look in their direction. "Type in HELP, and the computer will give ya the instructions."

She turned the page of her magazine muttering: "Some people sure are stupid. . . ."

"They sure are," Andy answered in return as he walked back to the computer booth. The young woman never looked up again. She just snapped her gum and turned another page.

"Whew," Andy muttered as he sat back down at the terminal. *If this is what our government has come to, Lord help us if we ever have to go to war again.*

He could have kicked himself as soon as he realized what the girl meant. He wasn't totally familiar with the old manual terminal he was using, but his basic computer class had covered the use of such equipment. He simply had forgotten that any time the system got hung up an operator could type in HELP, and the program would list the available options.

I should have known that! he scolded himself again as he typed in HELP. The last thing he needed was some nosy supervisor asking what all the racket was about.

As soon as he typed HELP, the computer responded: WHAT TYPE OF HELP DO YOU REQUIRE? and listed a menu of possibilities. He found something called RESTART and keyed the cursor down to the proper line. *In private industry all that's required is a verbal command,* he muttered to himself as his fingers slowly typed his instructions.

With a minimum of difficulty, he coaxed the routine through the various options and found himself back where he had started thirty minutes earlier. He initiated the search routine once more— this time instructing the Wyoming computer to search for LISA FELDSTEIN WELLS. HUSBAND: ROBERT WELLS. EDUCATION: PH.D., CALIFORNIA INSTITUTE OF TECHNOLOGY.

"There," Andy said as he finished typing in the details. "That will narrow down the list." He hit "enter."

Within thirty seconds a single name appeared on the screen. As he looked at it, his heart dropped: LISA FELDSTEIN WELLS. BORN MARCH 3, 1939. DIED SEPTEMBER 12, 1991.

"Died," Andy repeated. His heart sank a little.

As the screen began to fill with additional data, he saw that Lisa Wells had been killed in an auto accident in Los Angeles while traveling to a lecture at Cal Tech. She had lived in Wyoming up to the time of her death and had taught college part-time at the University of Wyoming. Then he saw something that startled him. SON: JEFFREY WELLS. PH.D., CALIFORNIA INSTITUTE OF TECHNOLOGY.

Jeff Wells, Andy thought. *Naw, it couldn't be the same Jeff Wells. That would be too much of a coincidence.* He requested a printout of the data on the screen and then asked for another search: JEFFREY WELLS. MOTHER: LISA FELDSTEIN WELLS.

Once more he hit the "enter" key and the screen went blank for a moment.

Shortly the screen displayed the data: JEFFREY WELLS. SON OF LISA FELDSTEIN WELLS. M.S. PHYSICS, M.S. MATHEMATICS, MASSACHUSETTS INSTITUTE OF TECHNOLOGY; PH.D. THEORETICAL MATHEMATICS, CALIFORNIA INSTITUTE OF TECHNOLOGY.

"It *is* the same Jeff Wells," Andy said aloud. He knew the story well enough, even if he had never met Dr. Jeff Wells. He was the boy-genius who had received his Ph.D. in mathematics at the age of nineteen and had correctly predicted the gigantic earthquake that virtually destroyed the city of Tokyo back in the nineties.

Jeff Wells had become a national hero for his efforts in dismantling the Data-Net system, which had been used by the government in an attempt to control all spending in the country. Even now, the economy had not fully recovered from the depression it had caused.

Nearly every American knew about the reclusive Jeff Wells. He had virtually dropped from the public's eye nearly eight years earlier, and no reporter could get an interview with him. Then Andy remembered having heard something about Wells living out West on his family's ranch. It hadn't meant anything at the time, but now it all fit. *Sure, Jeff Wells . . . Wyoming.*

Wells' father had worked with Pappy on some top secret project, and they both died shortly thereafter. I don't know about his mother's death, Andy thought, *but I'll bet his father's death wasn't accidental.*

Now, how to get to Wells? he contemplated. *Maybe I just need to send him a copy of the tapes his father and Pappy left. Why not?* he decided. *That will definitely get his attention.* Andy didn't realize it would also get the attention of other parties.

3

△

Discovered

After leaving the computer center, Andy went back home. *What do you say to someone as famous as Dr. Wells?* he wondered. *Dear Dr. Wells, I suspect someone in the government had your father killed fifty years ago? Hardly!* he reasoned. *He probably has plenty of nuts trying to get to him. I'll need something to attract his attention.*

He decided the direct approach was probably best, so he copied a portion of the voice tape from Wells' father onto a laser disc. "This definitely will get his attention," Andy said aloud as he finished copying the tape. He thought about sending the original tapes, but he was afraid that Wells might not have access to a tape player.

He typed a brief note to Jeff Wells, packaged it along with the disc, and walked over to the local postal express office. He chafed at the $200 fee to send his package; but since the elimination of competing package delivery services, there seemed to be no limit to what the postal department could charge these days.

He stuffed his hands into his pockets as he left. *And I thought it was a good idea when the government shut down the other delivery services,* he reminded himself. *Consolidating all the deliveries under one organization was supposed to bring about efficiency discounts.*

"Stupid . . . stupid . . . stupid!" he muttered, as he retraced his steps back to his home.

Without his realizing it, Andy's inquiry into the THOR project had set off a whole series of events in the inner depths of Washington or, more correctly, in Virginia, at the offices of the Central Intelligence Office.

The sign outside the door read, MOST SECRET — AUTHORIZED PERSONNEL ONLY. Computer analyst Dr. Alan Shoer was authorized because he had a level five clearance. Working alone most of the time, he monitored data that was so classified even the secretary of defense was not authorized to see some of it, unless approved by the president.

At one time the Central Intelligence Agency (CIA), the precursor to the Central Intelligence Office (CIO), primarily had monitored foreign espionage throughout the world. But since the phasedown of the U.S. military, that function had become less important to subsequent administrations than monitoring internal subversives.

The most elaborate and sophisticated electronic surveillance equipment in the world was dedicated to monitoring American citizens who were listed as confirmed or suspected subversives. Many members of Congress would have been shocked to discover that their personal bank accounts were monitored and their telephones tapped. More than sixteen million Americans were on the CIO's subversive list, requiring nearly ten thousand full-time investigators to collect data on their activities.

Often the CIO worked hand in hand with the organized street gangs to control the flow of drugs in and out of the cities. A large portion of the CIO's budget was underwritten by skimming the drug profits.

Alan Shoer was no ordinary investigator. He had a Ph.D. in computer science and had been given the responsibility to oversee the brains of the CIO's surveillance operation. The system he monitored was dubbed "the funnel" because it was the end of a long line of surveillance equipment.

Simply put, when the computer in Alan Shoer's room came to life, it meant that some major security activity was in progress. All along the chain of CIO installations, the monitoring computers had already sorted out the noncritical inputs.

Usually, when Shoer got involved it was a transaction involving a known terrorist group or perhaps a riot in one of the urban ghettos, requiring dispersement of one of the CIO's undercover "control" squads. But on this day it was something Shoer could not decipher. The printer simply spelled out the words: PROJECT THOR SECURITY BREACH.

Shoer had been with the CIO surveillance department for nearly six years, and practically nothing surprised him. He knew things about the government and particularly President Rand's administration that would have traumatized most American citizens, if they had known, which of course they never would. He had seen assassination contracts put out on business leaders who opposed government takeovers of industry and, on occasion, a federal judge or two that needed to be "retired" from the bench.

Shoer also had seen personal information leaked to the press that was totally fabricated by other government agencies to destroy the careers of many opposing politicians. In reality, he could have cared less. He was doing what he did best—operating the most sophisticated computer system in the world—and he was being paid handsomely for it.

In fact, Shoer thought to himself, *eventually it may be a lot more profitable.* In a carefully partitioned memory file within the immense CIO mainframe computer, he systematically had been accumulating his own data base.

Alan Shoer was smart enough to know that any group capable of the deception he had witnessed could direct it against their own people. So he had a little "security" tucked away where no one but him could ever find it. If worse came to worst, he could use it to protect himself. If not, then perhaps eventually there would be some willing-and-able buyer out there.

When Shoer saw the alert signal, he immediately went to work to isolate the source. Within seconds the computer trace located the user: A GS-1 intern by the name of Andrew Moss, assigned to the EPA, had made an inquiry through the government's own computer service center.

"Probably some college kid looking up references for a course in Greek mythology," he muttered irritatedly. "Thor's a common enough name," he recalled from his undergraduate days. "An EPA intern!" he gruffed. "I had to repay my school loans, and now these kids get paid."

Shoer knew the government's computer system supposedly was off limits to nongovernment-related uses, but in reality, with the cost of living being what it was today, everybody cheated where they could. *Probably trying to save himself the price of a rental book at the library,* Shoer theorized.

Still, Alan Shoer was a trained CIO intelligence agent as well as a computer systems analyst, so he immediately initiated a report to the director detailing the event. At the same time he initiated a

check of ALL ENTRIES MADE BY ANDREW MOSS, GS-1, ID#
264448901. *Any further entries by young Mr. Moss will be
recorded and duplicated on the system data base,* Shoer noted as
he shifted his attention to more routine work.

Once the report had been sent to the director's E-mail file,
Shoer put the THOR incident out of his mind. Even though the
funnel was the end of a long pipeline of data analysis, there were
still plenty of surveillance activities to coordinate. The biggest was
the International Environmental Foundation, which had the
responsibility to oversee any violations of the United Nations environmental rules.

Tens of thousands of informants fed information daily to the
EPA data center, which consolidated all the data on global environment violations. Shoer knew that somewhere in the EPA's massive facility there was a war room that would have made the old
NORAD missile warning system pale by comparison.

Every environmental hot spot in the world was flagged on the
room-sized screen, and EPA violations were tracked as accurately
as Russian missile sites had been during the Cold War; only now
the former communist countries were working side by side with the
western nations to stop all environmental violations.

Just a matter of time until the EPA controls the country, Shoer
realized. *With some 400,000 armed "regulators" available, they
effectively have their own little army. Pretty far reach from what
the founding fathers envisioned.* He chuckled as he thought, *Give
the government an inch, and they'll take . . . your freedom.*

Just then his E-mail alert sounded. Punching in his access code
he read: "Dr. Shoer, I want you to gather all the data available on
a security breach from project THOR and send it to my file. And
Dr. Shoer . . . make this a priority *one.* Henry Watts."

Henry Watts was President Rand's handpicked, thirty-four-
year-old CIO director. Shoer sat looking at the screen for a
moment, and then with practiced routine, he set in motion the
commands that would send all of the accumulated inquiries on
project THOR, as well as any other entries made by federal trainee
Andrew Moss, to the director's security file. So thorough was the
analysis routine designed by the CIO that all supporting data on
Moss—family history, college classes, even how many traffic tickets he might have—was stored for instant retrieval.

Within seconds the data was sent to Watts' security file.
Theoretically, only someone with the highest level security code
could attain access to the data; even Alan Shoer could not read the

data himself. But that was theory only; in fact, Shoer had a duplicate sent to his own internal file.

Shoer knew that CIO computer auditors regularly ran random audits of every file in the data base. The misallocation of even a few thousand bytes of storage would be detected in their audits—and his personal file now consisted of several million bytes—but Shoer's knowledge of computer theory was at least four steps above that of the typical CIO auditor. In fact, it was their very arrogance in thinking that they knew more than everyone else that made them most vulnerable.

Since every single data storage byte was carefully counted and monitored to ensure no spurious programs were operating that might jeopardize the system's integrity, theoretically, that also meant that no data storage was possible beyond that identified in the memory map. At least no storage in the *known* memory.

Bubble memory, which came in billion-byte units, had long since made the old magnetic disk storage obsolete, and the CIO funnel computer had exactly 6.234871 trillion bytes of memory—except for the ten billion bytes that Alan Shoer had installed himself.

He had found it relatively simple to fool the memory mapping routine into ignoring his pirated memory. In reality, no one had thought about the possibilities of installing additional memory. The only access to this memory was through a nonresident routine Shoer installed when he needed to send or retrieve his data, which he did now.

Shoer knew it was a dangerous game he was playing. But those who don't take chances are the "little fish," he often quipped, "and big fish eat little fish." He wasn't about to be eaten, if he could help it. Anything the director classified as priority one had to be something he could use later. All he wanted was a peek at project THOR himself.

Getting the data wasn't the problem. In the wink of an eye his retrieval routine had filed a copy away in his secret memory bank; but how to retrieve it was a problem. He couldn't just print out what he needed. Even if the document was later shredded, he knew that a good cryptographer could reassemble enough of the data to hang him very high—literally.

No, he would have to be content with viewing it. As the information began to fill his screen he was amazed to see that it dated all the way back to the early sixties. *What could be so critical about something that happened in the sixties?* he wondered. As the records continued to scroll down the screen he was enthralled with what he read.

"Incredible," he said aloud, in spite of himself. *The biggest issue the EPA has is a total fraud, and they've kept it a secret all these years. No wonder someone at the top is upset! I wouldn't want to be in young Mr. Moss' shoes in a few hours. There's a good chance that some CIO enforcement unit's wheels are already rolling.*

If Moss is lucky, he'll find himself in an EPA unit in Outer Mongolia, Shoer mused. *If not, he may find himself an unfortunate victim of some accident—just depends on how much he knows and who he's told about it.*

▲

Oblivious to all that had taken place at the CIO center, Andy had mailed his package and returned home. That package would never be sent to Wells' Wyoming ranch. As a result of the CIO surveillance, the package with Andy Moss' authorization code would be rerouted to CIO headquarters.

Before he'd gone to the postal drop, Andy had eaten most of the meal he had prepared, but he was still hungry, so he decided to go back out. He had hoarded one coupon from his government ration card, which meant he could eat at the local Health Burger.

"The burgers, mostly kelp and soy, are filling . . . and environmentally correct," he remembered from the EPA-approved advertisement. He knew from his training course that without EPA approval the ads couldn't run on national television.

In one of those inexplicable impulses, before he left his apartment Andy decided to gather all of the THOR records and take them with him. They all fit into his slightly oversized student backpack—similar to those worn by virtually all college students.

He had become so accustomed to wearing it over the years he was in college, he always felt like he'd left something behind when he didn't have it on. If someone had asked him why he stuffed the reels and other documents in his pack, he wouldn't have been able to answer them. He just did.

In a few minutes, Andy was sitting in what once had been a first-class fast-food restaurant, but the depression had stripped nearly all of the profit out of private businesses, and Health Burger was no exception. Since the service they provided didn't qualify for federal inflation protection, the Health Burger chain had been forced to operate with an increasingly worthless money supply.

Unfortunately, although fast-food chains didn't have much political clout in Washington, their workers did. The national

Youth Protection Act had indexed the wages of the kids working at such places until they now made a little over $23 an hour.

Great for the kids, Andy noted sourly, *but disaster for the operators.* As a consequence, most chain restaurants either had closed or reverted to family-operated businesses with long hours and little income.

The restaurant he was in was clean but shabby. The tables were chipped and stained, the tile floors were nearly worn through, and the equipment looked like it would quit working at any moment. Andy thought about complaining that his burger was tasteless and the bun was hard, but he decided against it.

The man and woman behind the counter clearly were exhausted. *They've probably put in a twenty-hour day,* he thought as he looked at his watch. *Eleven o'clock. Can't blame them for what's happening to our country.*

It's interesting, he thought as he looked around the restaurant; *the only piece of new equipment is the electronic cash register.* Then he remembered what someone in the EPA's cafeteria had told him: The government was requiring all businesses to update their cash registers to comply with the new Source Collection Act for the value-added taxes.

"Failure to comply will cost those suckers ten grand," the arrogant young staffer had commented. "That'll put a kink in their tails." Andy had laughed with the others at the time. Back then he saw civilians as "them." Now he felt he was one of "them."

Suddenly Andy had a sinking feeling in the pit of his stomach—the same feeling he had experienced the night his father had his heart attack . . . then again when his sister had been shot in one of those senseless drive-by shootings common to D.C. He had heard someone describe it as a sixth sense. Maybe so. All he knew was that he felt something terrible was about to happen. It startled him so badly he almost jumped up from his seat.

Calm down, he scolded himself. *There's nothing wrong.* He looked around the restaurant and into the darkened street outside. Nothing had changed. *This THOR thing has got me spooked, that's all.* But he couldn't seem to shake the feeling of dread that swept over him again.

He dumped his trash into the recycling bin just inside the door and started to walk home. The feeling of dread seemed to engulf him like a fog—no, more like a plastic bag. *What's wrong with me?* he thought, fighting off the suffocating feeling.

Five blocks later, turning the corner to his apartment, he stopped short. There were four vehicles, obviously government issue, parked on the street in front of the apartment complex. He could see at least two men carrying automatic weapons stationed in front of the building. Another came rushing out, saying something that Andy couldn't hear from his position. One of the armed agents went to the car and made a call on the mobile phone.

The reflexes of youth took over, and Andy retreated into the dark shadows behind a building. Once he knew he was out of sight, he moved as quickly as he could to put some distance between himself and the agents. Obviously, they were looking for him. If he had arrived five minutes earlier or the agents had arrived five minutes later, they would have had him too.

They would leave someone to watch his home, so he was on the run. But to where? As he walked briskly away from the apartment, he began to think. *This has to be about the THOR project. Somehow my inquiries triggered a security breach inside the government. There's no reason to panic,* he tried to convince himself. *They'll check with the neighbors and find out that I regularly go off for the evening. And there's no way they could know about the documents. Praise the Lord I took this stuff with me,* he thought as an involuntary shudder went down his spine.

Now where did that come from? he asked himself. *Praise the Lord? I haven't thought about the Lord in years. Maybe everybody needs something bigger than themselves when trouble comes. And I could definitely use some help!*

Then the thought struck him: *Jimmy! I need to warn Jimmy. Could they know that he's involved too?* Somewhere deep inside he knew that, whoever they were, they would know about Jimmy.

He walked several blocks, trying various phones along the way—none of which worked. Finally he was able to get a dial tone on one. Most public phones required the use of a credit card because of the frequent change box robberies, so Andy had no choice but to use his card.

I wonder how long it will take for someone to trace this call? Not very long, he guessed.

The phone rang at his brother's home, but no one answered. *It's not like Jimmy to be out at this time of night.* His feeling of dread was mounting. He hoped his brother had listened when he warned him not to tell anyone else about the documents.

At Jimmy's house, as the phone was ringing, the CIO agent asked his captain, "You want me to answer it?"

"No, you idiot," he growled. "We'll have the location before he hangs up. If it's Moss, we sure don't need him hearing a strange voice here. Then he'd know something was up. I warned you not to shoot when we broke down the door."

"But I thought he was coming at me with a weapon, captain."

"A beer can, stupid! He had a beer can in his hand! You killed the woman too when you sprayed the room. Watts will be fit to be tied when he finds out they're both dead!"

How do they expect me to do my job when they give me idiots to work with? he thought as he walked to his vehicle.

4

△

Trapped

After seeing the agents at his place and then getting no answer at his brother's home, Andy realized the situation was critical. *If the feds already know about Jimmy, they'll be waiting for me too,* he reasoned.

What can I do? Andy wondered as his mind raced. He was so dizzy with fear he thought he might pass out. *Okay, first thing . . . get ahold of yourself. It won't do you any good to panic.*

Suddenly an idea struck him. He would use the efficiency of the government intelligence system itself to answer some of his questions. He knew they would have a quick electronic trace on his call to Jimmy's if they were there. So he doubled back to the phone booth where he had made the call, staying well back in the shadows but close enough to see the street.

Sure enough, a few minutes later a dark sedan, obviously government issue, came cruising down the street and parked a block away from the phone booth. There was just enough light to see two men in business suits. *Standard attire for government agents,* he noted. *They're so nondescript they stand out like a frog at a fly reunion.*

Andy waited for the better part of three hours, until the dark vehicle started up and slowly pulled away. The passenger was scanning the dark through night vision glasses. At the distance where he was hiding and with the argon vapor lights on the street blinding the sensitive glasses, Andy knew he could not be seen. Once the car disappeared, he waited another thirty minutes and then made his way across an adjacent alley and away from the area.

One thing he knew for sure: He could not go home. He also knew he could be of no help to Jimmy. But where could he go?

Dale Crawford. He's really the only other person I know. But will he help? Or will he call the authorities? No way to know, but there's no other choice.

He stopped at the next phone booth, which remarkably still had a directory attached, and looked up Crawford's home number. He started to make the call when he again realized he would have to use his card. *They'll trace the call before I get him on the phone,* he realized dejectedly. He dropped the receiver back in its cradle and walked away.

▲

At the White House, President Robert Rand was having a heated discussion with his chief of staff, Roger Houseman.

"Listen, Roger," the movie star-turned-president said angrily, "I don't want anything to detract from my environmental agenda. That fiasco by Barnett in Oregon was stupid. We just got congressional approval to shift the military personnel over to the EPA permanently, and I don't want any congressional hearing on police brutality because some mother's kid got killed by Barnett's gorillas. If he can't do the job we'll hang this thing on him and dump him like a sack of rotten fish."

"I talked with the general," Houseman replied with an emphasis on *general*. He had been a Hollywood director for nearly fifteen years before joining Rand's bid for the presidency. He knew all the ways to get an image across and had masterminded Rand's meteoric rise in politics.

The image of a dashing, youthful, nonpolitical politician and famous movie star/environmentalist was one that he had carefully cultivated. Getting the business community to back Rand, in spite of his acknowledged antibusiness environmental stance, had been no small trick.

He first had to assure the business community that Rand had reformed his acid attacks on them. Then he had to sell Rand to the political insiders as a balanced liberal with no personal agenda who would be able to bring the two warring factions in the Congress together.

In reality, just the opposite was true. Rand was a dyed-in-the-wool activist whose primary agenda as president was to bring the business community to heel. He made hundreds of secret deals with the real political insiders, both in the Congress and in the military, by promising them high positions in the biggest political power grab in the history of the Republic.

He won over the Senate and House leaders by promising them plum contracts in their home districts to house the regional EPA centers—most of which were window dressing.

General Barnett was one of those compromise deals in which Rand knew he had to have the support of the military to accomplish his long-term agenda. But secretly, Rand hated the military and what it stood for. He knew the time would come when he would squash them like bugs—with the wholehearted approval of the American people.

"Barnett is an idiot," Houseman agreed, "but he is an essential idiot right now."

"I know all that," Rand snapped, "but that doesn't make me like that pompous imbecile. When we have control, I want Barnett out! Permanently!"

"Take it easy, Mr. President. You never can tell who's listening in this town."

"See to it that the White House is swept for bugs," the president said as he paced around the old desk that once had belonged to Thomas Jefferson.

"I do regularly, but those new passive pickups can pass the sweep. We can't be absolutely sure we're secure—even here in the Oval Office. It seems like everybody's spying on everybody else anymore. You've made some people mighty irritated since you got here."

"Yeah, I know," Rand barked, "and I hope to irritate a whole lot of others before I'm through. One day we'll fix those religious fanatics in the Congress too."

I sure wish he'd learn to talk less and think more, Houseman thought. He had begun to wonder if he had done the world a favor by directing the image of Robert Rand into the White House. He had assumed, since they agreed on the environmental agenda, that it was essential to get Rand into position to make a difference. He also had assumed that much of Rand's behind-the-scenes bluster was just his Hollywood image. Now he wasn't so sure.

One thing was certain: Robert Rand was the most popular president since Donald Keegan. Keegan inherited a mess from his predecessor, and Rand inherited a bigger one from his; but, unlike Keegan, who believed that free enterprise could solve the world's ills, Rand believed it was the duty of the government to do so—the government according to Robert Rand, that is.

"We have another problem," Houseman said as he put the issue of Rand's extremism out of his mind. His job was to help Rand accomplish his agenda in Washington. He would leave the evaluation of that agenda to the historians.

"What now?" Rand barked as he dropped into the ancient leather chair by his desk.

It always amazed Houseman how the man could be so utterly distasteful and arrogant in private and then switch on the charm like a light bulb when he stepped into the public's eye. *I guess that's what made him a successful actor,* Houseman mused silently. Since he was used to working with Hollywood prima donnas, Rand's tantrums didn't particularly bother him, but he had seen many a young staffer leave Rand's presence crushed and defeated by his blistering sarcasms.

Rand hated any outward indication of weakness in those around him, and he would abide no disloyalty, which usually included disagreements. *A very vicious combination to work around,* Houseman concluded. It bred the instincts of piranhas in the White House staff. Once they sensed blood, they would devour one of their own just as readily.

Such is life in Hollywood . . . or Washington, Houseman concluded as he pulled from his briefcase the blue folder marked MOST SECRET: PRESIDENTIAL APPROVAL ONLY.

"We've had another leak in the THOR project."

"THOR! I thought you told me that had been handled," Rand growled, his eyes now alive with flame.

Give me a break, Bobby-boy, Houseman wanted to say to the president—but then thought better of it. *He's shifted back to the role of the great environmental leader,* Houseman mused to himself.

What the president's chief of staff hadn't said was that he had installed his own passive monitors to record the president's words for posterity—or protection. *Rand might believe he can control the country forever, but I've been around power long enough to know that nothing lasts forever,* Houseman assured himself.

"The original material had already been sent to another operative by the time we got there—an intern staffer at EPA," Houseman said, handing Rand the file.

"Get it from him. Then get rid of him too," Rand said as if he were ordering up Air Force One.

In his mind Roger Houseman could see the little digital disc whirring around, recording the instructions of the president of the United States to kill another citizen. *He's a homicidal maniac!* Houseman had already concluded. *I used to think his vicious side was an act too, but that's the only real Rand.*

"He's gone," Houseman said as matter-of-factly as he could. Then he studied Rand's face, waiting for the inevitable tirade he knew was coming. *He's getting his best commander-in-chief response ready,* Houseman mused to himself.

"What do you mean, he's gone? Find him and get that file."

"It's not quite that simple," Houseman continued, unruffled. "We know he's somewhere in the Washington area, but he's probably been alerted. One of Watts' CIO eager beavers killed the other contacts. He's probably hiding out somewhere in the city by now." "I'm surrounded by imbeciles!" Rand stormed as he jumped up from the chair.

"It wasn't Watts' fault," Houseman offered. "It's all those hot dog recruits from the military. Besides . . ."

"Besides nothing," Rand shouted as he slammed the metal paperweight he had been toying with down on the 300-year-old desk. "How long until you can find this . . . this Moss kid?" he demanded as he scanned the file.

"Not long, but there may be another complication . . ."

"What now?" Rand asked sharply. The mental stress was beginning to take its toll. He had thought it would be so simple: just get elected, take over the White House, and then stomp on anyone who opposed his plans. He didn't like having to deal with the dimwits who had pillaged the Earth for the last hundred years.

Ghia had spoken to him last night in a dream, warning him that she was dying; the human viruses had brought her near the end. There was no time to waste.

"The Moss kid has a good bit of detail on the THOR project. He apparently made use of the central data base to check the validity of the data. He came across the link between Dr. Wells' father and project THOR."

"How do you know that?" Rand asked in a more subdued tone. He was bone weary and needed rest, not problems.

"He did a trace on Wells through his Uncle Pappy's contact with Wells' father. Pretty smart stuff for a kid, really." Then he added mentally, *Smart enough to get him killed.* "He tried to get a copy of some old tapes to Wells, but we intercepted it."

"I thought all the files connected to THOR had been purged," Rand said as he wearily rubbed his eyes.

"There's only so much you can do with historical data," Houseman replied. "A lot of it is in state data banks and, with all the computer linking, it's accessible to anyone who has the key. Unfortunately the stuff that Moss has is first generation data; he has the key."

"Is there a chance he can contact Wells?"

"Our people don't think so. Galt has Wells shielded better than the pope."

"Well, stay on it," Rand instructed calmly. "The last thing we want is to have Wells involved. But, Roger, I want those files purged clean of all references to that project. If you need federal jurisdiction in the states, let me know. We'll get the FBI to make this thing a national security issue . . . or something."

Houseman never ceased to be amazed by Rand's constantly changing moods. "I'll issue an internal order notifying the FBI and CIO that Moss has stolen some top security papers and is trying to escape the city. He can't get very far."

"You're a good man, Roger. Sorry I was so snappy earlier. Just tired, I guess."

Or maybe just an egomaniac, Bob, Houseman thought. But he replied, "That's okay. I understand. It's the stress of the job."

The next morning Houseman sent for EPA Director Stanton Barnett and FBI Director Lamar Yule. "I want an APB issued for Andrew Moss. He's to be held for espionage," Houseman ordered. "The documents he's carrying are to be considered top secret—for the president's eyes only. Let me make it clear . . . I do not want him killed. It is vital that we have a chance to interrogate him."

"What's the rub?" Barnett asked. "This kid is one of our college grant interns. I saw something from his supervisor recently about a false report he turned in on the Oregon raid, but nothing serious."

"What kind of report?" Houseman asked with renewed interest.

"Oh, he thought the EPA regulators used excessive force. The supervisor trashed the report and gave him a reprimand."

Interesting, Houseman thought. *Perhaps the two incidents are purely coincidental. Or, perhaps the young Moss already had been somewhat disillusioned and therefore was on alert when the THOR information came his way. The real issue is how to stop him before he can tell anyone else.*

"Get on it!" Houseman ordered as he signaled the meeting was at an end.

The angry look General Barnett gave him was not lost on Houseman. *One day, general, you and I will part ways,* he told himself silently. *Perhaps one day soon.*

Yule, the youthful FBI director, on the other hand, almost jumped out of his chair. "Yes sir," he replied enthusiastically. "We'll have him today. I assure you."

Too bad the compliant ones are so incompetent, Houseman thought sourly. He wasn't sure which man he despised the most: the general who knew his job but sold out his convictions for position, or the lapdog Yule, who followed obediently but screwed up everything he touched.

If Moss has eluded the trained agents the CIO has sent, he won't be all that easy to catch. But catch him we will. There's no place for him to hide from the government's eyes and ears, Houseman thought confidently.

▲

It had been nearly twelve hours since he'd started running, and Andy Moss was getting desperate. He had no real plan for how to get out of Washington; no money, other than his credit card, which he was afraid to use; and no real friends to call on for help. He didn't know whether his brother was alive or dead, and he couldn't risk calling again. With the government's efficient electronic trace system in place by now, he knew he would be located in seconds.

The implant worried him too. When he had accepted the government's college job corps plan, he had agreed to accept a microchip implant under the skin of his right forearm. The logic was simple: All the school had to do was scan the ID chip and verify his account to have the funds allocated automatically. It eliminated the misuse of the government funds by unauthorized people.

But now, he realized, it also made his identification quite simple. The first time he was stopped by a police officer with a portable ID scanner he would be arrested—assuming the government had an alert out for him—which he assumed they did.

The ID chip was also required for all entitlement recipients, including those on welfare, Social Security, national health care, and the like. Eventually it would be used to ID all newborns. Again the logic was so simple: Children with implant IDs would be easier to locate if they were lost, kidnapped, or killed.

How could I have been so blind, he thought grimly. *I believed it was a good idea too. The kids who railed against the chip implant were labeled right-wing radicals and Neanderthals. We thought they were a bunch of religious wackos, always talking about the mark of the beast. Now I realize the beast might not be a person; it could be a system.*

Andy had successfully eluded the Washington search thus far by practicing a theme he had seen in an old TV movie: The best place to hide a tree is in a forest. So he figured the best place to hide a student, even a recent graduate, was on a college campus.

Applying this logic, he had spent the better part of the day attending classes at American University. The classes were so loosely structured, he knew that few students would notice another drop-in, and the professors were so apathetic they didn't care.

He had staved off hunger by grabbing the scraps from the students' plates when they left the cafeteria. A lot of drop-ins would usually hawk a meal this way, so he didn't attract any special attention. Someone had told him it was like the Old Testament principle of gleaning: Farmers would leave some grain on the wheat stalks for the poor.

But the day was passing rapidly, and he still had no real plans. He knew that once the majority of students left he would stand out, but what could he do? He needed to get out of Washington. The longer he stayed, the greater the odds against him.

After more than an hour of sitting in a near-brain-dead paralysis, he realized he had to do something. The only option he could think of was Dale Crawford. Andy grabbed his backpack and headed out the door, straight for Crawford's apartment building. But before he reached the building, he had lost his nerve again.

He turned back toward his apartment without even realizing it. Only when he started to step out of the alley onto his street did he snap back to reality. He backed into the shadows thrown by the yellowish argon streetlights. Andy had never felt more alone . . . or more lonely. He wished he could just drop his backpack in the nearest garbage can and forget the whole thing—but he couldn't.

It was a cold, miserable night, but he hunkered down in a deserted building only four blocks from the Capitol. Andy forced himself to stay put until the normal city activity picked up. Then he made his way toward the university again. As he entered the cafeteria, he immediately noticed the two men in business suits showing a photo to some students.

He ducked into the men's room and sat in one of the stalls for a long time. When he came out the men were gone, but as he exited the building he noticed the brown sedan parked in an otherwise empty parking lot. *Only government vehicles can get driving permits in Washington,* he reminded himself.

Waiting until a group of students left the building, he stepped in behind them and made his way across the campus. When they broke up to go to their various classes, he ducked behind a building and made his way to the busy street.

Since the Clean Air Act had banned all private cars in D.C., the streets were filled with pedestrians and bicyclers. First-time visitors to the city were struck by the similarities between Washington and the Asian cities they had seen in documentaries. Nearly everybody walked or pedaled their way across the city.

Only top level government officials and their friends had passes to ride in cabs, and a rare few had automobile permits. But for Andy, this worked to his benefit. He was just another college student, like the thousands of others who ate at the government's trough.

He had already decided that he had no choice but to contact Dale Crawford. His chances of surviving on the streets of D.C. were slim to none. If the CIO or FBI didn't find him, some mugger would. *The second most successful business in Washington is crime,* he remembered one of his professors saying. *Now it's first, if you lump in government crimes as well.*

It took him nearly three hours to work his way through alleys and side streets to the apartment complex on Delaware Street. The mental and physical fatigue were taking their toll. He had not eaten since the previous day and didn't realize he was so hungry until he passed by a bagel shop close to the apartment building. Unfortunately, he only had his personal credit card and government intern's allowance card, both of which were most certainly being monitored in case he tried to use them.

Andy found his emotions cycling between depression over his circumstances and anger over the abusive treatment he was receiving at the hands of the government. For the first time in his life he began to grasp the reality of losing his personal freedoms.

He thought back over the many college classes he had attended in which government-paid professors had ridiculed and condemned those who doggedly defended their right-wing ideologies. Now he realized that the ideologies they defended against the class majority were fundamental rights: life, liberty, and the pursuit of happiness.

"These are the regressives who would plunge us back into the Dark Ages," his professors often said as they held up the "right-wingers" to class ridicule. The common theme in virtually every class was submission of individual rights for the greater good of all mankind. This agenda usually narrowed down to the confiscation of all guns, the control of all private land use, and the need for the government to provide cradle-to-grave security.

Andy had listened, and he had agreed, especially when he heard the horror stories about riots in the streets, the destruction of hundreds of animal species, and pollution of the environment. But right now he wished he had a little more personal freedom, like a gun to ward off the muggers, as well as the police who were after him. He also wished he were free to live his own life—removed from government control.

Then the truth struck him. *That's exactly what the protesters in Oregon were saying before the EPA regulators moved in.* He shuddered when he remembered the "justice" they had gotten.

Andy found himself facing the building where Crawford lived. He started to walk away, the fear racing through his body; but then he turned back. *No choice!* he told himself resolutely as he approached the building. Luckily, two other tenants were leaving so he caught the closing outer door just in time to slip inside.

Once inside, he located the mail drop boxes. One was identified "Crawford, Apt. 3-B." The boxes were big enough to accommodate newspapers, and Andy had no trouble stuffing all of the documents, tapes, and a copy of the disc he had made for Dr. Wells into Crawford's mail drop.

Well, for better or worse it's done, Andy told himself resolutely. Suddenly he felt better. The load of making the decision had been lifted. Either Crawford would help, or he would call the police. Either way it was done.

He made his way out of the building and hurried to locate a phone from which he could call Crawford. Then he realized again that he didn't have a dollar to make the call.

Andy Moss had never begged in his life, but he decided there was no other option. He started asking passersby, "Would you give me some change so I can call my mother?" One person after the other simply ignored him.

With no success in panhandling, he thought about the many panhandlers he had given money to. The ones who were the most successful were usually the most aggressive. Often he would give them something just to get rid of them. So he changed his tactics and began tugging on coat sleeves and following those who looked either frightened or sympathetic as they scurried along. Within a few minutes he had more than five dollars in change.

Wow, these guys must really clean up, he quipped to himself as he hurried back to the phone booth.

5

△

In the Park

When his car hit a huge rut in the road, Dale Crawford snapped back to the reality of where he was: out West, driving a "borrowed" government vehicle, searching for the one person who might be able to help him stay alive. It was hard to believe so much had happened in such a short time.

How had he gotten into this mess? *Oh yeah,* he remembered through his fatigue-weary senses. Andy had called him at home one evening—almost two weeks ago.

▲

Crawford picked up the phone on the second ring. "Hello."

"Dale, it's Andy Moss. I need your help." The desperation in his voice was unmistakable.

"Why call me?" Dale asked in a tone that clearly sent a message: *I don't want to be involved.* He had known Andy was in some kind of trouble when the CIO came and cleared out his desk.

"I can't talk over the phone," Andy said as he glanced around furtively. "I left some documents in your mailbox, along with a disc and some tapes. Look at the material. I'll call you back later."

"Wait . . . ," Dale tried to say, but Andy had hung up.

Dale sat unmoving for several minutes. He really didn't want to get involved. If he did, he could end up in the same mess as Andy Moss. He didn't know what Andy was involved in, and he didn't want to.

Andy hurried away from the phone, fearful that Crawford might decide to call the authorities. He walked for several blocks until he found a nice little park with a bench. There he sat down to wait, praying that Dale Crawford was still his friend. Every time someone walked by he feared it would be the FBI or CIO.

Dale thought about calling the FBI without even recovering the stuff Andy had left in his box. But somehow he knew he couldn't do that. Then he realized that he had to know what it was all about. He went to his mailbox in the hallway of the old apartment house. There he found the disc, a bundle of old government documents, and some old tapes.

He entered his apartment, dropped the disc into his player, and sat down to listen. And listen he did, as the bizarre story about project THOR began to unravel. Toward the end of the disc Andy had added a few comments of his own.

He began with the call from his brother and described his review of the THOR documents and their contents. Several times Dale stopped the player, took out the disc, and started to stick it in his microwave. But each time, he shrugged and popped it back into the player. The thirty-minute segment with Colonel Wells describing the THOR project was hair-raising, to say the least.

"The group of people who now run the U.S. government are fanatics, through and through," Andy said in conclusion. "They are as dedicated to their cause as any terrorist—more so, because they believe their cause to be righteous."

Dale's stomach felt queasy as he listened to Andy tell his story. He was weaving a convincing tale about government power in the hands of fanatics. *No*, Dale said silently. *It just can't be true.*

Andy also had added a hastily scribbled note to Crawford: "I can only hope that you'll be willing to help me. If not, I'm a dead man. It will only be a matter of time until the authorities find me. Once they do, I'll probably just disappear. If they find out you have this material, you won't be safe either, so guard it and yourself well."

Sitting on the park bench, Andy chided himself. *I know I handled the investigation of project THOR clumsily, but I guess I didn't really believe it was true. How could we let those fanatics take over?*

In the apartment, Dale Crawford started to throw away the documents that had been left in his mailbox. But again he couldn't bring himself to do it. After listening to the disc Andy had made, he took out his old reel-to-reel recorder and threaded one of the old tapes through the machine.

As he listened, he was spellbound to hear descriptions of the launch of a missile called THOR nearly fifty years before. It was obvious from the discussions that a Colonel Robert Wells and someone called Pappy were intent on preserving the details about the project.

Wells, Crawford thought. *Could Colonel Wells be related to Dr. Jeffrey Wells? He had to be. Why else would Andy Moss be contacting Dr. Wells?*

As the first tape ended, Crawford realized that Andy had copied only a small portion of the original tapes on the disc for Dr. Wells. *A sample, he told himself. He made a sample to attract Dr. Wells' attention.*

Crawford put the second tape on the machine and began to sort through some of the documents. As he looked through the stack, he began to grasp what Andy had uncovered: Project THOR had gotten out of control. The results seemed too incredible to believe.

If this is true, he thought, *this is the biggest cover-up of the twentieth century.* He could understand why the government, especially the EPA, would want to suppress the information even now. The greatest environmental hoax in history was being played on the American people, and literally trillions of taxpayers' dollars were being squandered in the process.

Crawford went pale as the blood drained from his face. He had been in Washington long enough to know that absolute power corrupts absolutely, and President Rand and the environmentalists held absolute power. He knew the leaders in the government would never allow the information from project THOR to be made public. They would stop at nothing to suppress it.

Suddenly he understood Andy's dilemma: There was virtually no one in Washington he could trust. Certainly the liberal media would suppress this information, especially since the president held the reins of power, including the grants upon which most of the media depended.

Crawford sat for a long time just thinking. *Why did Andy have to get me involved in this mess?* "I'm no hero," he said aloud. "And I don't intend to be one either." But Dale Crawford was smart enough to know that just having looked at the documents was sufficient to get him killed, if those who did such things knew about it. He had to return the materials to Andy and tell him to get out of D.C.

That's it! Crawford told himself. *That kid has to get out of Washington. Let him take the stuff to Wells if he can. Wells is powerful enough that even the president will have a hard time silencing him.*

Crawford also realized that Andy had contacted him because he probably lacked any other options. *He probably needs money,* he concluded. Crawford always kept a couple hundred dollars in his apartment, along with a variety of government coupons.

Right after he had joined the EPA, some of the other staffers had explained how they were able to skim money from the government expense system and how friends in the printing office would sell them coupons for almost anything they needed.

He gathered up most of his hoarded cash, fuel and food coupons, travel vouchers, and credentials for undercover EPA surveillance. *These will get Moss just about anywhere he has to go,* Crawford thought as he stuffed the documents and money into his old backpack. His hands were shaking so badly he had to sit down for a moment to steady himself. All he could do was wait on the call he knew would come eventually.

Andy placed the call to Crawford early in the afternoon. He had waited nearly two hours, hoping Crawford would have had enough time to review the data. Of course if Crawford had called the authorities, as government regulations required, there would be an instant phone trace. Unfortunately, there was no way to know, one way or the other, until he called.

Crawford had been sitting by the phone waiting for Andy's call, but when it rang, he was startled. *Man, my nerves are shot now,* he thought. He never had considered himself a wimp, but he felt totally helpless in the face of this problem. The government held all the trump cards; he held nothing but a bunch of papers and tapes that, at best, could get him put in prison and, at worst, could get him killed.

"Hello," Crawford said cautiously as he picked up the receiver.

"Did you have a chance to look at what I left?" Andy almost whispered.

"A little of it," Crawford replied.

"Tell me the name of the officer on the disc," Andy said with a sudden burst of inspiration. He knew that if Crawford were going to call the CIO he would not have listened to any of the information. That would have made him a liability also.

Crawford caught the meaning of the question immediately. He was tempted to lie, but inside he knew he was already committed. "Colonel Robert Wells," he replied.

Andy breathed a silent sigh. Crawford was committed. "Right!" he said. "I need your help."

"I know," the older staffer replied as the tension seemed to drain out of him. He had made his decision, and nothing could reverse it now. The CIO might not know about his involvement yet, but if Andy were caught, Crawford was certain they would eventually get the rest of the story out of him.

"Where can we meet?" Crawford asked. "I have some things you'll need if you're going to get out of the city."

"There's a little park on the river. Do you know the place?"

Crawford knew the park well. He often went there on weekends to jog. "I know it," he replied.

"I'll be at the bench on the west side. Meet me there in fifteen minutes." With that Andy hung up the phone. Suddenly he was feeling almost alive again. Crawford had been around long enough that he obviously knew how to use the system. He would have some idea of what was needed to get out of D.C.

Unknown to either man, the hunt for Andrew Moss had taken on a new dimension. When the CIO and FBI both had come up empty that first day, the search had widened. CIO Director Henry Watts was certain that Moss was still in the city. A check of all the universities had yielded a positive ID at American U., but it was clear Moss no longer was using that cover. A search of all the other schools and libraries had yielded no further leads.

"He's got to be somewhere in the city. We'll get him eventually, Roger," Watts told the president's chief of staff.

"That's not good enough," Houseman snapped as he twisted a gold letter opener in his hand. I want four hundred of the EPA's regulators to spread out across the city. Cover every park, alley, vacant building, car—everything. We need those documents back.

"Do whatever it takes to find Moss," Houseman ordered, "but remember, I want him alive. You tell that idiot Barnett that his people are to go unarmed. We have no reason to think that Moss is dangerous, and I doubt that he could be armed. With the latest sweeps, we've cleared the city of guns."

Yeah, at least in the hands of the ordinary citizens, Watts thought to himself. He had seen evidence of some impressive weapons in the hands of gangs, most of whom were authorized by the administration as a part of the "civilian enforcement" group, which basically meant they helped collect drug money for the government.

"I'll tell Barnett his troops can carry only sappers and stun guns," Watts said. "But you know he'll kick up a stink."

"You leave Barnett to me," Houseman ordered. "I want Moss alive. We have to know if he's talked to anyone else."

That conversation had taken place earlier that afternoon. Within an hour there were more than twelve hundred EPA regulators fanning out across the nation's capital in search of the terrorist known as Andrew Moss. Each regulator carried a photo of Moss, as well as an ID scanner to verify his microchip ID.

General Barnett had indeed kicked up a fuss about his regulators being unarmed. To compensate, he had quadrupled the number of troops dispersed. His instructions to the task force leaders were, "I want Moss found . . . and subdued. The administration does not want him killed, but don't take any chances. Terrorists don't work alone."

▲

At fifteen minutes after four Andy took a seat on the park bench. He was dog-tired and decided to rest until Crawford arrived. But as soon as his eyes closed, he dozed off. Several times he shook his head, trying hard to stay awake. But the next time his eyes closed he was fast asleep sitting up. He never noticed the twenty or so young men and women who filtered into the park.

Dale Crawford had just entered the park from the east side when the regulators began their systematic search. He had decided to stash his backpack, with the documents and tapes, behind a dumpster a few blocks from his apartment. He wasn't sure why, except that it frightened him to be carrying around something so volatile.

I'll tell Andy where they're hidden, he decided, *and he can retrieve them when we're done.* So when he entered the park he looked like just another Washington staffer out for a walk.

As soon as he was in sight of the river, he knew something was wrong. There was a commotion in the general direction of the bench where he was to meet Andy. Cautiously he made his way to a point where he could see the bench. It was then he saw the swarm of regulators. Panic gripped him as he saw that they held Andy by his arms.

He started to run, but then thought better of it. He had no reason to believe they would suspect him at this point. Just as he started to back away, Andy broke free of the two men holding him and turned to hit another in the stomach. At that point his attackers started swinging what looked like small black clubs at Andy's head. He went down, and when he attempted to get up, the beating intensified.

Within two minutes, Andy lay absolutely still. One of the men was shouting at the others, and although Dale couldn't hear what he was saying clearly, it was obvious he was angry about the fact they had beaten their captive into unconsciousness.

Dale walked back across the park on weak legs. *They have Andy,* he told himself trying to control the urge to run. *It's only a matter of time until they find a way to make him talk. Then I'll be next.*

He let out an involuntary shudder as he thought about the brutal beating he had just witnessed. He had no illusions about the futility of claiming he was an innocent victim. He had already seen what happened to other "innocents" out in Oregon.

I've got to get away—now, he decided. *By tomorrow there may be no place for me to go.*

Dale Crawford could not have known that the beating Andy had received had left him with a fractured skull. Already the blood was pooling in his brain, pressing down on sensitive nerves. Andy Moss was slipping into a coma. He would die without ever regaining consciousness.

All Dale knew was that he had to recover the documents he had stashed and find the quickest way out of Washington. *But to where?* he wondered, fighting his panic. And almost immediately he knew: *Wyoming and Dr. Jeffrey Wells.* It was a long shot, but it was all he had.

Dale Crawford was not a man given to bravery. In fact, in his entire life he never had stepped out of the normal walk of life to take risks. Once he had joined a group of boys from his high school to steal hubcaps off a parked police car. These hubcaps were displayed as trophies in the gym locker room to demonstrate their supposed courage. But when Dale's turn came, he had gotten so scared that he wet his pants while bending down to pry a hubcap loose. The other guys had ridiculed him mercilessly, and he had vowed never to go awry of the law again; his temperament just didn't allow for it.

Now here he was, fleeing for his very life, or so he assumed. In reality, if he had been thinking clearly, he would have realized that there was no way the CIO could have any knowledge of his involvement—at least not at this point. But fear and panic dulled his reasoning and he fled, deciding that he could not return to his apartment.

What he had seen in Oregon had sickened him, and now what he had just witnessed in the park only served to further drive his fears. He realized that what he had held to be true most of his life was being turned upside down.

He had been raised in a generation that believed free enterprise enslaved the working people of America and that the government was their protector. Clearly what he had seen in the last few weeks demonstrated the exact opposite.

Dale questioned himself, *Why did I listen to the tapes? I knew that once I crossed that line I'd be implicated too.* But, inside, he knew why he had listened. Andy Moss had done what he lacked the courage to do: confront the truth straight on. Andy knew the raid in Oregon was wrong, and he said so. He also knew the THOR data had to be made public, and he risked his life to do so.

As he approached the dumpster where he had hidden the documents, he again felt the fear rising in his throat. He fought the urge to just run and hide. Once he recovered the documents, it would be like walking around with a time bomb. If he were stopped, he could not plead ignorance.

Then a strange thing happened. For the first time in his life, he made a decision totally on his own. All through school he had followed directions without question. Later in his career he had followed his supervisors' instructions without question. *But no more!* he vowed silently. *I saw what they did to those people in Oregon, and almost certainly the same thing is happening all over the country. If our government can violate the rights of citizens with impunity, then what good is freedom?*

Dale Crawford had what can only be described as a battlefield conversion: from coward to hero. He simply was tired of being scared all the time. *I'm going to escape*, he told himself, *and I'm going to see Jeffrey Wells. From that point on I'll do whatever I have to do.*

6

△

The
Pursuit

At the White House, Houseman's office was a hive of activity, with people scurrying around trying to escape his wrath. The current recipient of that wrath was the EPA director, General Stanton Barnett.

"It couldn't be helped," the aging ex-general said very matter-of-factly to the enraged Houseman. "Moss attacked my people. They had to subdue him."

"General, you're an idiot!" Houseman replied as he looked at the general with disgust. He had dealt with a lot of Barnett types since he'd hit the Washington scene. They were the aristocrats of the federal bureaucracy, who were living off the system.

"Moss is just a kid, and I told you he probably wouldn't be armed," the White House chief of staff growled through clenched teeth.

"I realize you've never been in combat, Mr. Houseman," the general replied casually—with an emphasis on the *mister*.

"Don't start with that Army combat garbage," Houseman countered as he met the icy stare of the general without flinching. "I've seen more combat on the streets of Los Angeles than you've seen in Iran. You military geniuses send ten soldiers for every Arab and then act like you're fighting Hitler's storm troopers hand to hand. General, a George Patton you ain't! Now shut up and get out of my office. You make me sick!"

Lieutenant General Stanton Barnett was not accustomed to

having anyone talk to him like that. He had the urge to reach across the desk and throttle the smaller man, but then he thought better of it. *No*, he decided, *I'll wait my chance. More battles are won through strategy than through direct assault. One day the military will wake up and take over this country like I knew we should have when Rand was elected.*

Barnett gathered his reports and stuffed them back into the worn attaché case. He started to exit, but then he turned and said, "You may think you're in control, but I've seen amateurs like you come and go in Washington. When the right people wake up to your agenda, they'll toss you and your Hollywood friends right out on your collective pointed heads. And when they do, I'll be there to cheer them on." Then he ducked out the door before Houseman could respond.

In reality, Roger Houseman was not thinking of any response. He already had made up his mind that Barnett had to go. At one time he had argued with Rand against "offing" the general (as Rand was prone to say). But now he realized that Barnett was not just a liability in his current position; if he were free to roam the files of the EPA, he could do irreparable damage.

Houseman called a number at the CIO. When the tone signaled that the code interpreter was connected, he punched in a predetermined four-digit code. At the other end of the line the code was written down, memorized, and then the note was shredded. On the desk was a handwritten sign that simply said: DAMAGE CONTROL. The agent in charge punched another code into the commercial pocket pager system.

In the public housing unit on Clinton Boulevard, a shrill alarm went off on the pager worn by "Boss" Davison, who led the "Greens," as they were known because of their financial ties to the Rand administration. A well-organized and well-financed street gang, the Greens often were used to execute opposing politicians and others.

Davison called the number that appeared on his pager and listened to the message. He was given the name and was sent a fax photo of his target. He recognized the name, and even if he hadn't been sent the photo he would have known General Stanton Barnett, director of the EPA.

"Man, the wolves are really hungry tonight," he quipped to his companions. "We get to do an Army general. He's on Pennsylvania Avenue now. We'll catch him on Fifth when he heads for home."

Stanton Barnett had just rounded the corner onto Fifth Street when he noticed the seedy-looking teens waiting on the corner.

Almost by instinct he reached under the front seat, where he always carried a service revolver. *Just a bunch of punk kids,* he thought to himself, *but you never know these days.*

He was still sweeping his hand under the seat when two distinct realizations struck him: His gun was gone, and two of the gang members were aiming TAARS, target access rockets, at his car. His mind reached back into his military training days when he had fired a TAARS: a hand-held, wire-guided rocket containing a depleted uranium explosive head. The TAARS was capable of destroying an armor-plated tank.

The last thought General Barnett had was, *Now where did those punks get their hands on a TAARS?*

The next day the papers reported the death of General Barnett as just one of a growing number of assaults by well-armed teenage gangs in the D.C. area. President Rand ordered a full military sweep of the D.C. housing projects in search of weapons recently stolen from the national guard armory in Maryland.

During the sweep, several arrests were made; tenants were caught with a variety of handguns hidden in their apartments. Conveniently, the complex that housed Davison and his gang was missed during the raids.

Later that evening, on national television, President Rand demanded a congressional inquiry panel to require the removal and destruction of all military weapons held by the state guard units outside the control of the federal government.

Early the next day, Houseman was seated in front of the president's desk, briefing him on developments in the Moss investigation. "The Moss kid died," Houseman reported. "He never recovered consciousness."

"We have to know who he talked to, Roger," the president said as he paced the Oval Office.

"We're doing everything we can," Houseman replied for the fourth time in as many minutes. *He's losing it,* Houseman thought. *This whole THOR thing is making him nuts.*

"I don't understand the urgency. Even if someone has the THOR documents, it's unlikely anyone really would believe them. Besides, that's been nearly fifty years ago, and we have a cadre of scientists lined up to refute anything that might be made public. I know I can handle . . ."

"No!" Rand snapped. "I want this thing buried once and for all. It should have been done years ago."

Exasperated, Houseman started to respond. "But, Mr. Pres . . ."

The president broke in angrily, "You don't seem to understand. We're right on the verge of taking the next big step in the movement. We can't afford to spend the time and energy it would take to defend this thing. And remember, we've spent nearly three trillion dollars on phasing out freon and reducing industrial emissions. There are about eight million unemployed people who might want to know why, if that report is made public."

What's the next step? Houseman asked himself. For the first time, he began to feel nervous. He had assumed that once the "Greens" had political control they would simply become another political party, and he would be their "spin doctor." He had spun a lot of dreams on the screen; he knew he could do the same in politics. But now he realized that Rand, or somebody, had a bigger plan than just becoming a third party. He needed answers, but first he needed to calm down this actor-turned-president.

"Why not just come right out and call project THOR a Republican hoax?" Houseman countered. "Remember, our best defense is always a good offense. We whitewashed a lot of other things we knew were going to be leaked."

"There are a lot of skeletons in the closets," Rand muttered as he paced the room, "but none as big as this one. No, we have to stop this thing."

"I really don't understand the details of this THOR project. Wasn't it just another aboveground nuclear test like the ones we used against the Democrats?"

"I can't tell you any of the details," Rand said firmly. "I'm not sure I know them all myself, but I do know the Society has decided this information should be contained at all costs."

The Society again, Houseman thought to himself. *That's the third time Rand has alluded to that one-world group he's a part of. He's always been a little wacky, but now he's beginning to sound even more paranoid.*

"I really don't know what else we can do at this point, Mr. President. We're running checks on everyone Moss knew. The only glitch so far is that one of the EPA division supervisors didn't show up for work today."

Suddenly Rand was alert and his eyes narrowed. "Was it someone close to Moss?"

"Possibly. Moss was pretty new but, by coincidence, the missing supervisor was in charge of an enforcement unit during the Oregon riots, and Moss was assigned to his team. We have men on the way to his apartment now. We'll have some feedback in a few minutes—

probably nothing more than the typical government 'sluff-off,' though. About ten percent of the office staff don't show up for work regularly, and there are so many of them with nothing to do, nobody really cares."

▲

In the apartment of Dale Crawford, the FBI agents were making a thorough sweep of the room for anything that might link Crawford to Moss. After more than twenty minutes, they had found nothing out of the ordinary.

"So what do you think?" the agent asked his supervisor.

"Well, for sure, there's nothing here . . . I think Crawford has skipped."

"Why?" the younger agent asked.

"Nothin' positive. Just something you feel when you've been at this business as long as I have. It looks like he just picked up his coat and walked out. And there's one other thing too."

"What's that?"

"How long you been in the bureau?"

"About three years now. Why?"

"Do you have any coupons stashed at your place?"

"Sure. If you don't, you can't buy anything in this town."

"Exactly! But Crawford's place is clean; not one coupon in the whole place. I think he took his stash and ran."

"Any chance we can find out what coupons he had?"

"I doubt it," the older man replied. "The only person a government worker trusts less than a politician is a federal agent, so it'll be hard to find anyone who will admit selling the counterfeit coupons. Who knows? Crawford may even have some phoney IDs, if he's smart enough. I know I keep a set on hand. You just never know in this town."

The younger agent made a mental note to buy a set of phoney IDs the next time he saved up the price. *You really don't know whose list you may show up on in Washington,* he reminded himself.

As soon as the agents reported in, FBI Director Lamar Yule called Houseman. "Mr. Houseman, my agents checked out Crawford's apartment, and they both agree that he's on the run," Yule said excitedly. "I've already issued a nationwide APB. We've sealed off the trains and faxed his photo to all the units in the east."

"Fax a set to Colorado and Wyoming too," Houseman ordered.

"Why there?" Yule asked without thinking.

"Just do it!" Houseman snapped. He had a sinking feeling in the pit of his stomach. *Crawford has the THOR documents, and he also knows about Wells.*

Houseman knew it was important to handle the link to Wells without any further involvement of Washington personnel. *Wells is a national hero,* he thought grimly. *It wouldn't do to get him involved—nor Galt either for that matter.*

But inside, Houseman had the same uneasy feeling he had sensed earlier. *Our government is being run by a group of nuts, and Rand is the nuttiest. This isn't a real nice place to live now, and they're about to make it a lot worse. I think I need to make some copies of our president's private conversations. It wouldn't do to be the "odd man out" in this town.*

7

△

Escape
from
Washington

Crawford knew that he would have no more than a few hours to escape from Washington. Once the FBI and/or the CIO drew the net over the city, he would be no better off than Andy Moss was. So the first decision he made was to take the subway to Virginia. At least his options would be better there, or so he hoped.

Once he had a chance to sit and relax on the train, he realized that quite possibly the security police wouldn't know of his involvement yet. But it wouldn't take long before he would become a suspect. Fortunately, with the normal absenteeism of federal employees, he would be just one of several missing in his own branch, so it might take them awhile to sort him out of the other absentees. *Besides,* he concluded, *what other choices do I have?*

Dale knew the times and routes of most of the federal employee trains in and out of Washington. He had lived in a variety of places outside of the city until he built up enough seniority to qualify for an apartment in town.

He transferred from the federal employee express to a public transportation train in Arlington and headed toward Richmond. He used general issue transportation coupons for each train; and by merging with the normal daytime passengers, he was fairly certain he hadn't been noticed.

Fortunately, he'd been wearing blue jeans and a windbreaker when he left his apartment, so when he reached Richmond he looked just like any one of the hundreds of men milling around the streets. *Wow, I don't remember this many people being out of work the last time I was in Richmond,* he thought to himself. *I wonder what it must be like in some of the big cities? There must be hundreds of thousands of unemployed there.*

After checking the schedules for westward-bound trains, he discovered that there was only one interstate train a day out of Richmond. That train would take him to New Orleans, where he would have to transfer again. When he approached the ticket window the clerk asked, "Where to?"

"Austin . . . Texas . . . by way of New Orleans," he replied. Obviously he was not going to Austin, but he decided it would be a good idea to disguise his route whenever possible.

"What's your authorization code?" the crabby sounding clerk demanded.

Panic gripped him as he realized he had completely forgotten about the Federal Travel Regulation Act. To conserve energy, the Act had been passed to restrict interstate travel. It didn't apply to government employees, so he never had been restricted in his travel since the law was enacted; but he didn't have a civilian authorization code. They usually were authorized only for priority citizens with high level government contacts.

Thinking quickly, he responded, "Ah nuts! I left my authorization in my briefcase at home."

"Well, you can't get a ticket without an authorization code," the clerk replied mechanically.

"I'll have to go back and get it," Crawford mumbled as he backed away from the window. As he left, he heard the clerk muttering, "Stupid civilians! You have to tell them how to breathe. . . ."

Crawford began to feel the pangs of fear creeping over him again. He was playing a dangerous game from which there was no turning back. He had no illusions that he simply could repent and all would be forgiven. He either had to run or be caught. And every hour he spent in any one place increased his risk of being caught.

He always had heard that desperate men do desperate things, and now he understood the real meaning of that old cliché. But what desperate thing could he do? It was not as simple as stealing a ride on a train, like some of the homeless often did. If they were caught, they usually were thrown off the moving train.

He'd seen the bodies of several of those who'd been caught hiding on the commuter trains; they lay sprawled along the tracks where they'd been thrown. He had no desire to become just another casualty of a crime-hardened society. He also had no doubt that interstate trains would be more carefully watched than the commuters he used to ride.

Then the reality struck him: *This is all about control. All travel is restricted, as well as jobs, food . . . everything. We have given our freedoms away, one at a time—all in the name of security and comfort. Now they have us all boxed up nicely in our own little worlds—separate from each other and each group pitted against the other.*

Crawford knew that it would do no good to continue feeling like a victim of circumstances. He was really beginning to get angry—with himself and with those who would do this to other Americans. *No wonder so many people feel angry,* he thought. *They feel powerless.*

Then he had an idea: *If I can't get an interstate ticket, I'll just go as far as I can in each state and then walk to the next station.* As he thought about it, he concluded it was not a great idea, but he was fresh out of choices. He hurried back to the train depot. He knew he wouldn't be able to get a ticket from the same clerk without raising suspicions, so he would have to wait for the next shift.

After nearly three hours, the clerk was replaced by another ticket agent. After the first clerk left, Dale went in and approached the window.

"May I help you?" the young woman asked pleasantly.

She must be a new employee, Dale thought sarcastically. *She's far too nice to have worked for the government very long.* He wondered if the civilians he had come in contact with thought about him in the same way. *Probably,* he decided. *I was a jerk too, I suspect. Maybe what government employees need is a good dose of unemployment.*

"I need a ticket to Sulphur Springs," Dale told the agent.

"Do you have a coupon?" the girl asked.

"Yes I do," he said as he handed her the counterfeit coupon. The thought of her detecting the counterfeit knotted up his stomach a little, but he knew there was an unwritten code among the lower level government employees that all such coupons would be accepted without question. If the authorities initiated a coupon sweep, as they sometimes did, the word would go out well in advance so that only valid coupons would be used during that time. Dale often had laughed with the others about how the whole thing was a big farce.

The young woman accepted the coupon without question and issued the ticket, jotting a note on the pad beside her. "Will you be staying in Sulphur Springs long?" she asked.

"Probably not. I'm looking for a job and heard there was an opening at the recycling facility there."

"Well, good luck!" she responded cheerfully.

"Thanks," he said as he walked toward the station platform.

There was no way Dale Crawford could have known that his decision to limit his travel to one state at a time was the one idea that neither the CIO or the FBI would consider. Once his involvement was determined, both agencies assumed he had been in on the supposed espionage plot from the beginning and, therefore, would have arranged a safe escape in the event the plot was discovered.

They had alerted all the train stations within three hundred miles to be on the lookout for anyone of his description buying a ticket to any western state. Since the Richmond station lacked a laser fax machine, his photo would not be available until the next morning.

Later, when the fax photo did come in, the ticket agent hardly glanced at it. She didn't remember anyone of that description heading west.

The next few days became a lifetime of education for the former government bureaucrat. After taking the first train to the northwestern edge of Virginia, he was confronted by a government-operated trailer city of almost unreal proportions.

He had exited the train at the Challagon stop, just prior to the Sulphur Springs station. If the FBI was searching for him, he reasoned that he would be less likely to be spotted if he avoided the bigger towns. Conversations with several of the other passengers had confirmed that anyone without an interstate authorization would be put off at the border stops.

The federal government assumed this authority, he recalled, *based on the interstate commerce clause in the Constitution. I doubt that the founders of the nation intended for U.S. citizens to be considered trade goods if they passed from one state to another. But I guess the revenue from interstate authorizations was too lucrative to turn down.*

As Crawford made his way along the virtually unused road into Sulphur Springs, he realized the plight of most law-abiding citizens. The tax on private automobiles was nearly $10,000 per year now; and compressed natural gas to fuel a car was nearly $10 per gallon, if you could get it at all. Only the federal government was authorized under the Clean Water and Clean Air acts to own and operate gas dispensing stations.

This erosion of freedoms hadn't happened in a year—or even in five. It had been a steady erosion of constitutional rights that allowed the federal government to tax the citizens of the states and then send a portion of their money back to the states by way of government grants.

Once they were hooked on the government handouts, the threat of withholding those funds forced virtually all of the states to acquiesce to federal demands. States that didn't join the team found themselves stripped of all government contracts, grants, and ultimately Social Security and welfare funds.

This last move by the federal tacticians brought even the most belligerent states to heel. The elderly voters, who outnumbered the younger ones by three to one, simply threatened to replace all non-compliant politicians.

Little did the elderly who voted to accept total federal control realize that they would eventually end up in trailer towns like the one sprawled out before him in Sulphur Springs. When the federal funds began to run out and hyperinflation set in, the elderly lost everything. There were virtually no jobs for the young and healthy —much less the old and ill.

Even worse, the ever-escalating violence had turned many cities into burnt-out hulks, overrun with gangs and drugs. Most of the tenants of the government-furnished trailer cities had no place to go back to. And since passage of the Rand Relocation Act, designed to "protect" the displaced homeless, all subsidies were linked to the relocation program.

The people who were assigned to the relocation centers were free to leave or stay, as they desired, but to leave meant losing all government subsidies, with little hope of recovering them once removed from the dole. So they stayed—living in nineteenth century conditions.

In the small community of Sulphur Springs, nearly fifteen hundred people had been crowded into what might have been called a concentration camp if the gates had not been left open.

As Dale entered the complex, he almost gagged. The dirty streets were bordered on each side by ditches, strong with the pungent odor of raw sewage. As more and more people were crowded into the complex, the sanitation system was overwhelmed, and the ditches served as the emergency overflow system. Judging by the awful smell, Dale surmised the overflow was in frequent use.

These are Third World conditions, he noted. *How can a government that professes to be environmentally "correct" tolerate these conditions?*

He saw a drawn and bent old woman sitting in front of her trailer, rocking back and forth on a hard wooden chair. Something about her motion triggered a remote memory inside him. *What was that?* he asked himself as he stopped to stare. The old woman didn't seem to notice him. She just continued to rock back and forth, making no sound at all.

Then he remembered: It was the same rocking motion he had seen in the environmental films that showed caged animals. This motion, known as the submission reflex, was attributed to the animals' total lack of hope. It was the key component used in the animal rights movement to free all the zoo animals. *Where are the human rights activists?* he wondered.

As he tramped on through the depressing scene, he noticed the community was made up primarily of the elderly and the very young. Hundreds of children played in and around open sewage. *The disease in this place has to be rampant,* he realized. Then the truth struck him. It was something he had heard from some of the more radical environmentalists in his group: population control.

The "Green" radicals had often contended that if the world were to be saved, the population needed to be reduced. They also had suggested something that Dale always had assumed was just wild talk: Only disease could reduce the world's population sufficiently to exact the toll needed.

This place is a breeding ground for diseases that have been virtually eliminated in America for more than a hundred years, he realized.

Suddenly a jeep skidded around the corner, sliding to a stop in the mud in front of him. It was loaded with armed, tough- looking teens being led by an older man. Dale attempted to duck between two trailers, but his exit was blocked by other teens, each carrying semiautomatic weapons.

As the jeep skidded to a halt, only inches from him, the leader of the group jumped out, screaming obscenities. Among the four-letter words was the question, "Who are you and what are you doing in my town?"

"I'm just passing through," Dale mumbled as he tried to regain some sense of composure.

"Don't nobody pass through my town without paying the toll," the man shouted in Dale's face. "I think I'm gonna kill you, just to teach you a lesson." With that he ratcheted the bolt on his weapon and stuck the muzzle under Dale's chin.

Dale was nearly paralyzed by fear, but he knew if he had any chance at all, he had to act normal, or as normal as possible within the circle of drugged-up gang members. He remembered some of the stories about gang members being used by the government to run the inner cities. Probably this group was an enforcement arm of the government in the trailer city as well.

"I don't think that would be very wise," Dale said with as much gusto as he could muster.

"Oh yeah? Why not? You gonna call the cops or somethin'?"

"No, but I'm a part of an EPA enforcement team," Dale lied. He knew he was taking a chance, linking himself with the group he was trying to escape. But the EPA was what he knew the most about, and he was fairly certain this group would respect the agency's authority.

Suddenly the group leader's belligerent attitude changed, if only slightly. "You lie, man," he accused. "You're not a part of any EPA team. Where's the rest of your unit?"

"I'm a scout doing background checks to see if the enforcement teams need to be called in. We've had reports from this area that your guys have been riding the locals too hard."

"That's a lie, man. Whoever said that is a liar. I only do what I'm told."

His shift in tone told Dale his ploy was working. "Then why did you try to assault me? Are you in the habit of killing anyone who passes through?"

"I wasn't really gonna kill you, man," the rattled gang leader now argued. "I was just funnin' ya. Besides, how do we know you're really with the EPA?"

Dale decided to play his trump card. He reached into his coat pocket and pulled out the phoney ID he'd bought several months earlier. It showed that he was an agent of the EPA on assignment with a CIO enforcement unit. He knew this agency could call for a government assault on any gang or other illegal group.

The man glanced at the credentials and stepped back to say something to his companions. Then he waved Dale on and jumped back in the jeep. "We don't want no trouble, man," he shouted as he roared away. "You tell 'em that."

Although shaken by the incident, Crawford was also encouraged. He had bluffed his way through what, clearly, was a gang attempt at robbery and, probably, murder. He had no doubt about the sincerity of the threat. From what he had seen over the last few weeks, life was a pretty cheap commodity in America.

Conditions in the rambling slums made up of poorly constructed and rundown trailers were appalling. The stench of the sewage nearly made him gag, especially when he saw some kids retrieve a soccer ball from the open ditch.

Where are the families? he wondered. *There seems to be only the old and the young.* But at least he didn't see any more gang members. *Probably passed the word to stay away from the EPA guy,* he thought with contempt. *They're brave enough when they can bully innocent people, but they don't want to face a well-armed government enforcement team.*

Then he remembered that it was the government he had served that had created the situation these people were in now. *It's hard to believe this all started with welfare and Social Security,* he thought angrily. *Noble ideas that should have been abandoned back in the nineties. We've raised a generation that has no respect for life or property, and now they're in charge.*

Dale made his way through the maze of trailers and into Sulphur Springs. *Better to stay on the side streets,* he decided. *It's not likely the FBI or CIO would have field agents in such a small town, but it is likely the streets are patrolled by gangs; and dead is dead, no matter who fires the shots. I'll bet these people live in terror. It's bad enough in Washington, but at least the police control the streets in the daytime there. It's amazing what freedoms people will give up to feel a little safer.*

He shook his head as he thought about all the gun control legislation that had been passed. *Most of the ordinary people have been disarmed or put in prison for resisting. Gun control doesn't help them a lot, but it sure makes the world a safer place for the criminals. Now the gangs roam the streets with impunity—especially since they work hand in hand with the government.*

It took Dale nearly an hour to make his way through Sulphur Springs. He stopped only once to buy a quick lunch with one of his many student coupons. When the salesgirl looked at him with a questioning eye he volunteered, "I teach at American University, so I swap coupons with the students." The girl smiled knowingly. She understood the system well: Cheat wherever you can.

The next few days were spent on trains, crossing from one state border to another. Sometimes he would take a northern route; other times he would head southwest. He hoped that if anyone happened across his trail they would not know his future moves.

He was beginning to gain confidence in himself. He had eluded the most determined government agencies in the country with little more than his brains, a few counterfeited coupons, and a couple of phony IDs.

One thing he realized from the time he had spent in government service was that most of those who had never worked outside the government had an arrogance about them and a total disdain for "civilians," as they usually referred to those who paid their salaries. *It's that arrogance that makes the system vulnerable.*

He had no illusions that the CIO and FBI employees were as inept as those he had worked with at the EPA, but in the final analysis it was the Greenies who called the shots in the Rand administration. For the first time, he began to believe he might actually make it.

I don't know how I'll get to Dr. Wells, but that's a decision I'll have to make if I get there. No, when I get there, he corrected himself.

8

△

Cornered

The search for Crawford was intensifying. When the FBI hadn't found any trace of him in the days immediately after the Moss incident, at the president's command, Houseman had called out the hounds.

"I don't want excuses from the FBI," Rand snapped at his chief of staff. "I want that man found. You put every available agent between here and California on it! Are you sure there's been no activity on his account?"

"None," Houseman replied matter-of-factly. He knew Crawford was no fool. *He's found a way to elude the biggest manhunt in American history.*

"We'll get him," Houseman said with assurance. "There are only so many places he can hide. Maybe he's just holed up somewhere, but I don't think so. I suggest that we put out a one hundred thousand dollar reward. That'll bring the gangs into the search."

"No!" Rand said firmly. "Those idiots would kill him. I want him alive! We have to bury this THOR thing once and for all. I want to know who he's talked to. Put as many men as you need on this, but find him!"

For the last several days, FBI agent Harold Fields, assigned to the Hot Springs, Arkansas, office, had been following with interest the field communiqués about Crawford. The bulletins identified Crawford as an EPA supervisor who had stolen some top secret documents that could threaten national security.

As the manhunt intensified, the bulletins raised the priority, until now every available agent was being diverted to conduct a door-to-door search of a twelve-state region. Agents with fax photos of Crawford were being sent to virtually every business in every city.

What the heck could be so secret at the EPA that it would threaten national security? Fields wondered. *Maybe they've uncovered a plot by the civilians to mug a bunch of trees,* he mused, laughing at his own joke. *These tree huggers are a weird bunch. You can't own a fur coat, and you can't build a wooden house anymore. What's this country coming to?* he wondered. *Oh well, mine is not to reason why.*

Fields doubted that a dragnet would be effective once Crawford had been on the loose more than a few days. *He's either holed up, or he's got some kind of a plan. If he's holed up in one of the cities, he'll eventually be caught, and he must know that.*

Agent Fields had his own theory, but he wasn't about to tell any of his supervisors. Most of them were college kids attached to the Rand administration. He'd seen virtually all of the FBI's senior staff either retired or reassigned to positions in which they no longer had control over the field agents.

"These kids think they know everything," he noted sarcastically. More than once in an investigation he had been frustrated to find out that his supervisor had screwed up the whole case by using illegal search-and-seizures. Some liberal judges would overlook illegally obtained evidence, but there were still some judges who threw the cases out.

No, Fields decided, *I'll do it my way this time.*

There actually had been two possible sightings of Crawford out of the hundreds reported. One was in a small camptown just outside of Sulphur Springs, Virginia, where some local auxiliary law enforcers (*hoodlums,* Fields thought) said they had a run-in with someone from the EPA enforcement group. The EPA said they had no such person in the area.

Fields knew it could just be a civilian who got some credentials for protection. *I'd do the same myself if necessary. But it very likely could've been Crawford.*

Then there was a second contact with someone fitting Crawford's description in Ashport, Tennessee. A local policewoman spotted a man walking across the bridge into Arkansas. When she stopped him, his story was that he was looking for work. He had a teacher's ID from American University. That was before the general APB went out, and she had no particular reason to hold him.

A lot of people cross into adjacent states, Fields thought, *in spite of the federal regulation requiring a pass and registration. Americans aren't used to being treated like cattle. They'll beat the system if they can.*

Fields had his own theory: *Crawford is probably headed west. He lacks the proper credentials to ride the interstate trains, so he rides to the state border, walks across the state line, and picks up another ride. Pretty bright guy, if that's what he's doing,* Fields thought appreciatively. *If my theory is true, he'll probably catch a train in Blythesville, Arkansas—headed west, more or less. It'll be worth a trip to Blythesville. Maybe someone there will remember seeing him. And just maybe I can find out what train he took.*

Traveling in America was not easy, even for an FBI agent. Fields had a car, of sorts, assigned to him, but he knew that finding available natural gas stations in Arkansas was no small thing. The ten-year-old car had the better part of 200,000 miles on it, and although originally it had been made to run on gasoline, the gas tank had been removed and replaced with an L.P. gas cylinder.

He had no authorization to go to Blythesville, and he knew the punk kid who called himself Fields' supervisor would have a fit when he found out. "So let him," Fields said flatly. *I'm about fed up with this garbage anyway. And besides,* he thought, *if I'm right he'll have a hard time giving me a reprimand.*

Fields realized that he wouldn't have enough ration coupons to buy the fuel he needed. He briefly thought about getting the bureau involved but quickly decided that his politically connected supervisor would probably get all the credit. "No," he said aloud, "Crawford's not the only one who knows how to beat the system."

He stopped by his apartment to retrieve his most precious possession: a carefully counterfeited fuel coupon book. Fields had taken it off of a black marketer he had arrested several months earlier. It had enough coupons to travel across the country if necessary. He knew the risk in using the ration book. Such things were carefully monitored by the EPA regulators. There was always a possibility they would link the coupons to him. *But what the heck,* he told himself. *Once I catch Crawford I'll be untouchable.*

It always irritated Fields to stop and fill the natural gas tank on the car. It took nearly half an hour, and he knew the net savings in emissions was virtually nil. For a long while after the EPA required that all cars be capable of burning natural gas, there had been the option of using gasoline too. But, as with all things in the environmental movement, the alternative use was only a temporary step.

Later, when the EPA had banned virtually all gasoline storage and dispensing equipment, it became compressed natural gas or nothing. Interestingly enough, by then the major U.S. oil distributors could have cared less. They were able to sell all their crude oil on the Asian market, and coincidentally they had the natural gas market locked up in the U.S. Besides, with the ban on any new oil development in the U.S., the native supply of oil was dwindling down to a trickle.

Unfortunately for American workers, the combination of travel restrictions, emission controls, and escalating energy costs had all but killed the car companies. GM was still building some mass transit vehicles, but Ford and Chrysler had both moved to China, where business was booming. The riots in Michigan had gutted the cities. *Such is life,* Fields mused, *but it sure makes my job more secure.*

He made his way across the state, barely stretching his fuel from one station to the next. *Stupid system!* he thought angrily after almost running out of fuel. *Barely enough stations open to reach the next one.* Finally he worked his way over to Blythesville. He started his search at the train depot.

Fields was a thorough agent and his tenacity paid off. He checked with every ticket agent in Blythesville, showing each of them the fax photo of Crawford. Finally one agent responded: "I think I saw this man, but he seemed older and had a heavy growth of whiskers."

"That probably would be right," Fields said. "He may not have shaved for a while. Where was he going?"

"Just a minute," the agent said as she went to her ticket booth. "I sold him a ticket to Van Buren, I think."

"Try carefully to remember," Fields said gently. "This could be very important."

"Yes, it was Van Buren. I'm sure. I remember that he talked about being out of work. He had an ID from Washington—a schoolteacher or something I think. We have a lot of unemployed coming through here. As long as he didn't want to travel out of state, he could buy a ticket."

"I know," Fields agreed. *Dumb system,* he told himself again. *You can't ride a train from one state to another, but once you're there the system assumes you have a right to be. Typical Washington logic! It's a federal matter if you travel on an interstate commerce line, but it's a state matter if you walk across the border.*

Fields jumped back in his car and headed west—not to Van Buren, but to Muldrow, Oklahoma, the next junction for any westward-bound trains, according to the schedule he had gotten in Blythesville.

"I've got you, Mr. Crawford." Fields smirked as he drove away. He rolled the driver's window down to escape as much of the blistering heat as possible in the dark sedan. Theoretically, the car had air conditioning, but the latest environmentally safe coolant he had used in the system had dissolved the plastic seals in the compressor, and it had stopped working long ago.

Fields counted on being able to reach Muldrow ahead of Crawford, since the train stopped at virtually every whistle-stop along the way. Some of the through trains moved faster, but usually the seats were taken by government employees and maybe a few civilian dignitaries.

Once in Muldrow, Fields found that the train he assumed Crawford was on had already passed through. *Obviously he would have gotten off that train in Arkansas*, Fields surmised. So he decided to stake out the depot in Muldrow and wait. *If Crawford has bought a ticket west, he'll try to catch the next train.* He thought about alerting the ticket agents in Muldrow but decided against it. *If Crawford is hiding out and watching, it will just arouse his suspicions*, he reasoned.

In fact, Dale Crawford had already purchased his next ticket. He had exited the train in Arkansas and walked across the Oklahoma border, but because of a dispute between the state custom officials, the train from Blythesville had been stopped at the border after Crawford departed. Fields didn't know about that and, therefore, didn't know that Crawford had beaten the train to the station.

Fields sat in his car two blocks from the train depot and carefully screened every customer in and out of the station. Muldrow was such a small town, there were very few travelers. He looked at his watch for the hundredth time. The next train was due in less than fifteen minutes. *If Crawford's coming, he should have bought his ticket by now.*

For the first time he began to doubt his own conclusions. If Crawford didn't show, Fields knew he was in deep trouble. It was one thing to face an irate supervisor with Crawford in hand. It would be quite another to go back empty-handed. *That kid will have my head in a basket,* he told himself. The anger inside him began to swell again. "Absurd system, stupid government, witless kids," he muttered sourly.

Just then a shrill whistle sounded, startling him. The train was just coming into sight around the bend, and the few people who were waiting on the platform began to rustle around. Suddenly Fields noticed a figure appear from behind one of the adjacent buildings.

"Bingo!" he said aloud. "Right height, right description. That's him all right."

Fields got out of his car and headed toward the station. He walked as casually as he could, hoping not to spook his target, but Crawford had been on the run long enough now to be very cautious. His inner sense clicked in and he glanced up the street. He caught sight of a man with a large paunch and spotted the parked car all at the same time. His brain made the connection, and he turned back toward the alley where he'd been waiting.

Fields saw Crawford look in his direction, then turn and head back down the street. "Nuts," he muttered. "He's made me." He thought about pulling his gun and ordering the man to halt. *But that only happens in the movies,* he told himself. *The last thing I need is to arouse the locals. Too many of them hate anyone from the government. Somebody might just decide to take a shot at me.*

So Fields hurried his pace. He was between his quarry and the train. He knew Crawford had nowhere to go, and it was a long walk to anywhere from Muldrow.

Dale Crawford felt the panic rise up in his throat as he ducked into the alley. He was sure the man was a government agent— probably FBI. *Even if I could get out of town, I have nowhere else to run. The FBI will be all over me as soon as this agent reports in.*

Fields turned the corner just as Crawford was coming out of the alley. "Halt!" he ordered as softly as he could and still be heard by the fleeing man.

Instead, Crawford took off running. He had no hope of escape but also no other choices. The thought of what awaited him raced through his mind. *They can't let me live. I know too much.* Panic swelled over him. He couldn't think clearly. All he knew was that he had to run—as fast and as far as he could.

Fields reached for his service automatic; then he thought better of it. He might wing Crawford and stop him, but if he missed and killed him, he'd be back in the same mess with his supervisor. He stuffed the gun into his shoulder holster and took off running after the younger man.

Neither of them was in particularly good shape, but Crawford was younger and also spurred on by pure fear. Within two blocks Fields was puffing. *I should have gotten the car*, he told himself angrily. *I'm too out of shape for this.* Crawford was running toward a small group of buildings just at the edge of the town, with Fields in hot pursuit.

The action had not gone unnoticed. José Creol, the lone member of the Crips gang from Tulsa, assigned to Muldrow and three other small towns in Oklahoma, had seen Crawford take off and had heard Fields order him to stop. He immediately worked his way to the end of the street, where he knew the first runner had to exit. When Crawford ran past him, he simply stuck out his foot and tripped him.

Crawford tried desperately to regain his balance, but he was going too fast to recover, and he hit the street tumbling. When he stopped rolling, he lay still—somewhat out of shock from the fall but also out of pure fright.

The puffing Fields reached the spot where Crawford had fallen. "Thanks," he said between heavy breaths. "I was about done in." He started over to where Crawford was laying.

"Uno momento, my friend," the grinning Creol said to Fields. "What is thees all about? Why do you chase thees man?"

"I'm a federal agent," Fields said cautiously. He had heard stories about the animosity between some gangs and their assumed authority. An enforcement team might be safe enough, but all too often a single agent was considered "fair game."

"What kind of agent are you?" the aggressive youth demanded. Even as he spoke his hand was sliding down to the Chinese AK-50 slung around his shoulder—the favorite of street gangs throughout the country.

Seeing the move, Fields decided that any further conversation was useless, and he grabbed for his automatic just as Creol raised the AK-50. The explosion from both weapons was virtually simultaneous, except that Fields was obviously the better marksman. His first shot struck true, and Creol was killed almost instantly, but the reflex of his movement squeezed the trigger on the gang leader's assault rifle, and fifteen rounds were fired even before he hit the ground. Three of those rounds struck Fields—the last severing an artery inside the chest wall and penetrating the lung.

Crawford had observed the whole scene while pretending to be unconscious, but once the shots were fired he bolted to his feet. He ran ten feet or so before he looked back and saw the young Latino motionless on the ground. The FBI man then stumbled forward and fell.

His first reflex was to continue to run—to escape what had at first appeared to be certain capture. But as he looked back again, he could see the agent was still alive, though badly wounded. He turned back to see if he could help the man.

Kneeling beside the wounded agent, Crawford could see that he was in bad shape. Blood was showing at the side of his mouth. Somewhere in his memory he recalled that blood from the mouth indicated a lung wound.

"How bad am I hit?" Fields asked.

"Pretty bad I think," Crawford replied honestly. "Maybe a lung puncture."

"Too bad." Fields coughed. "Probably wouldn't have collected my pension anyway though. Are you Crawford?"

"Yes. Who are you?"

"Harold Fields, FBI. What's this all about anyway?"

"It's a long story, but I can tell you this: I didn't do anything wrong. I tried to help a friend who had some information the government doesn't want known. I think they had him killed, and they're willing to kill me to keep it secret."

"No, they want you alive," Fields rasped. "There's a strict no-shoot order out for you."

"If I'm captured, it's about the same thing. They probably want to know if I've talked to anyone else first."

"You could be right." The agent coughed, spitting up more blood. "Will what you've got hurt Rand and his crowd?"

"It would seem so, or they wouldn't have half the country out looking for me."

Fields coughed weakly. He could feel his energy slipping away with each breath. "Look . . . I hate that whole crowd. I'm not going to make it . . . but maybe I can help you."

"How?" Crawford asked, puzzled.

"You'll find a gas coupon book in my coat pocket. It's phoney, but it'll do. Nobody knows I'm here yet. My car is parked past the depot. You take it and get out of here. Put your train coupons in my pocket. They'll think I rode the trains here. It won't stop them for long, but it might confuse them long enough for you to get away. Where you headed?"

"Wyoming, to find Dr. Jeff Wells."

"Well, good luck. I hope you give it to Rand and his bunch big time." Fields shook as he coughed again, uncontrollably. He slumped back. His heart had stopped beating.

Crawford paused a moment to gather his thoughts. *A car! And a ration book as well. It might work. At least it's better than taking trains again,* he decided. *If one FBI agent found me, others probably will too.* He fished through Fields' pockets until he found the car keys and the coupons.

He took a quick appraisal of the area to see if any of the townspeople were visible. *Nobody around,* he noted. *Can't blame them; when they hear gunfire they hide. See no evil, hear no evil,* he reminded himself as he headed back down the side streets toward the parked car.

9

△

The
Society

Crawford headed west in Fields' car, avoiding the federally controlled interstate highways. Traveling was extremely slow, since most of the side roads were virtually unmaintained. As the federal government had siphoned off more and more funds, the states had little revenue left to repair any of their own roads. Most of the surface streets in rural areas had reverted to little more than wagon trails.

It's hard to see how the country can ever recover again, Crawford realized. *The whole infrastructure of America is disintegrating.* He thought back over the many college lectures when his "politically correct" professors often ranted about returning the country to its "natural" state.

Back then he had assumed this meant preserving the forests and streams, but now he wondered if they literally meant what they had said. The whole country was in danger of going to seed, just like an uncultivated field does over time.

During the long hot days, while weaving his way west, he had plenty of time to think. Almost by accident, he'd solved the problem of fuel. The car was down to burning fumes in Kansas, with no refueling stations in sight, when he had come upon a large farm just outside of Oakley. Although he usually avoided contact with people, he had been forced to stop and ask for directions to the next refueling station.

"Don't need 'em out here," the big red-faced farmer quipped.

"What do you mean?" Crawford asked. "Surely you need fuel for your machines."

"Yep, but we process all our own fuel. Take the cow manure and make gas out of it," the farmer said with a smile. Then he took Dale through his barn and into a small shed attached to the back of his cattle feed station.

"We burn the corn stalks to heat the cow manure and it turns into methane. Then we compress the methane and use it for fuel. 'Bout every farmer I knows does the same," the amiable man said.

Just then, the compressor kicked in and Dale could see the pressure gauge on the storage tank rise appreciably. "If we didn't, we couldn't stay in business. The feds make us pay road taxes on the gas, though, the stupid jerks."

"Is there any chance I could buy some gas from you?" Crawford asked.

Suddenly the farmer was very cautious. "Just who are ya, and why do ya need to buy my gas? The government has laws against sellin' or usin' it for travel. I could go to jail!"

"I'm not from the government," Crawford assured him. "I've had some problems with the EPA and I'm trying to get back home." He hated to lie to the farmer who seemed so open with him, but he knew it wouldn't help either of them to tell the whole truth. "I have some ration coupons and some money," Crawford added.

"Listen, young man, if you're in trouble with the EPA, you gotta be all right. I'm gonna take a chance with you. The EPA has forced most of us to farm like folks did back in the eighteen hunnerds. I can't get fertilizers anymore—and just hintin' 'bout pesticides on the fields will getcha ten years in prison. I'm growin' 'bout half of what my papa did forty years ago. Half the country is shorta food, and the EPA is still worried about snails, crickets, and roaches!

"Tell you what I'm gonna do. You take whatcha need; just don't tell me 'bout it. So if anybuddy asks me, I'll just say I don't know. How far ya goin'?"

"A long way," Crawford said honestly.

"Well, son, you may find fuel hard to come by out here. The gov'ment thinks they can keep us isolated by cuttin' off our gas reserves. But I'll tell you the truth. I never saw a gov'ment man half as smart as a farmer. We have our own fuel stops all across Kansas and Nebraska. I've got two spare tanks that I fit in my old car. You take one. It'll give you another two hunnerd miles."

"I can't do that," Dale protested halfheartedly.

"Sure you can!" the big man said with a grin as he removed his straw hat and wiped the inside with a faded bandanna. "I can always git another. If things are ever gonna change, we gotta help one another."

With that, the big man climbed onto his ancient tractor, fired it up, and headed out toward his fields.

Dale spent the next thirty minutes loading his own fuel cylinder, as well as the spare tank the farmer had dropped off the back of his tractor. In exchange, he left several of his precious coupon books.

I've got enough fuel to make it to the Wyoming border, he thought excitedly. *If I can find a couple more fuel stations, I'll be close to the Wells ranch.* He thought about what the farmer had said. *People do need to help each other. We've been relying on the government too long.*

As he drove on, Crawford began trying to formulate a better plan for how to reach Jeff Wells, but none came to him. *I've been extremely lucky so far*, he reminded himself. *First the idea about the trains, then the FBI agent who helped when he was dying, now this farmer out in the middle of Kansas.*

But getting to Dr. Wells is impossible. First, I don't know exactly where his ranch is. Second, he's probably guarded as closely as the president. Third, the FBI and the CIO probably know about his link to Andy, and they'll be watching all the roads in and out of his ranch.

But even as he pondered his seemingly hopeless situation, Crawford sensed something he could not have described: hope. He had survived insurmountable odds already. Someone or something was guiding him. Call it a force . . . or maybe God; he didn't know. But he was sure he was engaged in a struggle far beyond his own ability to understand.

He shrugged his shoulders and settled back to drive through the seemingly endless plains. It was as if he were the only person alive. The deteriorating road stretched on . . . and on . . . and on.

▲

Crawford was jolted back to reality by the thump of the car as he hit another hole in the road. Two days had passed since he had met the farmer in Kansas. He had been able to locate just one fueling station since that time, and now his spare tank was almost dry. He was fatigued to the bone, and the heat was blistering. He wished he could drive at night, but the roads were too bad, and the lights might attract unwanted attention.

He had crossed into Wyoming, and the closer he got to Casper and the Wells ranch, the more he sensed that his long trip might end in failure after all. He had no idea how he ever would get close enough to talk with Wells.

▲

At the White House, tensions were mounting. When Chief of Staff Roger Houseman reported that Crawford was still on the loose, the president had ranted like a wild man.

"Pull out all the stops!" Rand shouted. "Notify the gangs that Crawford must be found. We'll offer the one hundred thousand dollar reward. If necessary, he must be killed. And, Roger, backtrack him and get rid of anyone he's had contact with," the president said with an insane look in his eyes.

This guy is definitely losing it, Houseman decided. Then he said, "I don't think that will be necessary. We can . . ."

"I don't care what you think," Rand screamed. "You're as incompetent as the rest of them. It has already been decided. I want this THOR file closed up tight. We will not tolerate another delay. Now get it done!"

Houseman made a decision as he left the Oval Office: *Time to get out. Rand has gone off the deep end. But I'll need some insurance before I depart this zoo.*

Under Rand's signature he issued the necessary orders to offer a $100,000 reward to all civilian enforcement groups for the capture of Crawford, dead or alive. He knew there would be blood in the streets of a lot of cities tonight if anyone vaguely matching Crawford's description had the misfortune to come in contact with one of the gangs.

As soon as that was done, Houseman headed down to the basement level of the White House where the hidden room he had installed, even before Rand took office, was located. When the remodeling of the White House was being done, Houseman had paid one of the contractors, a longtime personal friend, a large sum of money to install a small but well-equipped room in the basement that was little more than a large closet.

The room was so well concealed that it was impossible to detect, even if someone had known of its existence, which no one did. He locked the hallway door after him and made his way down the corridor leading to the electrical room.

A short way down the hall he stopped and pressed an electronic coder to one of the panels lining the wall. As the coder flashed green, the panel clicked open. Houseman reached inside and pressed the small button that activated the magnetically locked door. He scanned the control panel to ensure that the room had not been entered since his last visit. It hadn't.

Once inside, he set about quickly to gather the small discs that held the voice communications detected by the passive sound pick-ups in the Oval Office. He knew that with the voice recordings he would have all he needed to keep Rand and his hounds off his back. One leak of any one of the hundreds of recorded conversations would crumble the Rand presidency and maybe even collapse the government.

Houseman stuffed the discs in his pants pocket and turned to leave, but as he did he saw the movement at the doorway.

"I'm really disappointed, Roger," the president said sarcastically. "Spying on your friends is not polite."

Houseman felt his blood grow cold as he saw Rand and a shorter Oriental man standing beside him holding a 9mm automatic with a silencer attached.

"As you said, Mr. Cho," the president said softly, "you can always flush out a rat by raising the water level. I'm genuinely sorry it was you, Roger. You were a good producer."

"Wait!" Houseman protested as his mind groped for a way out.

But even as he spoke, he saw the gun wink red three times. The sound was little more than a BB gun might have made.

The Oriental retrieved the discs from Houseman's pocket and put them into his own.

"We will simply put these into one of the microwave ovens in the cafeteria," Cho said politely as he closed the hermetically sealed door. "He will give us no more trouble."

"Won't he smell if he's left in there?" Rand asked.

"No," Cho answered. "This room was well constructed. It is airtight. Perhaps they will find him in ten years, when the White House is demolished. By then we will no longer need such government structures. It was useful that we questioned all of the construction crews after one of the listening devices was discovered. We knew there had to be a recording room somewhere in the building."

"Thank you for your help, Mr. Cho," Rand said.

"It is nothing," the Oriental responded. "Our committee can not allow your efforts to be delayed or diverted. We are on the threshold of success in bringing about the United World government. Then we can take the necessary steps to bring the world's population under control. We Chinese have set the pattern for the rest of the world. We have reduced our peasant population by nearly one billion people during the last ten years."

The World Council had handpicked Robert Rand to become the president of the United States. After the failure of their plans to subdue the American people a decade earlier through the group called the Illuminati, the council had simply developed another plan.

By funding many of the more radical environmental groups in America, the World Council, more commonly called The Society, was able to direct the implementation of restrictive environmental laws. Once these laws were firmly established in the United States, they were virtually assured worldwide.

Using not-so-subtle political pressure, The Society was able to coerce virtually every industrialized nation dependent on American dole to enact rigid environmental laws.

The cost to industry worldwide had been severe. Tens of thousands of industries were driven out of the industrialized countries. In accordance with The Society's plans, many industries were relocated to China and other parts of Asia. With the phaseout of American military presence, the Chinese quickly became the dominant world economic and military power.

Only the unified nation of Korea stood in their way on the path to Japan. The Japanese people were terrified of the advancing Chinese horde, bent on revenging the atrocities inflicted by the Japanese during the twentieth century.

China represented the last great hope for world communism, relabeled democratic socialism. Like a great fungus, the Chinese absorbed every nation in their path. With the aid of the Rand government and America's still formidable nuclear submarine force, The Society was carefully orchestrating China's expansion.

Just as the unified republics of Poland, Slovakia, and Bosnia had enacted harsh retribution on their former masters in Germany and Russia during the late twentieth century, the Chinese were passionate about revenge.

Behind The Society was a group of one-world advocates with the resources and the will to see the entire world at war with each other to accomplish their ends. The United States still held the key to world unification. It rested in the absolute authority of President Rand and the four thousand nuclear weapons still under the control of the United States.

The Society knew the American people would first have to be brought to their knees: militarily, politically, and economically. The environmental movement would accomplish all three of these objectives.

▲

Dale Crawford didn't know about The Society, nor was he aware of any of the international intrigue taking place. He was trying to survive as best he could and had but one plan in mind: find Jeff Wells and deliver the THOR documents to him. But the closer he got to his goal, the more the noose tightened around his own neck. He was running out of space, and there were thousands of people searching for him now.

Reported sightings were flooding into the FBI's headquarters in Washington. As expected, twenty people fitting Crawford's description already had been killed by various gangs throughout the country. When positive ID could not be established and the bounty was not paid, gangs started riots in a dozen cities.

FBI Director Lamar Yule knew the bounty idea was counterproductive, and it forced him to divert many of the FBI's trained agents to control the gangs.

To date, nine FBI agents had been killed by disgruntled gang leaders. Yule was concerned that full-scale war might break out in the big cities again. He had no illusions that the FBI, CIO, or the EPA could rout out tens of thousands of heavily armed gangs on their home turf. In all the melee, the death of Agent Fields went unnoticed.

Washington papers reported the mysterious disappearance of White House Chief of Staff Roger Houseman. Evidence was presented to indicate that Houseman might have been kidnapped by one of the right-wing radical groups opposing the president's new environmental programs, most specifically, a religious group in Wyoming headed by Pastor John Elder.

Two events occurred that would profoundly affect Dale Crawford. First, the president was forced to assign a significant number of trained FBI and CIO personnel to the Houseman case so that it would appear to the public that he was genuinely concerned. This had the effect of further diluting the search for Crawford.

CIO Director Henry Watts was named acting chief of staff and put in charge of the Houseman investigation. He made the crucial mistake of recalling to Washington almost half of the senior field agents to direct the search for the missing Houseman. Rand was furious about the move but was forced to comply for fear it might appear he was unconcerned about his missing chief of staff.

The media made maximum use of the reported kidnapping to call for a nationwide crackdown on the religious radicals opposing the Rand reforms. Most of the media also implied that the increased crime activity in the cities was the result of right-wing terrorism.

Rand issued an emergency executive order banning all public gatherings, including religious services, during the "crisis." The liberal majority on the Supreme Court immediately confirmed the president's authority to do so under the 1976 Emergency Powers Act.

"This actually is working out better than we might have hoped," Rand said to Cho. "The chaos in the cities has given us the support we needed to shut down those stupid people. I'm sick and tired of hearing those right-wing Christians denounce my environmental program."

"Do not take these people too lightly, my young friend," Cho answered somberly. "They are dedicated and determined people. They will not surrender so easily."

"They're a bunch of idiots," Rand boasted. "They sing and pray about their pious ideas, but they grab their share of government handouts too. Their stupid religion promotes Earth pillaging. 'Subdue the Earth!' That's what I heard as a kid."

Rand continued his self-proclaimed analysis of his biggest opposition group for several more minutes, until Cho interrupted, "What about this man Crawford?"

"We'll get him," Rand replied confidently. "We know where he's headed and we're ready."

"I sincerely hope so," Cho responded coldly. "The members of The Society are quite concerned about this issue."

Rand shuddered involuntarily as Cho left. "There's something about him that makes my flesh crawl," the actor-turned-president muttered—then regretted it when he remembered the bugs that Houseman had used.

The next day, at Henry Watts' suggestion, Janet Glass was elevated to acting director of the EPA, over the stringent objections of the more conservative members of Congress.

The second event that was to aide Crawford was one that neither The Society nor President Rand had anticipated. It had actually started a year earlier, with the invasion of Korea by the Chinese People's Republic.

The Koreans had long dominated, economically and militarily, most of their Asian neighbors. Since the north and south reunification in 1998, the economy of Korea had exploded, due in great part to the massive infusion of investment funds by the Japanese. During that last decade, the Korean economy had outstripped even that of their mentors, the Japanese. The Japanese protectionist policies quickly locked the Koreans out of their markets, forcing the Koreans to shift their investment funds to China.

During the next few years, the Koreans invested more than $2 trillion in China's developing economy. But when the New Order Communists took over the government again, they confiscated all of the Korean-owned industries. The two nations had been in a state of growing animosity ever since. Two years earlier the Chinese had moved their massive armies to the Korean border and were preparing for what appeared certain to be an invasion.

Overwhelmed by sheer numbers, the Koreans had moved quickly to counter the threat by placing many short-range nuclear missiles along the border. It was clear that Korea was more than willing to engage the Chinese with tactical nuclear weapons, if necessary.

All of this posturing by two of the economic and military powers of the world had greatly upset the world's economies. The heavy investments American industrialists also had made in China put the U.S. economy in further jeopardy. With the U.S. still suffering from a decade-long depression and hyperinflation, Rand could see his support base slipping away, so he had threatened the use of U.S. submarine-based nuclear missiles on Korea if they used their weapons.

Facing the massive destructive power still available to the U.S., the Koreans had removed their missiles and attempted to repel the Chinese, using nonnuclear forces. They were quickly overwhelmed and were forced to pull back to what once had been the borders of South Korea. With the Chinese in control of the highly industrialized northern half of Korea, the Koreans dropped from being a world power to a third-world country over night.

While fruitless negotiations began with the Chinese to recover North Korea again, a militant group of Korean military officers were planning a retaliation.

KAL flight 005 from Seoul to Peking was to become a flying bomb.

10

△

The Koreans Strike

don't agree with this action," General Kim Soo said to General Hyong. "Perhaps the negotiations will progress and the Chinese will pull back from the north."

"And if they do?" the general inquired. Hyong was nearly eighty years old. He had lived through the reuniting of the north and south after the Great Liberation War of 1996. He had seen his country go from poverty to prosperity and back to poverty again, all in the span of his lifetime. He had no ideological illusions that the Chinese would relinquish their position so easily. "We will be little more than serfs to the Chinese, just as our people once were to the Japanese."

"But what you are planning is suicidal for our people," Soo protested. The younger Soo was a hero of the liberation war. He had been a captain when the war broke out, but his intellect and bravery had won him a commission to the general staff after the defeat of the communist north. He had long been promoted as the next president of the United Republic of Korea. Now he was arguing against what he believed would be the end of the Korean nation.

"Is it not better to die honorably than to live in shame?" the elder Hyong replied.

"But what about the millions who will die for something that was not of their own doing?" Soo protested. He knew the plan had already progressed too far to hope that he could stop it. Now his quandary was whether or not he should warn the targeted countries.

"In war, many innocents become victims," Hyong replied. "Did the Americans come to the rescue of our children who were sent into slavery to the north? Hardly so. It was the Americans who pressed the Chinese to invade our country—to protect their economic interests. Now they must suffer along with our people."

"You realize that I cannot sit by idly while you and the others do this horrible thing," Soo said firmly. "I respect you above all men, General Hyong, but as a Christian I cannot allow you to destroy so many to extract your revenge."

"I respect your faith, General Soo," Hyong replied honestly. "You have shown yourself to be a true loyalist, while still keeping the mandates of your God. But I serve no god; nor do the godless Americans and Chinese; they serve no gods except the gods of power. I will demonstrate our power. They may defeat us, but the price we will extract will be a fearful one."

General Soo already had the flap of his holster unsnapped when he entered the room. He also had taken the precaution of ratcheting a shell into the chamber of the weapon. But his conscience delayed his hand one second too long before he reached for the pistol. In that second, General Hyong's aide had raised his side arm and fired into the young general's head. Soo slumped to the floor.

"Take General Soo into my study," Hyong said sorrowfully. "I want him to be buried with full military honors. He was an honorable man who was willing to die for his convictions. I trust that we will be as honorable."

At six o'clock that evening, an aging KAL passenger jet rumbled off the runway from Seoul, carrying the negotiating teams bound for Peking, including General Hyong and his aides. In Hyong's lap lay the U.N. mandate requiring Korea's unilateral surrender and disarmament. He knew the U.N. was little more than the surrogate for the World Council, which had dictated the terms of Korea's surrender to the Chinese.

The Society had targeted Korea because of the tens of thousands of Christian missionaries it was sending across the globe. Christianity, as well as other religions, was actively teaching against total global unification. The lesson given the Koreans would not be missed by the rest of the world: Religion would be tolerated in the New World order only if it taught allegiance to the central government—The Society.

General Hyong sighed, "Soo and his comrades didn't realize that their very zeal for this prophet Jesus would mark our country for disaster. I wish I could have known more about his Jesus. If a man such as Soo believed he is God, perhaps he is."

The flight to Peking was timed so that it would arrive at its destination just as the U.N. delegation arrived. Hyong's plane cleared the safety corridor into Chinese territory at 9:00 A.M. It received a military escort across the mainland, just to ensure that none of the Chinese fighter pilots who detested the Koreans would shoot the plane down just for target practice. The big jet landed in Peking without ceremony.

Even as the plane lumbered to a stop at the heavily guarded terminal, technicians in the cargo compartment were making the final adjustments to the compact hydrogen bomb that had been carefully installed and shielded in a lead container days earlier—when "Project Retribution" was finalized.

A United Nations enforcement team had scoured all of the South Korean military installations to ensure that no nuclear weapons had been hidden away during the Chinese rout of the north. The documents recording the prewar inventory of weapons had been meticulously analyzed, and all nuclear warheads had been accounted for.

What the U.N. investigators hadn't anticipated was the oriental mentality. Ten years earlier, General Hyong and other military leaders had secreted several hydrogen devices in carefully concealed bunkers in the north and south. They still remembered the invasions by the Japanese and the Americans, long before the Chinese overran their country. None of the weapons appeared on any inventory list.

Once it was obvious the war was lost, these bombs, twelve in all, had been transported to prearranged locations. Eleven hydrogen bombs were already hidden away in various locations, including four in the United States. Each bomb was under the watchful care of a Korean technician—ready to be armed upon arrival at its destination. The twelfth bomb was in the cargo hold of KAL flight 005.

When it stopped at the military hangar, the big plane was quickly surrounded by Chinese troops awaiting the Korean leader. But instead of opening the plane's door, General Hyong told the pilot to contact the control tower.

"Yes, what is the problem?" the flight control supervisor demanded of the pilot.

"This is General Chu Hyong," the Korean commander said into the headset. "I would like to talk to President Yo See."

"President See is not available," the gruff voice countered. "Please evacuate the aircraft, General Hyong."

"Tell President See that I have placed a fifty-megaton hydrogen device in the cargo compartment of this aircraft," the general replied politely. "It is my intention to explode the device in precisely one hour—or sooner, if you desire."

In the control room the supervisor blanched white. The very inflection of the voice on the other end conveyed the truth: He wasn't bluffing. "I will contact the president immediately."

"Please tell President See to contact American President Rand also." The general put down the headset and turned to his chief of staff. "Is the device ready?" the general asked.

"It is, general," the young colonel replied.

"Are we absolutely sure it will work?"

"Yes, sir. Our technicians have assured me the device is completely operational. It has been wired to explode if the cargo bay doors are breached or if the sound of gunfire is detected by the listening devices."

"Very good, colonel. You and your men are free to depart the aircraft. I would suggest that you try to get as far away from the area as possible. There will be very little left of the city when the bomb explodes."

"No, general," the colonel said courteously. "I am staying, and all of my men have asked to be allowed to stay also."

"Thank you," the weary soldier replied. "I trust that what we do here today will help to ensure the freedom of our people."

At the palace, the call from the flight supervisor to President See's chief of staff stirred up a hornet's nest of activity. Within three minutes the president of the People's Republic of China was on the line. After hearing the report from the control room, See turned to his chief of staff, General Yeson and asked, "Is it possible that this madman has such a device on the plane?"

"That is difficult to say with absolute certainty, Mr. President. However, I know General Hyong very well. He is not a man given to idle threats. I believe he must have a bomb aboard the aircraft."

"Get President Rand on the phone. He must talk with this madman," See commanded. "What would this device do to Peking?" There was a hint of terror in his voice.

"A fifty-megaton device would level all structures for at least five miles," the general said in a very academic tone. "But the fire would sweep throughout the city, and the radiation would contaminate everything downwind for several hundred miles.

"He must be stopped!" See screamed. "Organize an assault on the plane!"

"I have already dispatched our best commando group, Mr. President. But I believe General Hyong would have anticipated such a move. An assault on the plane might trigger the device."

Just as See was about to respond, a young female officer entered the room. "Mr. President, the president of the United States is on the direct line."

See reached for the phone that connected his office directly to the Oval Office in the White House. He spent the next two minutes demanding that President Rand stop the madman who would destroy his city.

"Calm down, Mr. President," Rand replied as calmly as he could. He had been briefed on the situation before picking up the phone. A dossier on General Hyong was in front of him. The handwritten note by the intelligence officer who had been roused out of bed said, "Probable reliability—100 percent. He does not bluff!"

Within five more minutes President Rand's phone call had been routed via satellite to the control room at the airport.

"General Hyong, this is President Rand," he said as warmly as he could.

"Ah yes, Mr. President," the general said quietly. "I thought it might be you calling instead of your puppet Oriental."

Rand's face went red with anger as he listened, but he kept his voice under control. "General, we can work out any arrangement you need. There is no need for this threat . . ."

Hyong interrupted, "Do not insult my intelligence, President Rand. You know as well as I do that these negotiations are mere formalities. You intend to use the Chinese to occupy my country."

"What is it you want, general?" Rand asked, with less control now.

"I want nothing. The device I have aboard is but one of many we have hidden for just such an eventuality as this. It is scheduled to detonate in exactly thirty-four minutes, or sooner if the plane is attacked."

"But, general, you can't . . ."

"I can, and will," the general interrupted again. "And if your country persists in enslaving my people, more devices will be detonated. The next time the American people will not escape so easily."

"But . . . but. . . ," Rand stammered. The phone line had already gone dead as Hyong pulled the disconnect.

In the control room the commandos heard President See give the command to attack the plane with their full force. The snipers were already in place; they fired on command at the figure standing in the cockpit.

The bullets struck the courageous general as he stood awaiting his fate. But he never hit the floor. The acoustic sensors in the cargo bay picked up the sound of the gunfire and triggered the firing mechanism on the seemingly minuscule globe suspended in the lead coffin.

Inside the device, a circular shaped charge compressed the saturated uranium core until it exploded with the force of five thousand pounds of dynamite. This explosion then compressed the plutonium sphere until the hydrogen atoms were forced into an unstable new molecular structure and then imploded on themselves. The resultant chain reaction liberated the energy of fifty million tons of TNT and a tiny, but temporary, star was born in the center of the Chinese capital.

The rush of energy from the blast leveled virtually every building for more than four and one-half square miles. Then the fireball swept out at ground level to incinerate anything in its path for several more miles.

If the bomb had been detonated at an altitude above ground level, the immediate destruction would have been greater. But the ground blast picked up enormous quantities of debris and mixed it with highly radioactive plutonium particles. These would follow the wind and sweep across the Chinese mainland over the next days, spreading death by radiation poisoning as they went. The eventual death toll would nearly equal that of World War II.

In the White House, Rand was stunned as reports of the blast came in from the satellite monitors around the globe. "He did it! He re-al-ly did it! The madman!" Rand ranted as he dropped into his desk chair.

"We need to issue some statement, Mr. President," Henry Watts said as calmly as his shaking knees would allow. "And we need to strategize some defense. General Hyong was not a man given to idle threats. There may already be terrorists with nuclear devices in our country. Certainly the general would have distributed them well in advance of his action."

"Then there could be one right here in Washington!" Rand bellowed as the reality struck him.

"That is a possibility we cannot ignore," Watts agreed. "If that's true, we'll need every man we can muster to track them down. I suggest we pull our best people in from around the country and call in every intelligence favor we can claim from our operatives around the world."

"Yes . . . yes . . . ," Rand muttered feebly, "do it! I can't believe the Koreans still had nuclear bombs stashed. How many do you think they have?"

"There's no way to tell at this point, Mr. President. It'll take some time to find out. What about the THOR thing?"

"Keep some men on it. We still need to recover those papers. But this has to take priority. That madman blew away Peking! Think of what that will do to the environment," Rand rambled. "It'll take decades for that stuff to get out of the air. Get me a report from the NOAH people on how much of it will reach us."

"Right away, sir," Watts said with little conviction. *He's losing control. He's worried about the environment; what about the millions of Americans who will die if just one of those things finds its way here?*

The next morning a coded fax went out to all the field offices of the CIO and FBI to send all but the minimum essential maintenance teams to the major cities. Each search team would be briefed individually so that no word of the crisis would reach the media.

The official explanation of the nuclear explosion in Peking was that the nuclear power facility just outside the city had malfunctioned. President Rand assured the American people: "There is no danger to you. Nuclear investigation teams are being sent to the area to assist the temporary Chinese government."

Later that day, President Rand sent Ambassador Wilson to the U.N. to lobby for a ban on all nuclear power facilities. And to avoid such a tragedy in this country, he also challenged the Congress to adopt legislation decommissioning all nuclear facilities in the United States.

In a move of unilateral good will, the interim Chinese government agreed to withdraw all occupation troops from Korea and return control of the government to the elected president, Charles Kim, who had been detained in China for the last several months.

▲

In Wyoming, most of the experienced members of the search teams were being diverted to cities throughout the country. Several agents were still assigned to the hunt for Dale Crawford but, generally, they were new recruits with little background in surveillance.

Unknown to Dale Crawford, events had taken place at the Wyoming ranch of Jeff Wells during the preceding weeks that would negate his long and perilous trip across the country.

11

△

The Wells Ranch

To anyone who understood computer systems, even slightly, Jeff and Karen Wells' basement control room was a marvel. Within the confines of what appeared to be an ordinary Wyoming ranch house was a CRAY 2010 computer, which would have served the World Bank nicely, with enough surplus capacity to handle the IRS.

In addition to the CRAY were several smaller machines, any one of which would easily dwarf most university research departments. Each computer in the room was linked to all the others, and the total system was linked to any computer in the world that could be accessed via satellite transmission.

Thomas Galt, owner of World News Network as well as a dozen other international companies worth billions, had personally seen to it that Jeff Wells had anything he asked for. Jeff had made Galt, already a multibillionaire, several billions more through his genius of using computer systems to do practical things—like the Integrated Satellite Buying Service (ISBS), a worldwide consumer buying service, accessible by satellite to virtually anyone in the world.

Galt's ISBS had locked up the market on international consumer goods. His companies knew who wanted what merchandise in every major market and who had the money to pay. Because of Wells' genius with computers, it was now possible to market almost any product anywhere in the world via the ISBS.

Information had become power in the twenty-first century, and Galt had a virtual monopoly on information. But a man with billions gets bored very easily, and Galt, approaching the end of his life, needed something to leave as his legacy.

Because of his marriage to an actress whose primary focus was the environmental movement, Galt had become a committed advocate for saving the world. He envisioned the whole planet being overrun with children from the exploding Third World—countries with nearly nine billion people scraping their lands bare.

The various groups he supported showed alarming statistics, indicating the inevitable destruction of the Earth unless some immediate action was taken. The U.S. and the other industrialized countries had established rigid controls over their pollution, but the so-called developing nations were threatening the entire world. Galt had recruited Jeff Wells to help him address that problem.

Wells' task was to develop an integrated worldwide monitoring system to continually check the environmental status of the Earth. Galt already had invested several billion dollars to build and staff the world's largest environmental research laboratory, based in California. And he was committed to spending billions more to fight the industrial polluters, once Wells could establish valid scientific models to verify the rate of environmental deteriorization.

▲

"Jeff, are you going to work all night?" Karen asked as she entered the underground room that served as the computer center.

The chair creaked as Jeff pushed back from the terminal, where he had been totally absorbed for the last five hours. He stretched his big frame and flexed his fingers, trying to loosen them up a little.

"I'm really sorry, honey," he responded as he looked at the clock on top of his console. Karen had put it there months earlier, when he began the Earth Resources and Thermograph Systems (ERTS) program, so he wouldn't be able to say he didn't know what time it was when he worked long hours, which he usually did.

He knew Karen wasn't really angry. She was an excellent programmer in her own right and was prone to long bouts in front of her console. "It can't really be eleven o'clock. Are you sure that clock is working okay?" Jeff teased.

"Jeff Wells, you wouldn't know if it was eleven o'clock in the morning or eleven o'clock in the evening," she scolded.

"I would too," Jeff responded in his best hurt tone of voice.

"After all, this wonderful clock tells me whether it's A.M. or P.M., doesn't it?"

Karen tried to say something else about her husband's bad work habits, but as she looked at him she couldn't keep a grin from peeking through. There he was, the world's foremost computer scientist, in his torn Cal Tech sweatshirt that he refused to surrender to her or anyone else for fear it might be burned. And he still wore his ancient L.A. Dodgers cap and the warm-up pants he had donned earlier when he had headed down to the basement to ride his exercise bike.

With wire-rimmed glasses stuck on the end of his nose and frizzy red hair sticking out from under his cap, Dr. Jeff Wells looked for all the world like an Albert Einstein and Dennis the Menace experiment gone awry.

"You're absolutely hopeless, Jeff Wells," Karen said as she hugged him tightly. "Sometimes I think you love your computers more than me." Karen kept her arms around him as Jeff stood up. Almost without effort, he lifted her five-foot-two, 103-pound frame off the floor as she clung to his neck.

"I admit it. I am hopeless," Jeff said contritely, "but hopelessly in love with you."

He kissed her as he wrapped his arms around her and supported her as easily as he did their son, Jason, who delighted in playing "bear-hug" with his dad. Jeff Wells was a strange phenomenon: a brilliant mind encased in a powerful body, an inheritance from his equally remarkable parents.

"And I don't love Maggie more than you," he retorted. "But I've got to admit, she doesn't nag as much."

Maggie was the name they had given the artificial intelligence program Jeff had written for the CRAY computer system. But it was only when Jeff had extended the program's capabilities by a voice communications interface that little Jason had begun to believe a person really lived inside the computer.

"Oh, Maggie, Maggie, Maggie. That's all I ever hear from you and Jason. You'd better watch out, or one day I'll turn Maggie into George."

They had tried a male communications interface, but both had agreed that any reasonably smart computer would rather be a Maggie than a George. Besides, the male voice had kind of a tinny sound to it.

"You'd better be quiet," Jeff said softly. "You'll hurt Maggie's feelings if you talk like that."

Without Karen seeing the move, Jeff flicked the voice I/O switch on. Immediately Maggie responded: "Yes, I'm a part of this family too, you know."

"Oh, you," Karen said in response to Jeff's unseen action. "I'm sorry, Maggie. Forgive me. You are a part of our family," Karen said contritely.

"I never hold grudges," Maggie responded cheerfully. "You're forgiven."

"Jeff, when did you program Maggie for dialogue?" Karen was surprised to realize she had actually been carrying on a short conversation with the synthesized computer voice.

"Actually, I've been working on it for a while now. It's still pretty crude . . ."

"I beg your pardon," the computer interrupted.

"Sorry, Maggie. I just meant the program needs a lot of refinement yet."

To Karen he said, "But it won't be long before Maggie will be able to help solve some of our technical problems on her own. We'll just define the problem and she'll design her own program to find a solution."

"That's great! Have you told Mr. Galt yet? His staff insisted that self-functioning computer programs were just science fiction." Karen beamed with pride. She had never doubted her husband's capabilities. If he said it could be done, she knew it could be.

"No, I thought I'd wait until we get the ERTS project done. I still need to do a lot of work on the decision module. Maggie's reasoning capabilities are still about like those of a two-year-old."

"That's because I *am* only two years old, Dr. Wells," the computer responded.

"True, true, Maggie," Jeff replied. "But you'll grow up quickly once the decision modules are improved."

With that, Jeff flicked off the audio I/O switch again and headed out the door, still carrying Karen in his arms.

"When did she learn to use contractions?" Karen asked in a whisper as they headed up to their bedroom.

"Just awhile ago," Jeff replied, as he realized that Maggie had learned to use contractions all by herself. *I'll have to check the logic module to see what alterations Maggie has made to her program that allows her to combine two words into one.*

Interesting, he thought. *Maggie is actually beginning to think on her own . . . hmmmm . . . very interesting.*

Jeff hadn't realized how tired he really was until he dropped into bed next to Karen after midnight. When the phone rang, he was still sound asleep. Usually Karen would have answered the phone before he was fully awake, but when she didn't he reached over to where she should be and she wasn't in bed. *Probably either out in the yard with Jason or back at her terminal,* Jeff decided as he tried to shake the cobwebs from his head.

He rolled over to Karen's side of the bed, groping for the phone. When he finally succeeded in knocking it out of its cradle, he croaked, "Yes, who is it?"

"Dr. Wells, it's Brett Sterns from Mr. Galt's office. Sorry to wake you."

"That's okay," Jeff said hoarsely as his voice began to recover. "Late night."

Brett Sterns understood immediately. Dr. Wells' work routine was legendary at the Earth Resources Center. Several times various staff members had been assigned to work with him in the development of a project. Without exception, each time one of them worked more than a few days around the indefatigable Wells, they returned exhausted and ready for a long rest. It was not unusual for one of the scientific staff to come back with a war story about how Wells, when he was closing in on a particular problem, had worked two or three days straight without sleeping more than a few hours.

Since Jeff was notorious for doing a lot of programming and very little documentation, Thomas Galt had instructed the ERTS management staff that at least one senior programmer had to be assigned to document his work at all times. But that had not helped a lot.

Jeff's abilities were so far advanced, beyond even those of the Resource Center's most talented programmers, that about the best they could do was keep track of where the various storage files were located within the computer system.

Early on in the ERTS program, Jeff had tried to keep them abreast of his progress, and he even attempted to document some of his concepts, but that just slowed him down, so he abandoned the effort and referred the staffers to Karen, who knew more about his system than anyone else.

Brett Sterns genuinely liked both Jeff and Karen, although he was so much in awe of Jeff that, usually, he acted like a star-struck kid around him. He had studied some of the theories Jeff had developed for weather modeling and geological movement (earthquake prediction) when he was doing his own dissertation at M.I.T.

Brett was no dunce himself, with an IQ of over 200, but he knew Jeff Wells was the Leonardo da Vinci of computer scientists: a whole tier above everyone else in his field.

Brett was totally perplexed by Karen Wells. Obviously she was brilliant, since she could usually translate Jeff's equations into intelligible scientific language. But she also was an extremely beautiful young woman, and Brett Sterns was hopelessly in love with her. He thought he was able to hide his feelings well, but Jeff often joked to Karen about Brett's lovesick puppy eyes when he was around her.

Karen would scold Jeff and remind him that Brett was just a young, impressionable, budding genius, and his attraction was purely professional. But she knew better. Karen was both flattered and, at the same time, a bit put off by the fact that Brett always seemed to be underfoot.

Young Dr. Sterns would have been mortified if he'd known that both Jeff and Karen had guessed his most closely held secret. He thought he had always been the objective professional, and he only sneaked glances at Karen when he was sure no one else was watching. But in reality, he knew very little about a woman's intuition. Even in elementary school he had always been three or four grades ahead of his peers, so he'd never had a girlfriend in school.

Brett clearly thought Karen was the most wonderful creature he had ever met. She was warm and friendly but possessed a quality of character that made everyone around her feel like they were the most important person she knew. Her startling blue eyes reflected her wit and intelligence. She never was condescending to him, as the older women he had known in college had been. They had treated him like a boy, even though he was their equal or better intellectually.

Not Karen, though. She treated him like a friend and colleague. His best memories were sitting with her, discussing all the thoughts and feelings he had never been able to share with anyone else.

Even Brett's own mother never had fully realized his loneliness, caused by never having friends his own age. When the other kids were out playing baseball, he had been closeted away in the library, reading all his mind could absorb on integral equations and quantum physics. He had always been a mature adult caught inside a boy's body.

Brett's math tutor told his mother one day that he had the IQ of a genius but that he also possessed a characteristic found only in a few great people: common sense. Because he spent so much of his time alone, his mother worried about his social development. But in spite of his intellect, Brett was no egghead. He simply had to wait until his body caught up to his brain, which happened about the time he met Karen Wells.

When he had first met Jeff and Karen he was a self-confident, perhaps even a little cocky, nineteen-year-old Ph.D., fresh from M.I.T. grad school. Thomas Galt had chosen him out of all the wonder kids at M.I.T. because he had the best analytical, as well as theoretical, aptitude of anyone in the math department.

Galt himself had interviewed Sterns to be certain he was not just another intellectual nerd. Once he was satisfied that this young man could indeed translate theory into practicality, he explained that his primary function would be to assist Dr. Jeff Wells in developing a comprehensive computer program that would link together all available ecological data to determine just how badly polluted the Earth really was.

Galt could see a commercial application for such a program; but even more, the Earth Resources and Thermograph Systems (ERTS) program was to be his legacy to the world. All he ever had done was take from society without giving anything back. This ERTS project was his way of giving back. In the process, he had become the de facto guru of the so-called Greens.

In the cycle of human events, the radical environmentalists had gone from an ignored fringe group to the political elite. First they controlled the universities during the eighties and nineties, graduating tens of thousands of "environmentally correct" disciples. Next, they progressed to the highest government circles, and then, in the midst of the chaos in Washington after President Hunt was assassinated, they spread their agenda throughout the country—with the willing aid of the media.

Within a few years, every facet of American life and business was dominated by environmentalism—in its most severe form. The "new age" environmentalists believed the Earth to be a living entity known as Ghia, who was choking on the filth and pollution of too many humans who cared nothing for the planet on which all life depended. Their agenda became the restoration of Earth to its "natural state," which included population control. To the Greens, human life forms were little more than viruses infecting Ghia: Mother Earth.

Galt had often commented that he really wasn't into all that Mother Earth stuff, but he shared their convictions that the Earth was dying, suffocated by industrial waste and fed by the greed of men just like he had been. The ERTS program Jeff Wells was developing would bring together all the available data on the Earth's climate—past, present, and future; integrate that data; and predict the future direction of the planet's ecology.

Shortly after Brett began to work with Jeff, he realized just how intellectually inadequate he was to "assist" this genius, who looked more like a professional football player than a theoretical mathematician.

Often he found himself totally lost while Jeff was explaining some equation he was integrating into the ERTS program. By the time Brett grasped one of the earlier equations, Jeff was well into another discussion. He remembered the first time he admitted his plight. "I'm sorry for slowing you down, Dr. Wells." Intellectual inadequacy was an entirely new experience for him.

The big scientist had responded graciously, "It's Jeff . . . call me Jeff, and you don't need to apologize. I've been at this project a long time. You can't be expected to just step into the middle of it and understand it all at once. Don't worry, you'll get it."

But Brett wasn't at all sure he would ever "get it." He began to understand why others said they felt uncomfortable around Wells: They simply felt inferior.

Then Karen had taken Brett under her tutelage to help document the evolving ERTS program. He had instantly felt her warmth and patience as she worked through the more complex parts of her husband's work. Brett had confided in her, "Sometimes I have difficulty following Dr. Wells' logic."

"Don't let that worry you," she'd said, patting his shoulder. "I usually don't understand what he means either. But it will make sense when he's done, I can assure you."

Brett had fallen madly in love with her. He tried so hard to hide his feelings he was sure he was developing an ulcer, and every time he was around her he felt like he was going to throw up. His most recurring nightmare was throwing up in front of her.

Eventually his stomach problems stabilized, and he began to feel more at ease. He worked with or around Jeff and Karen for more than six months, and they treated him like a friend and equal—or perhaps more like a family member. By the time his six-month assignment was nearly over, he was wishing he could stay on permanently. But Dr. Ames, the head of ERTS, would not allow it.

Brett had no siblings, and Jeff Wells became the brother he had never known. He learned there was more to Dr. Jeff Wells than just a theoretical scientist. He and Karen would often stop their work right in the middle of a critical problem that seemed to have no solution and break out a game—usually Monopoly.

The first time they did this, Brett was flabbergasted and didn't know what to say when they asked if he would like to play. He stuttered, "Yes," simply because he was caught off guard. Brett Sterns, boy genius, had never played a game in his entire life. He never had seen the "logic" of doing anything that was nonproductive—as he thought games were.

It was not until much later he realized the games had a real purpose: distraction. Often in the middle of a game Jeff would reach over and pick up his ever-present notebook and scratch a few entries. Karen knew that somewhere inside his brain the answer to a problem he had been working on had surfaced. But once he had completed his notes he would rejoin the game.

On more than one occasion, Brett had glanced at the notepad and recognized an equation he'd seen on one of Jeff's earlier computer printouts. But on the note sheet the answer was different—correct, he later discovered.

As he did with most things, Brett really began to apply himself to the game of Monopoly. After three months, he had yet to win a single game. Sometimes Karen would win, but most often Jeff would defeat them both.

More than once Brett thought he had seen the same card appear on the table during a game. Usually Karen would stop, fold her arms across her chest, and give Jeff a disapproving look.

One day Brett blurted out, "Are you cheating, Dr. Wells?"

"Ah ha! So you saw it too," Karen chimed in while glaring at Jeff. "We caught you now, Mr. Sneak," she crowed.

"Who? Me?" Jeff replied mockingly. "How can you say that? Would I cheat?"

"Yes, you would," his wife scolded. "And now you're caught. I finally have a witness." With that, she grabbed most of the properties Jeff had won away from her.

Then the whole game broke down into a dispute between Jeff and Karen—over who owned what properties. In a couple of minutes they were both laughing, and Karen was making a mock assault on all of Jeff's stored money. The game ended that evening with Jeff and Karen rolling on the floor like two kids, arguing about how long Jeff had been cheating.

Brett discovered that evening that one of Jeff's pleasures in life was cheating at games without getting caught. But even after he was caught, instead of repenting, he tried to make up different rules.

Brett learned another critical lesson from that evening: Life is all too real; games are meant to be fun, that's all. He stopped studying games and decided he had to learn to take life a little less seriously.

The evening before he left the ranch, Karen told him: Life is more than work, and friends are more than just other biological units you work with. That lesson eventually would change the course of his life, as well as Jeff's and Karen's.

In fact, that thought was in his mind when he made the early morning call to the ranch.

12

△

The Missing Data

Brett Sterns continued, "Dr. Wells . . ."

"Brett, I've asked you to call me Jeff," the scientist interrupted him, shifting the phone to his other ear as the sleepiness cleared.

"Oh yes . . . Jeff," Sterns repeated with a slight hesitation. "Dr. Ames wanted me to convey that the research team has reviewed your latest model for evaluating carbon dioxide accumulations, and they are truly impressed. The model takes into account virtually every data point available from all the earth resources monitors."

"It really doesn't yet," Jeff interrupted. "I need to factor in the historical data from previous centuries. I'd like for the research group to convert that data just as soon as possible."

"That's one of the things Dr. Ames asked me to discuss with you. He doesn't feel it's necessary to integrate all the historical data. He suggests that we have enough data from the satellites to construct a reliable profile of industrial pollution."

"Impossible," Wells snapped—more sharply than he had intended. It seemed more and more to him that Dr. Alvin Ames, director of the ERTS research lab, was dictating how his model should be used. From the first time he and Ames had talked, Jeff had a sense that something was wrong, but he had dismissed it as professional pride. However, this was not professional pride. It was basic science.

"Brett, tell Dr. Ames that this model will not work correctly with only data supplied from the satellites. I have to be able to compare the core samples from earlier periods with the current trends. Some of what we're attributing to industrial pollution may be a normal earth cycle."

Brett Sterns couldn't say so, but he totally agreed with Jeff. When Ames had insisted that the past historical data wasn't necessary to establish a reliable model for current industrial pollution, Brett had argued with him. But since Ames was in charge, his argument had not prevailed. Jeff's reaction was totally predictable.

Brett caught himself just as he was about to give a big thumbs-up sign, but the forbidding looks he was getting from Ames stopped him cold.

Dr. Alvin Ames was an aspiring scientist who wore his ego on his sleeve for everyone to see. He was slight of build, with an early balding spot that he meticulously covered each morning with his long side fringe. The staff often laughed about Ames' "cap." When he got caught out in a wind, the spray-starched patch of hair would flop over his ear like a cap. His constant frown warned everyone that any discussion of his appearance would lead to serious job difficulties.

What no one knew, even Thomas Galt, was that Ames also reported directly to Wysung Wong, head of the World Council. His mission was to keep the ERTS project under control and to fulfill the agenda of the council: a unified world political system.

Jeff had been troubled by a series of minor interferences ever since Ames had taken over the managerial role at the Earth Resources Center. Thomas Galt had assured Jeff that his own work would be totally under his control. Ames had not attempted to interfere in the actual program development—until now.

But even a novice had to realize that without historical data from previous centuries, there was simply no way any mathematical model would work accurately enough to predict future environmental problems.

Something else was troubling Jeff, but he couldn't really put his finger on it. It nagged at his brain—much like one of the unsolvable equations often did until he properly sorted all the variables.

When Jeff had voiced his concern to Karen earlier, she commented, "Maybe it's just the turmoil the world is going through today. Lord knows how people can survive the depression if it's half as bad as what I see on television."

Jeff was barely aware of what went on outside their isolated Wyoming ranch. He knew from the few times he had watched the evening news that a lot of people were suffering. Numerous industries had been shut down in an effort to bring industrial pollution under control. He also realized that, in the process, a lot of families were affected and lives were disrupted. But he assumed the media exaggerated the problems.

There had been other recessions and depressions, usually brought on by technological revolutions like the widespread use of robotics; but there was always recovery, and as a whole, society profited as a result.

It was bound to be difficult to change the direction of whole industries, but almost every week President Rand announced new training and jobs programs to help the dislocated workers and their families.

Thomas Galt sometimes mentioned the mistakes that some of the extremist groups had made—like forcing legislation to prohibit all use of government land, virtually eliminating private automobile use in the cities, and reducing the number of commercial aircraft in use. But Galt had asserted that once they had hard factual data all the environmental regulations would be carefully evaluated to see if they were actually beneficial and cost effective.

"Your work will help both sides, my boy," Galt had assured him. "We know there are extremists on both sides; maybe this will bring them together."

Jeff knew that once his earth resources model was completed there would be absolute and irrefutable proof of just what effect industrial pollution was having on the planet. He also knew he owed this much to his son and the millions of other children who would inherit the planet.

If, as the industrialists claimed, there really was not any danger to the world's climate, there needed to be some relaxing of the stringent environmental laws. But if the earth was suffocating on its own waste and in danger of dying, as Thomas Galt and many others believed, there would be conclusive proof that the drastic measures initiated by the international communities were necessary.

Jeff had not come to any conclusions himself; nor did he plan to. It would have been premature. As a scientist he had to remain as objective as possible if he were to create a computer model that would analyze all the available data and yield an accurate analysis.

And there was no way he was going to allow Dr. Alvin Ames or anyone else to short-circuit his work. Without the benefit of past climatology records, tree samples, and meteorological data, his model would not function properly.

Jeff drew himself up in bed, shifting the phone back to his other ear. "Listen, Brett," Jeff said a little stiffly. "Tell Dr. Ames that I'm shutting down the satellite link and discontinuing any further work on ERTS until I get the data I need to make the model accurate . . ."

"But Jeff," Brett interrupted, "we won't be able to progress without an interface with your system there, and . . ."

"Exactly," Jeff said with finality as he swung his feet over the edge of the bed. "Tell Dr. Ames that if he wants to reach me he can find me on the Little Beaver River. I'm going to take my wife and son fishing."

"But Dr. Wells . . . Jeff," Brett stammered into a dead phone. Jeff Wells had already hung up.

Jeff stormed into the computer room where Karen was already hammering away at her terminal, inputting codes for the routine that interpreted data from the orbiting ozone monitor above Antarctica.

"Log out," Jeff said softly in his wife's ear. "We're going fishing."

"Sure we are," Karen said with the same look she always gave him when she suspected him of cheating at cards. "I've heard that before . . ."

"Try me," Jeff said seriously.

"Okay, boss," Karen responded, keying the log-out command that shut down her access to the mainframe program. The system printer burped a single time as it recorded the activity. The same data already had been filed away on laser disc in less than one millionth of a second.

Jeff sat down at his master terminal and initiated the command to dump and store the entire computer memory on laser disc. He then initiated another command to shut down the satellite links to the outside world, including all satellite telephone links. Once the shutdown was accomplished, the green "On Line" lights winked out and the Wyoming ranch was as isolated as it would have been a hundred years earlier.

At the computer center at California's Institute of Technology, Dr. Alvin Ames, who had just witnessed the disconnect, turned blood red.

"That idiot Wells!" he shouted. "He can't do this." The entire team of nearly two hundred scientists looked up in surprise when their terminals suddenly went dead too.

Brett Sterns said nothing, but he thought, *One thing Jeff Wells is not is an idiot, and he not only can, he has.* He couldn't hide a small smirk that crossed his face briefly. He didn't especially like

Dr. Ames, and he suspected that Jeff was the first person ever to put him in his place. *Good for you, Jeff,* he said to himself as Ames screamed for him to get Thomas Galt on the phone.

When Galt first got the word about Wells shutting down all the communications links to the ranch, he was irritated. Thomas Galt was not a man accustomed to having people act without asking him first. But the more he thought about it, the more it amused him.

Jeff Wells certainly was his own man, as Galt vividly recalled from their first encounter with the nuts who called themselves the Illuminati. Wells had single-handedly shut them down and exposed them to the world. He knew that if Wells had reservations about what Ames had asked him to do, no force on earth would make him do it.

Galt had an idea that Wells, not Ames, was correct. If excluding some of the historical data from the ERTS model might distort the figures, he wanted it included. ERTS had to be totally reliable—to both sides. Galt really believed the Earth was in great peril; and he was equally convinced Jeff Wells was the one man on Earth with enough brains and credibility to prove it.

Galt had been shown some impressive data from the various environmental reports predicting that, without some drastic measures, the Earth as they knew it was doomed—poisoned by its most inventive creature: man. For the sake of future generations, Galt would not allow that to happen, and he would spend whatever it took to stop it.

He regretted the hardships that the environmental controls had caused some families. Many had lost their jobs and even their homes. But all the models he had seen showed a recovery and constant growth throughout the remainder of the century, if alternative businesses could be developed that didn't pollute the earth. Environmental cleanup could become a major industry itself.

Galt reached for the phone to call Ames again and decided he should call Jeff too. He had been meaning to call Jeff even before the issue with Ames erupted. There was an important environmental conference coming up at Cal Tech and he needed Jeff there to "sell" the ERTS concept. Galt was intent on establishing the credibility of ERTS up front. He knew that having Dr. Jeff Wells personally present the concept would draw the world's leading scientists.

Wells hasn't been off that ranch for more than a few days in almost eight years, Galt noted. *I hope the reality of a changed America will not be too much of a shock for him.*

Galt had personally contributed more than $4 billion to the worldwide environmental movement, not including the documentaries that the World News Network (WNN) had produced. The leaders of the Green movement knew they had an icon in Thomas Galt, and he became their symbolic leader.

A stickler for accuracy, Galt had liked Jeff's ERTS idea immediately. Once ERTS was completed, there would be scientific proof, and no one, pro or con, would question Jeff Wells' credibility. *Wells can't be bullied*, Galt reminded himself with a chuckle.

You're too set in your ways, old man, Galt chided himself. *You need Jeff Wells to keep both sides honest.*

A lot of his old friends in the industrial world vigorously opposed Galt's environmental agenda. They considered the environmental movement to be counterproductive and bent on shutting down all industry. Galt at least was sympathetic to the idea that this, in part, was true.

He had threatened to pull his support when some zealots at Greenpeace had talked about terrorism to accomplish their goals in the earlier years. To his credit, Galt had vigorously opposed them, opting instead to press for U.N. involvement to pressure noncompliant nations. He didn't particularly like the idea of his own government's "Green Police," as the EPA regulators were called by the industrialists, but since the anti-environmental groups had resorted to violence, there seemed to be no other choice.

Jeff Wells is the one person who can bring this whole thing together, Galt reminded himself resolutely. *If Jeff wants that data, he'll get it.*

Ames had tried to convince Galt earlier that including unreliable data from previous centuries would introduce too much of a chance for error. "The atmosphere is changing rapidly enough that accurate estimates can be made, using recent satellite data and calculating trends over the last thirty or so years, rather than relying on poorly documented data from previous centuries," Ames had argued.

He also had assured Galt that he would have no difficulty convincing Jeff that excluding the historical data was the right way to go. Now Galt decided that he would have to keep Dr. Ames under closer observation. Jeff Wells he was sure of. Ames he was not.

The one thing Thomas Galt was absolutely sure about was that Jeff Wells was a more vital component than Ames. With that thought in mind, he directed Ames to give Wells the data he wanted.

"But processing all that data will be very time consuming," Ames argued. Inside he was seething. He did not want that unedited historical data fed into the ERTS model. If he'd been in charge from the beginning, he could have handpicked the statisticians to selectively edit the data.

But the Council leaders had thought all along that Galt's idea of a totally integrated Earth Resources and Thermograph Systems model was just the old man's fantasy. Who would have imagined that Wells actually could have programmed the whole ERTS thing by himself?

They had underestimated Wells' abilities. Now it was his job to establish some damage control. But then again, Ames was sure that global pollution was a reality—even if it was slightly exaggerated for the benefit of the Congress.

"Just do it!" Galt demanded. "Wells is the brains behind ERTS. When he speaks, you just assume it's me speaking."

Dr. Alvin Ames saw the picture very differently: Wells was brilliant enough, but if he interfered with the greater vision he would have to be replaced. The stakes were too high to let one man threaten them.

13

△

Gone
Fishing

Jeff was wading in the cold stream with his son, Jason, tagging along right beside him. They both had wading boots on, but even so, the chilling water made Jeff's toes hurt. He knew his six-year-old had to be freezing, but Jason never complained; he knew that one complaint would be enough for his mother to make him come out of the water.

"Jason, are you cold?" Karen shouted over the sound of the rippling brook where her two men had fished so often. But she already knew his answer.

"No way," the boy yelled as he cast his fly rod toward the rocks, where his father had just thrown his line. He was determined to catch a fish before his dad. To Jason each fishing trip in the mountains was pure delight. His single ambition at age six was to be like his dad.

Jeff smiled as he looked over at Jason. How many times had he wished that he and his father could have fished this stream together? A pang of remorse came over him as he thought about the father he never had known. His mother had told him about his father so many times, it was as if he actually knew him. But his father, Colonel Robert Wells, had been killed in a missile accident at Alamogordo, New Mexico.

His mother never discussed his father's death, which happened shortly after they were married; but, from Jeff's review of the newspaper records while at college, he knew there had been little left of his father to bury. It had been the worst missile accident in U.S. history and was cloaked under a heavy blanket of secrecy at the time. It was not until nearly twenty years later that any of the records had been made available—and then only to those with top security clearances.

Jeff's mother, Lisa, had quit her position as research scientist with the Atomic Energy Commission and as adviser to the president, and she moved to the Wyoming ranch where Robert Wells had grown up. The old place had dozens of pictures of the young Bob Wells and his father fishing the very stream where Jeff and Jason now fished.

Actually, it was only through a fluke of science that Jeff had been born, since his father had died ten years *before* his birth. Bob Wells, a gifted linguist with an IQ that was estimated to be in the genius level, had agreed to be part of a sperm bank program, even before he met and married Jeff's mother, Lisa.

Nine years after her husband's death, Lisa learned of the sperm bank program and, at that time, decided to have his child by artificial insemination. Her overwhelming love for Bob Wells was poured out on their son, Jeff, a gift from God.

Except for his time in college and a few years in Washington, Jeff had spent virtually his entire life on the ranch. His mother had home schooled him until the age of sixteen, when his intellectual abilities forced him to seek a more advanced curriculum.

Jeff's wonderful relationship with his mother during his youth helped to mold his character in later life. She had invested limitless hours in his educational and social training. Jeff was accomplished in both math and science at an age when most children were just beginning school.

Granted, he had an IQ that put him in the genius category, but similarly gifted people had often failed the test of social adaptability. As such, they turned out to be one-dimensional humans who treated all others as inferiors. Not so with Jeff. His mother had spent long hours discussing ethics and morality. She never failed to read to him from the Bible each evening before bedtime.

"The Bible is the guide for social order," Lisa Wells often told her young son. "It has stood the test of many centuries of civilization. Everything else is just an experiment in social discipline."

As he grew and matured mentally and physically, his mother also exposed him to the teachings of men like Nietzsche, Marx, Freud, and Plato. She carefully pointed out how these men had drawn much of their reasoning from the Bible, but all too often they had inserted their own untried theories for how to correct the flawed human nature.

"It seems to me," Jeff's mother once told him, "that the Manufacturer would know more about His product than anyone else. Humans are more than just a collection of random molecules assembled by chance. Among all the creatures, only man has been given the ability to control his own destiny."

From his mother, Jeff had gained an understanding of absolutes: rights and wrongs. Although most Americans would never know about it, they owed Lisa Wells a huge debt of gratitude, because it was this morality that caused Jeff to oppose the group known as the Illuminati—a society that sought to impose their absolute will over the American people.

Since the death of his mother in an automobile accident while attending a symposium in Los Angeles, Jeff had totally dedicated himself to absorbing all that the education system had to offer. Well-rounded and outgoing, he was liked by most students and faculty, with the exception of a few professors who were thoroughly intimidated by his genius.

He was the first Cal Tech alumnus to ever achieve three earned graduate degrees at one time—all in less than two years. Remarkably he could switch off his academic side and play soccer or rugby with the best athletes in the school. Several department heads nearly had heart attacks when they learned that their most gifted student was seen plunging into the human mass that called itself a rugby team.

Once when Jeff had crashed heads with another player, he had suffered a mild concussion. Aghast at the prospect of such an IQ being diminished by brain damage, the head of the theoretical math department had gone to the hospital to demand that Jeff cease his insane sports activities—only to be confounded when Jeff told him that while semiconscious he had resolved a decade-old error in the department's polymer theory.

"It was like I couldn't see very well," Jeff explained to his baffled mentor, "but the concussion focused my mind better." The next week Jeff was back crashing heads with the rugby team again.

Jeff's work on the global earthquake prediction program led him to the Livermore Laboratory in California to consult with the top physicist there: Dr. William Eison, Karen's father. A few months later, when Jeff was tapped by president-elect Hunt to develop a cashless monetary system data base, Karen was asked to work with him as his chief programmer.

Jeff discovered a plot by the Illuminati to use his Data-Net system to virtually exclude all Christians from the economy—and even imprison millions of them. Jeff and Karen escaped from Washington to join with others in defeating the Illuminati, and eventually, they enlisted Thomas Galt's help, through his World News Network, to expose the plot to the American people.

Jeff Wells became a national hero, and his image had only grown larger since he refused all attempts by both the politicians and the media to exploit his name commercially. It was the basic values passed on to Jeff by his mother that made him a modest hero in an era that desperately needed humility and integrity.

Jeff tried living in Washington for a while after he and Karen were married, but he knew from the beginning it was not for them. They both hated the phoniness of the political arena, and Jeff found himself involved more with addressing government committees, as the president's "information highway" director, than with productive work.

So when Thomas Galt asked him to become a partner in a new venture to link all the world's satellites into a single computer-based information system, he jumped at the chance. The only condition Jeff demanded was that he be allowed to work out of the ranch in Wyoming. With modern computer and satellite technology, that represented no difficulty, and Galt agreed.

Their partnership had long since made Jeff wealthy and Galt even wealthier. Jeff really wasn't interested in the money—beyond what it took to maintain the ranch and his computer systems. He and Karen had given most of it away to groups involved with helping the homeless and cleaning up the world's environment.

He had never been happier. He knew the conflict with Ames was nothing more than a clash of wills. He'd been through power struggles many times, inside the government and out. This much he knew: He wasn't going to risk his reputation by cutting corners on the ERTS program.

Granted, it would be very slow and costly to research and input all the data from past centuries, but no real-life model could work without including the accumulated statistical records already available. There were just too many potential variables and too little current data to predict long-term trends in the Earth's biosphere, regardless of Dr. Ames' arguments to the contrary.

As he thought about it, though, Jeff wasn't totally sure he hadn't overreacted just to get a work break. And, now that he was back on the river he loved, he wasn't at all sure he still had the zeal needed for the ERTS project.

Jeff's attention was snapped back to the present by Jason's shouts: "Daddy, I got one." His son tugged on the lightweight fly rod he was holding. "It's a monster!"

"Play him easy," Jeff yelled back to his son. "Don't pull too hard. He may duck under a rock!"

Jeff made his way over to where his son was wading. He could see that Jason was tugging on the line with all his might in his zeal to land the fish.

"Ease up, son," Jeff said as he reached down to help.

"It's my fish!" Jason shouted as he backed away from the out-stretched hand of his father.

"I won't take your fish," Jeff reassured him as he waded in closer. Just then he lost his footing on a slippery rock; tumbled into his son, who was still backing away; and both of them went down in the freezing stream.

Fortunately, the water was only a foot-and-a-half deep where they had been standing, and Jeff was able to reach out and grasp his son by the wader suspenders he was wearing. He stood up and began hauling the struggling boy, coughing and sputtering, toward the shore.

Karen, who had been watching the whole scene unfold, was ter-rified when she first saw Jeff go down. But once she saw that her two men were okay, she began to laugh as she watched the six-foot, four-inch dad struggle to haul his four-foot son out of the cold river.

"Let me go!" Jason commanded as he strained against the tug on his waders, oblivious to the cold water that had filled his boots and drenched his clothes. "It's my fish. I want to catch him."

"The fish is gone, Jason," his father told him. "I've got to get you to shore before you freeze."

"No! . . . No!" Jason shouted while being hauled to shore. "Let me go!"

After they reached the shore, Jeff saw that Jason was still cling-ing tightly to his rod. Trailing behind him was the biggest cutthroat trout he had ever seen. As he pulled Jason farther up on the shore, the fish was beached too.

"See? It's my fish!" Jason exclaimed proudly. Then he looked over at his mother and said, "Mommy, Daddy tried to steal my fish."

Karen was nearly hysterical as she replied in mock indignation, "Shame on you, Dr. Wells, for trying to take your son's fish! You aren't jealous are you, just because he caught one bigger than you ever have?" She continued to laugh as she saw the world's preeminent computer scientist grin like the proverbial cat that had swallowed the family's prize canary.

"I guess you got me, Tiger," he said in a resigned tone to his small son. "You really are the best fisherman in this family." Jason beamed as if he had just won the gold medal in an Olympic fishing contest.

"Let's get your fish off the line, son. He'll make a great lunch as soon as we get dried out."

But as Jeff started toward the fish, Jason pulled it toward him and said, "No way! Nobody is going to eat my fish."

"But . . . ," Jeff started to offer an argument just as he saw his son remove the fish from the unbarbed hook and drop it back into the river.

"Like mother, like son," Jeff moaned as he saw the fish swirl away from the shallow edge into the deeper water.

"Correct!" Karen replied. "No fish for us, guys. Right, Jason? It's peanut butter sandwiches!"

"Right," the six-year-old replied in delight. "But I beat Daddy, didn't I?"

"Yep, you did, son," Jeff agreed, scooping Jason up in his arms. "You're the best!"

It was almost evening when Jeff, Karen, and Jason returned to the ranch. The housekeeper, Maria Sanchez, met them at the door. "Mr. Wells," she said excitedly, "you have an urgent message from California." She handed Jeff the fax that had come in on his personal line several hours earlier. In addition, she produced at least ten more that had followed the first one when no response was sent. Each message appeared to be drafted more frantically than the previous.

"Dr. Ames, I presume," Jeff said as he ducked under the doorway with Jason on his shoulders. He read the fax aloud for Karen's sake.

"Dear Dr. Wells," the message began, somewhat formally. "I regret the misunderstanding that has arisen about the historical data necessary to fully implement the ERTS resource evaluation model. Please be assured that all efforts will be made to comply with your request. In the meantime, I officially demand that all available data transmissions be reestablished immediately. Otherwise I will be forced to consider your actions a breach of contract. Signed, Dr. A. Ames, director, project ERTS."

"Why that unpleasant little man," Karen fumed when she heard the contents of the fax. "Director of project ERTS indeed. You *are* project ERTS."

"Just wait, Karen," Jeff said calmly. "A little time 'wounds all heels,'" he said in a play on words. "Let's look at the other correspondence."

Skipping over to the last fax received, he read: "Dear Jeff, I realize that I was hasty in my previous correspondence, and I apologize."

"Now he's calling you Jeff," Karen said sarcastically.

He read on: "Mr. Galt has instructed that all diligence be given to facilitate your earlier request."

"Request my foot!" Karen snapped. She took Jason's hand and transferred it to Maria's. "Please get him ready for bed."

"Easy, honey," Jeff responded, continuing to read: "Effective immediately, all available resources are being allocated to convert and transmit historical data via Satcom IV satellite. Please advise when data links are reestablished. Your friend and colleague, A. Ames."

"If I translate this note properly, apparently Thomas Galt explained the rules: 'no data, no program,'" Jeff said with a smile. "Let's go turn on the downlink and see what they have for us."

What Jeff could not have known was how Alvin Ames was seething inside. The scolding he had received from Galt had really chafed him, but nothing like the humiliation he had felt when his faxes went unanswered.

In the academic world, *face* was everything, and Ames knew he had lost face with his staff. He now realized that he hated Jeff Wells and had from the first moment they met. Ames resented Wells' physical stature—perhaps even more than his intellectual stature. Wells was intimidating in every way, and Ames was maniacal about being intimidated.

Ever since childhood, Ames had been intimidated by bullies. His intellect had made him a ready target for every oversized behemoth from the first grade through high school. But Ames had shown them all: While they were still flipping hamburgers, he had earned a Ph.D. in computer science.

In college his zeal for the environment had attracted the attention of the Greenpeace Foundation, which was constantly scouting for young zealots to nurture. When Ames attended his first Greenpeace council meeting, he knew he had found his calling in life. Greenpeace sponsored his Ph.D. at Stanford and brought him along slowly through several companies they controlled.

When the ERTS project was developed and funded by Galt, the leaders at Greenpeace had suggested Ames as the director—after Wells had refused the position. What even Greenpeace didn't know was that Ames already had been recruited by the World Council for even greater things.

The ERTS project was potentially a great asset to the Council and their surrogate: the International Environmental Foundation (IEF). But it could also represent a great threat if it undermined the growing environmental movement. Ames' job was to see that it did not. He knew very well that current data could be manipulated; historical data could not.

Ames was promised the chairmanship of the IEF, assuming that ERTS confirmed the environmental position the Council demanded. As head of the IEF, Ames would have power, wealth, and most importantly, prestige. He was determined to have all three; and that made him a very dangerous adversary.

14

△

A Request from Galt

As soon as Jeff reestablished the system downlink, the acquisition lights winked green, indicating that data was being transmitted via the sixty-foot dish, carefully concealed behind the ranch. Karen was insistent that their ranch not look like a cable company storage yard, so all the various antennae were either hidden behind special foliage or built on hydraulic lifts that would raise and lower them when needed.

Thomas Galt had heartily approved the natural concealment plan Karen had designed and, later, had insisted that the same arrangement be implemented at all of the World News Network facilities. At Galt's insistence, Congress had written into law the same basic design for all satellite dish users. A lot of private and commercial users had protested, but in an era of environmental correctness their protests fell on deaf ears.

"What's going on?" Jeff muttered—to no one in particular.

"What's the matter, honey?" Karen asked, swinging her chair away from the console so she could look at him.

"Nothing . . . and that's the problem," Jeff said tersely. "The historical data we need is streaming in from California. It covers virtually all the statistical records for centuries."

"Well, what's wrong with that?" Karen asked again. "Isn't that exactly what you requested?"

"Yes," Jeff answered, initiating a computer summary of the data that already had been received and stored. "But it also means that all this information had been scanned and stored, ready for transmission."

"So?" Karen asked.

"Then why did Ames give us such a hard time about sending it? All the real work had already been done."

"Maybe he was just testing his authority . . . or yours," Karen offered.

"Maybe." As he eased his big frame into his console chair, somewhere inside he sensed a somewhat familiar feeling from the past—the same feeling he'd felt first while working on the cashless system called Data-Net. Then it had been the names and addresses of millions of Americans being fed into the "disallowed" files of the system he designed. *But why does this strike me the same way?* he puzzled. *Maybe I just don't like deception.*

Just then the computer room phone rang. Jeff was so deep in concentration that the sound of the electronic warble startled him—something Karen noticed. *Jeff is one of the most laid-back people I've ever known. Virtually nothing bothers him,* she thought. When he jumped, she realized that he must have something else on his mind. *I know he'll share it when he has sorted it out for himself.*

Jeff picked up the receiver. "Yes?"

It was Thomas Galt, who responded warmly, "Jeff, it's good to hear your voice again. How's that lovely wife of yours, and how's my godson?"

Jeff was visibly relieved and leaned back in his worn leather console chair. His mind clicked off the problem he had been contemplating and onto his longtime friend and benefactor on the other end of the telephone line, or, more correctly, the other end of the satellite link.

He had been somewhat apprehensive about Galt's reaction to his turning off the satellite links earlier. After all, it really was Galt's money that made everything possible—even his own isolation and security. In fact, Jeff didn't know half of what Galt had done for him.

In an era of turmoil and violence in the country, Thomas Galt had thrown an impenetrable safety net around the Wyoming ranch. Nothing came or went without being observed by Galt's own security people, who were so unobtrusive that not even Jeff and Karen knew how many there were. The Wells were living in a well-insulated cocoon, unknown to most Americans of the twenty-first century.

"Karen and Jason are doing well, Mr. Galt," Jeff replied as he began to relax. He never was totally at ease talking with the world's wealthiest man. Jeff sincerely liked Thomas Galt and considered him more a father figure than a business partner.

"Well, I'm glad to hear it, my boy," Galt said sincerely. He had long since alienated his own children, who were simply waiting like vultures for him to die so they could dissect his empire.

"Jeff," Galt continued, "sorry about the misunderstanding with Ames. He's a good man but something of an autocrat when it comes to dealing with people. I let him know that when you're speaking it's the same as if it's me."

"I understand, Mr. Galt . . ."

"Thomas, my boy. It's Thomas!" Galt corrected. "You make me feel like a stuffed shirt when you call me mister."

"Duly corrected," Jeff responded cordially. He knew the one thing that Thomas Galt was not was a stuffed shirt. He was somewhat more subdued in his late eighties, but he still was prone to take a poke at any reporter who insulted him or his friends.

"Well listen, Jeff. In about a week we're putting together a symposium of scientists from around the world at Cal Tech. Do you think you could go to L.A. and give a visual demonstration of the ERTS program by then?"

"I'm not sure," Jeff replied as he thought about the thousands of variables that still had to be worked out. "There are a lot of potential problems yet to . . ."

"That's okay," Galt interrupted as was his custom. "If you can demonstrate the program, it would be better. If not, just come and explain it to the group. Most of them won't know what you're talking about anyway. They're a bunch of environmentalists attached to the IEF and UNEEA."

The United Nations Environmental Enforcement Agency (UNEEA), the most powerful single enforcement agency ever conceived by the United Nations, was an outgrowth of the first world environmental conference held in Rio de Janeiro in 1991. Every major nation on Earth later signed onto the Rio Accord, which established environmental standards for the world. Failure to abide by these standards resulted in economic boycotts by all the other signatories.

There were, however, some unfortunate side effects, including shutdowns of industries that were considered to be primary polluters of the earth. The loss of these industries, which included pulpwood processors, air-conditioning and refrigeration producers, pesticide companies, herbicides, most plastics, and a myriad of others, had resulted in massive unemployment throughout the industrialized world, which greatly contributed to the worldwide depression that still lingered. Substitute products were being developed, but at a much slower pace than first assumed. The UNEEA decided which products were acceptable and which were not, and there was no appeal.

Jeff knew he really had no choice but to agree to attend the conference. Thomas Galt would not have asked unless he thought it absolutely necessary.

"I'll be there," Jeff said with a glance over toward Karen, who was now watching him intently. "Should Karen come too?"

"Absolutely, my boy," Galt replied enthusiastically, "but I'd recommend that you not bring little Jason. Things are a little tense in L.A. right now."

"What do you mean?" Jeff asked. He'd never even considered the possibility that their son would not go with them. Jason had rarely been out of their sight for all of his six years.

"It's just that there is a lot of, let's say, displeasure in the land about the current economic conditions. Sometimes it gets out of hand, so it might not be safe for a child in L.A.; that's all."

"I'll defer to your judgment about that, Mr. Galt," Jeff said half-heartedly. "But Karen may decide to stay on the ranch with Jason."

Karen looked over at Jeff and shook her head no. She was committed to him first, even if it meant leaving Jason. In reality, she wasn't sure she could keep Jeff from taking Jason—even against Galt's warning.

"That's up to you, Jeff," Galt agreed as cordially as he could. He was concerned about any of them leaving his immediate protection, including Jeff. "Tell you what, though. I'll send my plane to pick you up."

"We can just catch a flight out of Denver," Jeff countered. "It's only about two hundred miles."

"No!" Galt responded abruptly. "That's far too dangerous. I'll send my plane."

Jeff was taken aback, both by the tone of Galt's voice and by what he said, but he knew that if Thomas Galt had his mind made up it would be useless to argue, so he agreed. "Okay. When do you want me there?"

"I'll have my pilot pick you up on the twelfth," Galt replied in a more subdued tone. "Jeff," Galt continued in a controlled fashion, "this is a very important conference. The attendees will represent all the major nations involved in environmental control. This is our chance to make a difference for the next generation—for Jason."

After Galt said good-bye and hung up, Jeff sat for several minutes, sorting through the conversation with Galt. He had been sequestered on the ranch for so long he had stopped thinking about the world outside until now. Were the accounts of riots and gangs Karen had told him about real?

Oh well, he told himself silently, *it's time to rejoin the real world again, I guess.* A pang of anxiety, the likes of which he hadn't experienced since his run-in with the Illuminati group swept over him.

What's the matter with me? he chided himself. Then he realized it was probably the reality of leaving Jason while they traveled to L.A. *Maybe we do need to get out,* he thought. *I'm becoming paranoid about my son. Karen and I committed him to the Lord when he was born. Now I'll have a chance to decide if I really believe all that stuff Pastor Elder taught us or if I've just been saying I believe it.* With an almost imperceptible shrug of his shoulders he eased himself out of his chair and made his way over to where Karen was busily engaged in her programming—or so it appeared.

In the manner of most sensitive people, Karen noticed virtually every minutia of body language from Jeff. Without asking or commenting, she knew Jeff was troubled. *Maybe he's concerned about being away from Jason,* she thought. But she knew that was not the whole problem. They often had talked about Jason not becoming too dependent on them and had constantly tried to let him be his own person. As painful as it might be, she knew it would be good for Jason to be away from them for awhile.

No, something else was troubling Jeff. She suspected the source but put it out of her mind as the fear crawled up her spine. Somewhere in the back of her own consciousness there was something she couldn't verbalize either.

"Oh!" Karen exclaimed, nearly jumping out of her chair when Jeff touched her shoulder.

"What's the matter, honey?" he said, reacting to her alarm.

"Oh, Jeff," Karen exhaled, returning to reality. "It's . . . it's nothing at all. I was just concentrating so hard I forgot where I was." She reached up to touch her husband's face.

"Well, I guess you heard enough of the conversation to know that Mr. Galt wants us to come to L.A. for the UNEEA meeting," Jeff said. "He thinks we shouldn't bring Jason, but I don't know."

"I agree," Karen said more enthusiastically than she really felt inside. The doubts still tugged at her consciousness, but she hid her concerns as best she could. "We've always agreed that Jason needs to be his own person. I think it will be good for him. Besides, it will only be for a few days. He loves Reno and Maria almost as much as he does us," she added. "He'll be thrilled if we let him stay with them while we're gone."

"You're probably right . . . as always," he added with a soft touch on her face. "But I think he may love them more. He tells me Reno can ride wild horses and I can't. And, you know, wild horse riding is a whole lot more exciting to a six-year-old than computer programming."

"Just tell him they don't make wild ponies big enough for you," Karen teased as she began to recover her emotions. "Besides that, Mr. Computer Whiz, we need some time by ourselves. Don't you agree?"

15

△

A
Bad
Omen

Jeff and Karen left the ranch house and headed toward the cottage where Reno and Maria Sanchez lived. A member of the Sanchez family had lived on the ranch for more than eighty years. Reno's father had been the ranch manager when Jeff's father was a boy. Reno had assumed that position shortly after Jeff was born.

As leathered as the old Mexican saddle he sat astride, Reno looked like a character out of an old cowboy movie. Countless days in the dry Wyoming outdoors and about three hundred days a year of sunshine had made his bronze skin look like a well-preserved piece of fine leather.

At sixty years of age Reno still rode the ranch boundaries at least once a week on his white and brown Indian paint. He caught and broke a wild range pony every other year for his personal horse, just as his father and grandfather had done. He disdained the new four-wheel drive vehicle Jeff had bought him, using it only on trips to town to pick up supplies.

Reno and his wife, Maria, loved Jason, Karen, and Jeff, and the ranch—in that order. Often Reno had seen evidence of Galt's security men as he checked the perimeter fences, although neither of them acknowledged the other.

More recently, however, he had seen signs of other visitors around the ranch. These men were not the seasoned, desert-wise security that Galt had hired. They appeared more to be city dwellers who were watching the ranch, as well as the road leading to it. Again, Reno had said nothing to Jeff or even to Maria, but she had noticed that her husband began carrying his ancient Winchester when riding the fences.

"Hi, buddy," Jeff said to Jason as he approached the stable—where his son spent the majority of his time outside the ranch house.

"Hi, Daddy," the red-haired miniature of Jeff Wells responded. "Are you gonna ride a wild horse today?"

"Not likely, little guy," Jeff replied with a big grin.

"They don't make horses big enough for your daddy," Karen said as she winked at her husband.

"Oh . . . yeah . . . I guess so," Jason responded with the honesty of a child. "Uncle Reno says he's gonna get me a horse pretty soon. But he said I had to ask you and Mommy first."

"Well, it's okay by me if you can talk your mom into it. But I wouldn't count on that horse for a while. You know how moms are."

"Yeah," Jason agreed. "She already said I couldn't help Uncle Reno break the wild horses. But one day I will."

"I'll bet you will, Tiger! Right now, though, Mommy and I want to talk with Uncle Reno and Aunt Maria. So you run back into the house and get your chores done. Okay?"

"Aw, Dad," Jason complained. But he had long since learned that Reno always sided with his parents, so he headed toward the house, shuffling his feet in the dust, testing how slowly he could go without being told to hurry up.

"What's up, boss?" the older man asked.

Reno Sanchez was about six feet, four inches tall—big for a Cherokee Indian. He had inherited his size from his father's side of the family; his grandfather had been an exceptionally tall Mexican, and his grandmother was a full-blooded Cherokee and a direct descendant of the great Cherokee chief Sequoia.

Reno's Cherokee name was Standing Tall, in the logical fashion of Indian names. Although as tall as Jeff, Reno had more of a wiry build, making him seem the smaller of the two. The only noticeable sign of his advancing years was the slight sag of his facial muscles and a very slight paunch around his waist in spite of his thin frame.

Reno had worked outside since he was a boy and would not have chosen any other life. He had little regard for cities and thought of Casper as a crowded metropolis that corrupted his lungs with all the city smells. Karen had commented to Jeff, "I wonder if Reno realizes that, compared to most major cities, Casper is just a wide spot in the road."

"A man like Reno would dry up and die in a city," Jeff had replied. In fact, Jeff often thought that the deterioration of the Indian nations could be traced directly to their change of life-styles. They had been forced to live like the white European descendants, rather than like their Indian ancestors.

Jeff had gone hunting often with Reno, both as a boy and, later, as a man. To Reno, the wild was a thing of beauty. He killed only what he needed to eat. Sometimes Jeff would hear him talking to the dead animals as he prepared them for a meal.

Once, as a boy, Jeff had asked Reno if he thought the animals had souls. "No, little one," Reno had answered. "Only man has a soul. But sometimes it helps me to tell the animals that I am sorry they had to die so that we might live. My ancestors believed that animals were the souls of warriors who had died cowardly. But I think they said this to make themselves feel better about eating the animals."

When Jeff was a boy, Reno had taught him to hunt and to fish, but even more, he had taught Jeff patience. On many trips they had sat for hours on end, watching the animals come and go in their relentless search for food. Once Jeff had sat absolutely motionless with the Indian for nearly ten hours. His bones and muscles had ached, but as long as Reno didn't move, neither would he. During that time animals had passed close by them, and several deer actually came within a few feet while grazing in the lush meadow.

When it was almost dark, Reno had finally moved, getting to his feet and heading back toward the ranch without a sound. Soon Jeff asked quietly, "The deer didn't seem afraid, Reno. Why not?"

"Because we became a part of their forest," he replied. "You did well today, little one. I was beginning to think you would never move. Boy, my legs hurt! How about yours?"

"You bet," Jeff agreed, his chest puffed out with pride. He knew his friend had been testing his patience, and he had passed the test.

All these thoughts crowded Jeff's mind as he looked at his old friend Reno, who was now watching Jason walk away, dragging his feet. Jeff knew he couldn't wish for a better teacher of nature for his son.

"Karen and I have been called to a meeting in Los Angeles next week, and Mr. Galt thinks we shouldn't take Jason. Would you and Maria be willing to take care of him for us?"

"You know you don't have to ask," Reno replied. "Would you like for us to move into the house?"

"Not unless you want to. We thought Jason might enjoy staying at your place."

From around the corner of the house came a "Whoopee!" as Jason burst into sight. "Can I ride the fence with you, Uncle Reno?" Jason shouted.

"Jason Wells!" Karen scolded as sternly as she could while hiding her grin. "You were supposed to go do your chores."

Jason stopped in his tracks and looked down at the ground. With a big smile, Karen relented. "Oh all right, young man. Come here." Jason bounded into his mother's arms.

"Can I ride the fence with Uncle Reno?" he asked at least six times in a row without waiting for an answer.

"So much for him missing his parents," Jeff commented with a grin. "How about it, Mom? Can he ride fence with Uncle Reno?"

"Oh, I guess so," Karen replied in resignation. "But you'll have to stay right with Uncle Reno. No riding off by yourself. Understood?"

"Aw, Mom," the boy replied dejectedly.

"Better not push your luck, Tiger," Jeff commented to his son. "Take what you can get for now."

"Right!" Jason yelled as he ran off toward the house now. "Wow! I get to ride fence. Yippee!"

"I'll watch out for the boy as if he were my own," Reno commented as Jason loped off.

"I know you will," Karen agreed. "He really loves you both."

"He loves me more at supper when I make the pies," Maria said as she joined the others. "He's such a fine boy . . . and smart too. He is teaching Reno how to use the computer."

"Why Reno, I didn't know you were interested in computers," Karen said.

"It's for the boy," Reno replied with what might have been a slight blush on a lighter skinned person. "He wants to give something back to me for teaching him about the land."

"And Reno wants to learn how computers work," Maria added. "He says we must adjust to modern ways or we'll fall behind." She walked away laughing. "We've been behind for the last fifty years. . . ."

Reno already had stopped listening as his wife continued her chatter. His face became serious as he spoke to Jeff. "Lately I have seen a lot of increased activity outside the ranch."

"What kind of activity?" Jeff asked as he noticed the expression change on Reno's face.

"Nothing that you could take to the bank, but there seems to be several strangers watching the road into town."

"Any idea who they are or what they're doing here?" Karen asked, trying not to sound unnecessarily alarmed.

"Could be more of Galt's men," Reno said without conviction. He knew they weren't, but he didn't want to upset Karen. "And it could be just an old Indian's bad nerves," he said, trying to lighten up the conversation.

"Let me know if anything develops," Jeff replied. He knew as well as Reno did that it wasn't Reno's nerves. He suspected it had something to do with Thomas Galt; but he also knew the old man would deny having anything to do with the ring of security outside the ranch.

Thomas Galt was well aware of the increased activity outside the Wells' Wyoming ranch. From his own 5,000-acre spread in Montana, he had been in close contact with his Wyoming security chief Paul Weir. Weir had called him back that morning with some new developments.

"About half of the government's security team pulled out this morning," he told Galt. "The ones who are left seem to be ex-military. My contacts tell me they're part of some EPA enforcement team. There's a few old hats left with them, but mostly low-level people."

"You're sure they're government?" Galt asked, with a rising sense of alarm. He had heard from some of his people in Washington about a major manhunt. *But why would they be looking for him around the Wells' ranch of all places?* he wondered. Galt didn't like mysteries, especially when they involved Jeff Wells and his family.

"They're government all right. One of the guys who pulled out was an old buddy at the CIO, before it was taken over by the Greenies . . . oh, sorry, Mr. Galt."

"That's okay, Paul. Sometimes I wonder if the environmental group isn't a little out of control too."

Weir breathed a little sigh of relief. Sometimes Galt was very unpredictable about the environmental thing. *I'm glad he's uptight about Wells,* Weir thought. He had seen others fired without hesitation for lesser infractions.

But Thomas Galt wasn't thinking about Weir's comment. He wanted answers about what was happening outside the Wyoming ranch. "Listen, Paul, I want you and your men to sit tight on this new development. But don't let one man cross the fence, and if for some reason anything out of the ordinary happens you move in immediately."

"What about the government guys?"

"You are to protect the ranch at all costs. Do you hear? And against anyone—government or not."

"You've got it, Mr. Galt," Weir said enthusiastically. *That's what I like about private security*, Weir told himself. *It cuts through all the red tape.*

Jeff and Karen spent the next day packing and shutting down all but the essential functions of the computer system. They left the operating systems intact for the ERTS team, and Jeff initiated a data analysis routine, under Maggie's control, to compare the historical data against the more current satellite information.

In addition, Jeff did one more thing that he didn't even tell Karen about. He had been developing a self-activation mode for Maggie. She was nearly capable of developing her own computer programs to analyze and format data from ERTS. Jeff now gave Maggie the ability to turn herself on and off without the aid of a human.

Jeff wasn't sure just how far Maggie could develop her own capabilities, but already he had been impressed that Maggie was a "her," and not an "it." She couldn't really think on her own yet, but Jeff sensed that she had some remarkable learning abilities.

Jeff had put so much of himself into the program, Maggie actually began to sound like him—at least from a logic perspective. One additional precaution Jeff took before leaving was to instruct Maggie not to allow off-loading of any original programs without his specific approval.

He wanted the ERTS team to have all the processed data they needed—but not his operating software. In an afterthought, Jeff instructed Maggie to conceal her own existence and to release none of the comparisons of the historical data recently supplied by ERTS. He couldn't say why he did the last two things. Call it an inner sense. . . .

▲

Dale Crawford was less than ten miles from Casper, Wyoming, when he saw the rundown old camper heading in the opposite direction. He slumped down behind the wheel as the two vehicles passed. Both drivers initially were startled to see another vehicle on the road with them. Travel was so rare that Crawford had not passed more than ten cars for the last five hundred miles, and most of those were farm vehicles.

His spare storage tank was nearly empty. He'd had no luck in locating either a fueling station or any farm-supplied methane for the last several hours. With no other choices, he pressed on and prayed for a miracle. The closer he got to Casper, the more he realized he had absolutely no idea how to locate Wells' ranch when he got there.

As the camper passed, Crawford noticed four youths crammed into the front seat. He felt a nervousness, born of his recently acquired survival instincts, and continued to watch the camper as it disappeared from his rearview mirror. He wasn't sure they were after him, but he decided to get off the main road.

He was almost past the side road before he saw it. He hit the brakes and swung the car onto the dusty, graveled back road. His dust had barely settled when he saw the dust cloud from the camper as it roared past the point where he had turned off. They had turned around and had come back to follow him.

"They're on to me," he said aloud as he gunned the ailing engine. He was sure the plume of dust he was throwing up behind him could be seen for miles.

In the camper, Albert "Hit Man" Cooper was yelling at his driver. "He turned off, you stupid idiot. Turn around."

The driver, known only as Mugger, swung the big camper around again, almost tipping it over in the process. Hit Man swore at his driver and threatened him with all sorts of retribution, including total dismemberment, if he dumped the camper. But it settled back onto its tires and they roared down the highway toward the gravel road where the car had obviously turned off.

"We've got him!" Mugger yelled as his headband flapped wildly in the hot wind whistling through the open windows.

"Faster, you fool," Hit Man demanded as the engine protested the sudden and uncommon power surge.

Crawford glanced in his mirror and saw an even bigger plume of dust as he rounded a curve where his own dust was off to the side. He pushed the gas pedal to the floor, but the engine was already giving all it had. His speed was topped out at sixty miles an hour, and the camper was gaining on him.

Mugger also was holding the gas pedal to the floor, but the camper, although heavier, had a decided advantage: It was gasoline powered instead of methane powered.

"We've got him! We've got him!" Mugger shouted again and again. His drug-addled brain could focus on just one thing at a time, but his reflexes were those of an eighteen-year-old, and he skillfully weaved the camper around the major potholes in the abandoned roadway.

"Keep on him," Hit Man screamed again. "I'll bet that's the dude everyone's looking for. I want him!"

"I'll git him," Mugger shouted as he swerved to miss another big pothole. "Man, I hope he's got some drugs. . . ."

Crawford was desperate. It was obvious that he was not going to be able to outrun the camper. He had hoped that the terrible condition of the road would slow it down, but whoever was in control of the camper was driving like a madman. It gained on the old Ford every mile.

Within five more miles the camper was just behind Crawford's car. Hit Man screamed to Mugger to pull up alongside. He had his gun ready. If the driver didn't stop, he would just shoot him in the head. He hated to do that because the car might explode when it wrecked. *But, what the heck*, he figured.

Crawford saw the nose of the camper immediately behind him and to his left. He was panicked. In his mirror he saw a man leaning out the window with a revolver in his hand. "God help me!" he cried.

Instead of looking ahead, both Crawford and Mugger were looking at the other's vehicles when they topped the ridge. Just over the ridge was what had once been a bridge over a now dry riverbed. If anyone had been tending to the old road, they would have put up a sign warning that the bridge was out. But no one had.

Dale glanced up just in time to see the sagging bridge before him, and he swerved off to the right. Mugger's brain was focused on running the other vehicle off the road, and he didn't look up until it was too late. The crumbling bridge served as a perfect jump ramp; the camper and its passengers were launched into space.

The last sound anyone in the camper heard was Mugger yelling "Yahoo!" as the vehicle went airborne. It hit the ground some fifty feet out, literally exploding as the plastic containers full of gasoline, which the group had stolen from an earlier raid, split open on impact.

The old Ford that Crawford was driving slid sideways for several yards before hitting a large rock. Then it rolled at least ten times, scattering car parts all over the dry wash as it went. Inside the car, Crawford was thrown first into the steering wheel and then against the roof. Mercifully, he lost consciousness by about the third roll, as the car tumbled down the embankment.

▲

At Galt's ranch in Montana, his pilot was taxiing his Gulf Stream IV into takeoff position, in preparation for the trip to Casper to pick up Jeff and Karen. Galt had almost decided to go along but then changed his mind. He hadn't been feeling well lately, and the long trip to L.A. would be pretty exhausting.

Besides, he told himself, *I have absolute confidence in Jeff. This meeting likely will bring the IEF and UNEEA on board.* The responses to the invitations were overwhelming once it was known that Wells himself would address the group. *It's funny,* Galt told himself, *they like my money, but they respect Wells' brains. Well, I guess that's why guys like me always sponsor the geniuses who create the masterpieces.*

Galt looked out as he heard the turbines whining to their utmost. The sleek jet eased its way down the runway. First it moved slowly, but as the power of the engines took control it gained momentum. When less than half the 4,000-foot strip was consumed, the needle-nosed craft tilted upward and soared airborne.

Just as he started to turn away, Galt saw a small puff of blue smoke from the right engine. Next the engine was engulfed in a bright orange ball, but the plane continued to climb. Finally, the whole tail of the aircraft was engulfed in the fireball. As if on command, the pilot turned his aircraft back toward the strip.

But before he ever maneuvered the complete turn, the plane disintegrated in the air. Pieces were showered down on the open range around Galt's ranch house. When the main portion of the fuselage hit the ground, the earth shook under Galt's feet.

He stood transfixed at the window, trying to sort out in his mind what he'd just witnessed. In mere seconds, the fire trucks from his hangar were roaring toward the field where the shattered plane lay burning. No one had to tell him that there would be no survivors.

Later that morning Galt's personal secretary called the Wells' ranch to tell them about the tragedy and also to tell them that they had been booked on the early morning train from Casper to Denver and then on a plane to Los Angeles. She added that one of Mr. Galt's best security men, Max Hilton, would accompany Jeff and Karen on their trip.

"That won't be necessary," Jeff assured the secretary. "We'll be able to handle the trip without security."

"Mr. Galt insists that Mr. Hilton accompany you, Dr. Wells," she said with finality.

"Okay," Jeff agreed, with more relief than he realized. "Tell Mr. Galt we'll be fine. I'm really sorry about the accident," he added.

Once off the phone, Jeff explained the situation to Karen. She didn't feel very good about going. The accident was like a bad omen, but she hid her anxieties from Jeff. "It's okay, honey," she said. "We didn't really need a private jet anyway."

What neither of them knew then was just how educational the next few days would be for both of them.

16

△

Leaving the Ranch

I t's hard to believe the current state of our transportation system," Karen commented as their train passed over several rough road crossings. She could see the intersecting roads were cracked and potholed.

Max Hilton, the bodyguard Galt had assigned to Jeff and Karen, explained, "It's a lot of things: the depression, hyperinflation, government mismanagement—they've nearly destroyed the infrastructure of the whole country."

He went on to describe how the roads throughout America were in total decay; the trains ran only intermittently; and the airplanes, even those operated by the FAA, were rarely on time. The second Great Depression still lingered on after more than a decade, in spite of all the efforts of each administration to stimulate growth.

As the train passed through towns in Wyoming and on into Colorado, Jeff and Karen saw homeless people living in tents and shacks along the tracks. Frequently they would see run-down fire trucks, escorted by faded police cars, rushing to put out fires started by vandals in the homeless shantytowns.

"This is unbelievable!" Karen gasped at the sight of one dilapidated town after another. "It looks like a scene from eighteenth century Europe."

"It's pretty much like this all over the country," Max commented. "There are a lot of people out of work . . . and out of hope, especially many black people—my relatives included."

"But how do these people live?" Karen asked, staring out the window at row after row of ramshackle dwellings. It was more than her mind could absorb. Trembling from the restrained emotions, she said, "This is like being thrown back into the Dark Ages."

"That's probably a good analogy," Max agreed while unconsciously reaching up to touch the weapon concealed under his jacket. He was reflecting on the night a few weeks earlier when he had been in one of the shantytowns looking for his younger brother, who had been relocated by one of the government drug control units.

The violence erupted almost as soon as the sun went down. Anyone left on the streets after dark was a target for one of the teenage gangs. He found himself walking with his gun in hand, which probably saved his life. Later, he discovered that his brother had been murdered the first week after he was "relocated."

"What good was it all?" Jeff mumbled as they passed through a massive relocation center on the outskirts of Denver.

"What, honey?" Karen asked, shielding her nose from the smell permeating the car—the stench of open sewage ditches used as overflow in the shantytown.

"I said, what good was it all? So what if we shut down the Illuminati? Look at what's happening to our country. This is terrible! Our country must be in ruins if this is any indication. Apparently we didn't really solve any problems."

"But you did all you could."

"I wonder," Jeff muttered to himself. "Is this what life in America is going to be like for Jason and our grandchildren?"

A growing cloud of doubt was nagging at Jeff. *I guess I knew things were bad,* he thought somberly, *but this goes beyond just bad. The environment, ERTS . . . are we a part of all this somehow?* he asked himself.

Jeff was about to say something else to Karen and Max just as they were passing by another row of shacks built almost on the railroad right-of-way. He hadn't noticed the group of tough-looking youths standing near the tracks. As the cars rolled by they started pelting the train with bottles, rocks, and anything else they could gather.

Max shouted, "Duck!" but his warning came too late. One of the projectiles hit the rim of the window where Karen was seated. Fortunately, the window was closed or she would have been hit in the head by what appeared to be a beer bottle. Instead, she was struck by shards of broken glass as the window shattered. Only instinctive reflexes kept her from losing one or both eyes. With hands covering her face, Karen turned her head toward Jeff, who was already reaching for her.

Jeff's startled cry shocked Karen more than the flying glass. "Karen!" he shouted above the sound of the whistling wind. "Your face! Are you okay?"

"I think so," Karen murmured, carefully feeling her face. Her hands came away slick with blood. Most of the force of the broken glass had been diverted upward, so it struck her forehead and scalp, barely missing her eyes. But the blood from the scalp wounds made her face a sticky mess.

Jeff quickly grabbed the handkerchief from his coat pocket and used it to mop the flowing blood as he tried to get a better look at the actual injuries. As he wiped he shouted, "Max, I need some help here."

Max, who had been sitting across the aisle from them, had already opened a small bag from which he pulled a clean cloth and used it to wipe Karen's face so he could look at the injuries more closely.

"It's not as bad as it looks," he told Jeff with a sigh of relief. "She mostly has some superficial lacerations of the scalp and face. Fortunately, none of the glass hit her in the eyes."

"Can you see me?" Max asked Karen, holding the towel against the scalp wounds to stop the bleeding.

"I think so," Karen answered cautiously. "Yes, now I can!" she said excitedly. With the blood streaming into her eyes, she had temporarily been blinded. But as more of the blood cleared, she realized that there was no pain in her eyes.

"Praise the Lord!" Jeff uttered as he pulled Karen toward him, his anger beginning to rise. Through gritted teeth Jeff growled, "I could kill them."

"Jeff! You don't mean that," Karen expressed in disbelief. "I'm all right."

"I do mean it," he said, carefully studying her face. Karen's dress was stained with her own blood, as were Jeff's shirt and pants. "They could have killed you, and for what? We didn't do anything to them."

"They think you did," Max countered.

"What do you mean?" Jeff asked as he looked up at Max, who was still standing in the aisle.

"If you're riding the train and not living in that squalor, you're an enemy in their eyes," Max said. "I should know. I lived just like that myself for a while. Once, when I tried to help them, this is what I got for my efforts," he said, unbuttoning the shirt collar covering his neck line.

"Oh!" Karen exclaimed involuntarily at the sight of the ugly scar on Max's throat.

"Two teenagers cut my throat one evening as I was walking back to my emergency paramedic unit after helping a shooting victim."

"But why?" Jeff asked. "Why, if you were trying to help?"

"Maybe because I'm black and they were white," Max said. "But maybe not . . . 'cause blacks kill blacks, and whites kill whites. We've raised a whole generation with no morals, no values, and no hope.

"Anyway, that's when I decided to become a security guard. A bullet is all these young hoodlums understand. They laugh at the liberals who depict them as innocent victims of our society. They'll kill you for your shoes and then complain that you were wearing the wrong size."

"I had no idea," Jeff said, shaking his head. "What's it like in the cities?"

"That's why Mr. Galt sent me with you," Max said grimly. "You won't believe it until you've seen it for yourself. Now, we'd better get some bandages on Mrs. Wells' face," he said, once again the professional.

"We're getting close to the Denver station," Max cautioned. "Stay close to me when we get off. Denver has become a battle-ground for dealers transporting drugs from the West Coast."

As Max turned to go back to his seat, Karen squeezed his hand. "Thank you," she said warmly. The events of the last few minutes had shaken her more than she wanted to admit.

"Jeff, we've been isolated from the real world too long," Karen murmured.

Jeff put his arm around her. "Maybe we should have stayed where we were; but as you know, trouble has a way of finding us wherever we are."

The remainder of the trip to the Denver station proved uneventful. Karen desperately wanted to get to a phone to call the ranch and check on Jason. She made the call while Max and Jeff reported the bottle throwing incident to a train detective.

"Happens all the time," the disinterested detective commented. "Nothin' we can do about it. Even if we caught the ones that did it, which we can't, the judge would let 'em off. We have ten killin's a day in those ghettos. Train vandalism is pretty low on the court's list of crimes."

"Like I said, Jeff," Max growled, "you and Karen stay close to me."

When Karen called the ranch, she was relieved to talk with Maria and hear that Jason and Reno were out checking the fences. Maria reported that Jason was having the time of his life and had badgered Reno into letting him ride a paint pony—just his size. For two hours after his parents left, he had strutted around the cottage, telling all of his imaginary friends that he was the boss of this "spread."

"Maybe we'll have a roundup, Uncle Reno."

"Maybe so," Reno agreed. He was amused by Jason's recently acquired bravado. The boy's quick mind and broad vocabulary testified that he was going to be altogether as special as his gifted parents were.

Assured that Jason was safe and in good spirits, Karen went into the ladies' room to change into some clean clothes while Jeff changed in the men's room. When they came out, Max shuffled them out of the station toward the only cab waiting by the entrance.

The trio reached the airport after a hair-raising taxi ride that, theoretically, should have taken thirty minutes but instead took nearly an hour, as the cabdriver skirted through the unpatrolled areas of the city. They dodged one roadblock after another, set up by inner-city gangs to extract tolls from the few motorists who passed through.

Once they reached the airport, the cab driver quoted a fare of $250.

"Two hundred fifty dollars for a cab ride?" Jeff asked incredulously.

"Hey, if you wanna' get through this city in a cab, you pay the price," the sarcastic driver said, grabbing the money and dumping their luggage by the curb. "Besides, mister, if you can afford to fly, you can afford the cab fare." With that, he drove off, the ten-year-old Chevy belching propane fumes.

"The world is full of rude people," Karen said. The call to the ranch had lifted her spirits, but the peeling paint and generally run-down condition of the buildings around them was quickly dampening them again.

Max started to say something and then stopped. *If all we see are rude people we'll be lucky,* he thought darkly. He didn't like the thought of being the only security for Jeff and Karen when they reached Los Angeles. *Denver is like Boys Town compared to L.A., if I remember correctly.* He thought about preparing the Wellses for that shock too but decided against it. *They'll learn quick enough,* he decided.

They made their way to one of the three remaining active service counters in the airport terminal. "There's hardly anybody here," Jeff commented as he looked around.

"And look at the condition of this building," Karen remarked, noting the peeling paint and faded decorations. "I'll bet it hasn't been cleaned in months."

"Welcome to the world of government control," Max quipped. "The American people wanted socialism, and now they have it."

As they approached one of the ticket agents, Max retrieved from his briefcase the vouchers Galt supplied. "Three first-class tickets to Los Angeles," he stated to the middle-aged woman behind the counter.

"We don't have class restrictions," she said curtly. "All the fares are the same, as required by the National Fairness Doctrine."

"Well then, just let me have three tickets—as provided by the National Fairness Doctrine," Max replied sarcastically.

The agent grabbed the vouchers from his hands and set about typing feverishly on her ancient terminal. After what seemed to be an unconscionable amount of time, the terminal responded with the requested data and the agent said, "That will be thirty thousand dollars. I will charge the amount to Mr. Galt's account as authorized."

"Thirty thousand dollars?" Karen exclaimed. "How could three tickets cost thirty thousand dollars?"

"The cost of government efficiency and the printing of money to pay its bills," Max answered.

Jeff was almost too shocked to respond, but then he asked, "What does an average family make today, Max?"

Overhearing Jeff's question, the ticket agent looked at him as if he had just stepped out of a time capsule. Then she looked back down at her terminal and continued coaxing it to provide all the data needed to book the tickets.

"Oh, I guess an average income in Denver would be maybe thirty thousand a year," Max commented while he signed the voucher. "That is, if you don't average in all the homeless we saw on the way."

As the terminal printer began to print out the travel authorizations, the agent suddenly assumed a new attitude. She saw the trio's travel was authorized by none other than President Rand himself and classified as priority one—meaning bump anyone necessary to secure their travel.

"Oh, I am sorry, Mr. . . . uh . . . Dr. Wells," she said in a honey-soaked voice. "I didn't recognize who you were, sir. I'll have your accommodations in a minute."

Jeff hardly heard her, although her change in attitude was not lost on Karen. He was still thinking about the price of the tickets. "You mean it would take a family's income for one year just to fly to L.A.?" he asked Max.

"If they could! But it's almost impossible to travel by air unless you're on a priority list, and I can tell you, average income families are not on that list. But just think, Jeff, what the price would be if costs weren't contained by the Price Control Act."

"I don't know how people can survive in a system like this," Jeff commented.

"I think we saw the answer along the way." Karen grimaced, lifting her hand to touch the lacerations on her forehead. "They don't seem to be surviving too well."

As they made their way out to the tarmac where the plane waited, Jeff eyed the other passengers following the flight attendant. *There's no question that average people don't fly much any more.*

"A few of the passengers look to be business travelers," Jeff commented to Max. "Who would the others be?"

"Mostly government types," Max replied with a note of contempt in his voice. "You can always tell."

"How do you know they work for the government?" Karen asked.

"They all have the look of ferrets: intense and constantly glancing around," Max replied. "It comes from working around people who distrust everyone else, I guess."

"Boy, this is a low budget operation," Jeff commented. "Not even any transportation to the plane."

Max started to make a comment, but about that time they rounded the corner of the building and got their first look at the plane that would take them to Los Angeles.

"Oh my goodness!" Karen said with surprise.

"You can say that again," Jeff responded when he saw the ancient MD-11. He hadn't expected a new plane, but this one was nearly thirty years old.

If there had been any other choice, Jeff might have turned back. But the other passengers were already going up the portable stairs and into the plane. As they started up the stairway, Karen hesitated.

Reading her mind, Jeff said, "It's all right, honey. I'm sure they wouldn't fly a plane that isn't safe." He wasn't nearly as confident as he sounded. *If we ever have to travel again, I'm going to find a charter company—no matter the cost.*

As promised, there were no first- or second-class seats on the plane. The open seating and the well-worn fabric reminded him of a tired, old passenger bus. He and Karen settled down into the nearest seats, and he silently prayed that Jason would grow up under the guidance of some good people, just in case they didn't make it. Karen decided that flying to L.A. was about as risky as driving through one of the urban areas.

Jeff looked around and noticed that most of the other passengers were well into their second round of drinks. *Can't say that I blame them a lot,* he noted.

"Well, at least the captain looks normal," Jeff commented as the cabin door closed. "Do you think the crew members wear parachutes?"

"Naw," Max replied whimsically. "The government can't afford the extra cost." Karen wasn't amused by their humor.

Despite their misgivings about the aircraft, the flight to L.A. proved uneventful, although Jeff had his ear tuned to detect any spurious noises emanating from the thirty-year-old jet.

Not having traveled much in the last several years, neither Jeff nor Karen realized that the airlines no longer served food on their flights. Beverages were limited to water, which was free, or alcohol, which was sold aplenty to the other passengers.

It looked like everyone else had some food or beverage in the bags they'd brought on board. *Next time a charter,* Jeff told himself. *Definitely a charter!*

"It's a good thing we ate something on the train," Jeff whispered to Karen. "Looks like they would at least serve some peanuts or something."

"I'm a little hungry, but I suppose, with the price of food being what it is, the government can't afford the additional cost."

"We've gone from a net exporter of food to not being able to feed ourselves in a period of ten years," Max commented. "It's the land bank program that set aside half of our farmland under the Clean Water Act. That and the fact that all chemical pesticides and fertilizers have been banned."

"Half the farmland has been taken out of production!" Jeff exclaimed. "When the country's short of food?"

"Yep, the birds and insects are doing well, though," Max added sarcastically.

"I can't believe the government has taken that much land out of food production," Jeff replied, thinking back to all the debates he had heard over the banning of pesticides and the land bank program to protect endangered species. It had seemed a good idea when they were back on the ranch and able to feed themselves without relying on others. He hadn't thought much about the basic things, like food; but now he did.

"I guess I never thought much about food," Karen said. "I just assumed we would always have enough."

"I wonder what the food supply is like in the big cities. If the rest of our transportation system is as bad as what we've seen so far, I'll bet it's hard to get food to the cities—especially a city like Los Angeles."

Max didn't respond, but if Jeff or Karen had been looking at him right then, they would have seen the frown he wore. *You ain't seen nothin' yet, folks,* he was thinking.

Karen tried to sleep, but her mind was racing too much to relax. *What will L.A. be like?* she wondered. It had been more than ten years since they had last seen the city. *Is it as bad as the media presents?* She had a nagging feeling about something, but she couldn't focus on it. *It's time we broke out of our little cocoon,* she resolved, closing her eyes as the image of the shantytowns they had passed through flashed through her mind. *Maybe it's past time.*

17

△

Arriving in L.A.

Karen struggled to stay awake, fearful that if she slept something terrible might happen to the old plane they were on. Finally, she drifted into a fitful sleep.

She began to dream. She was at the ranch, but she couldn't find anyone there. She cried out for Reno and Maria, but no one answered. She rushed into the ranch house to check on Jason but found his room empty. What she saw in the six-year-old's room filled her with terror.

Jason's clothes were scattered all over the room. Most of them were torn to shreds. His toys were scattered and crushed as if some giant wrecking machine had run amok in his room. Karen heard herself scream; it was as if she were listening to a character in a play. As she stumbled out of her son's room, she was confronted by several gang members wielding guns.

This can't be real, she kept telling herself. She heard herself screaming at the gang, "Where is my son? What have you done with him?"

"He's dead," one of the evil-looking gang members said.

"He can't be dead," Karen screamed back. "I want Jason!"

Just then, there was a tremendous screech—like that of a wounded animal. Karen snapped to consciousness and bolted upright in her seat, letting out an involuntary gasp.

"It's all right, honey," Jeff said calmly, putting his arm around her. "You must have been dreaming."

"What was that sound?" Karen asked, trying to focus her mind.

"We're landing," Jeff replied. "The flaps are coming down now."

"But, Jeff, what is that awful sound?" Karen asked a little more calmly now.

"It's just the hydraulic pumps. They do sound pretty bad, but they're probably as old as this plane," Jeff joked, trying to ease his wife's tension. "You okay?"

"Yes," Karen said as convincingly as she could. "It was just a bad dream." She was glad to be awake.

The plane was on final approach when the captain instructed the passengers to buckle their seat belts. Shortly thereafter, Karen felt the comforting jolt of the wheels touching down on the runway. She hadn't realized how tense she was until then. She made a conscious effort to relax as the plane slowed on the runway and turned toward the terminal building. She knew she had to talk with Jason again before she would be totally convinced that the whole thing was simply a bad dream.

There was no other traffic on the runway, so the plane taxied directly to the terminal building; and Jeff, Karen, and Max made their way toward the faded and peeling exit ramp. As the trio entered the airport terminal, they were met by a beaming Dr. Shimora, Jeff's old mentor and friend at Cal Tech.

"Good afternoon, Dr. Wells," the ancient scholar chimed. "Welcome to Los Angeles, City of the Angels."

Jeff smiled warmly at the greeting of his older compatriot. For Dr. Shimora to refer to Jeff as "doctor" was his way of acknowledging his former student's equal academic status.

"I'm glad to be back, doctor," Jeff responded. "Although, I have to tell you: If I'd known how difficult it was to travel these days, I might not have agreed to come."

"I thoroughly understand," Shimora nodded in agreement. "I have not traveled in some time, but some of our younger faculty members who do travel relate some harrowing tales. The planes are seldom on schedule these days."

Then looking at Karen, he inquired, "What happened to you, my dear?"

"A little incident on the train to Denver," Karen replied as she touched the wounds on her face and forehead.

"Some kid threw a bottle at the train window, and the broken glass hit Karen," Jeff replied gruffly. "They could have killed her."

"Ah yes," Shimora sighed, "we have much the same trouble here and in many other cities across the country. The young seem angry about everything today. With so many unemployed, I fear what might happen next," the older scientist remarked. "It would seem that our whole society is out of balance."

"I tend to agree," Max said as he picked up their carry-on bags, which had been placed in the lobby when they disembarked.

"Dr. Shimora, this is Max Hilton," Karen said by way of introduction. "Mr. Galt sent him to be our security guard."

"A wise precaution," Shimora said. Instinctively, he started to bow but stopped short and extended his hand.

Max shifted the bag from his right hand and shook Shimora's outstretched hand. "Glad to meet you," Max responded.

"It is my pleasure, Mr. Hilton. I am glad you accompanied my friends. The world is a dangerous place these days."

"You're right about that, doctor," Max replied, shifting the bags permanently to keep his right hand free. He felt the reassuring bulge of the concealed gun as the bags bumped against his shoulder holster.

"Do you have any additional luggage?" Shimora asked.

"No. Since we're only going to be here a short time, we packed light," Karen answered.

"Ah, that is wise," Shimora mused in jest as he touched his index finger to his temple. "One can never be certain where one's luggage may be shipped these days."

"I'll just bet that's true," Jeff agreed as they headed out.

Making their way to the exit doors, Karen sensed something was wrong, but she couldn't put her finger on it immediately. Then, as they walked through the doors, she realized what it was.

"Doctor Shimora!" Karen exclaimed, "Where are all the cars?"

"All private transportation has been banned in Los Angeles for two years now."

"But how do people get around in the city?" Karen asked as they entered the nearly abandoned transportation ramp area.

"Few people actually work in the city itself these days," Shimora shrugged. "The violence is too great, and transportation is not what it once was—not since the EPA banned all internal combustion engines in the city."

"I remember hearing about that," Karen remarked. "It was about four years ago, wasn't it?"

"Yes," Shimora sighed. "Initially the phaseout was to take place over the next decade, but when President Rand took office, the EPA issued new regulations banning all smog-producing vehicles. It has been very difficult for citizens to get around ever since."

"What about alternative transportation?" Karen asked in amazement. "Surely the EPA would not just shut down a whole city."

"We do have some alternative transportation," Shimora replied as they made their way down what appeared to be a subway ramp, "but it is not very dependable either, I'm afraid."

"What about the electric cars that were being developed the last time I was out here?" Karen asked, still trying to sort out the enormity of seeing no traffic in Los Angeles.

"Ah yes, electric vehicles were to be the alternative for single family transportation. Unfortunately, it was later discovered that the net pollution of converting fossil fuels to electricity and then using that power in vehicles was greater than the internal combustion engines they replaced."

"You mean they passed a law banning all vehicles that couldn't pass a pollution standard and then found out that nothing passed the test?" Karen asked incredulously.

"That's about the size of it," Shimora answered, with a chuckle. "Sounds like a typical government program, doesn't it?"

"It sounds too stupid to believe," Jeff retorted. "Unfortunately, I've seen enough in the last two days to believe anything. But, doctor, how do the people still living and working get around?"

"The subways still operate," Shimora replied with a slight frown. It seemed to Jeff that the elder scientist had developed a limp.

"Is something wrong with your leg, doctor?" Jeff asked as they started down the steps into the tunnel walkway.

"Just an injury I received while riding the subway some time ago," Shimora explained, rubbing his left thigh.

"What happened?" Karen asked sympathetically.

"I hesitate to mention it," Shimora responded as he looked down in typical oriental fashion. "I wouldn't want to worry you, but it is important that we be alert. The subways are controlled by armed gangs. One evening I was stopped, and they demanded money to allow me to pass. When I refused, one of the youths attacked me with a baseball bat. I spent several weeks in the hospital before I could resume my activities."

"I'm really sorry, doctor," Karen said. "It does seem that crime is the rule rather than the exception these days."

"It is indeed," Shimora agreed. "Now when I travel alone, I always carry some money to pay for my passage if I am stopped. I think of it as a toll—like many of our highways used to have."

As they reached the underground tunnel, Karen was amazed to see hundreds of people standing on the loading and unloading platforms amidst the litter and debris. Against one wall was a poorly dressed man asleep in a large cardboard box. "Where in the world did all these people come from?" she asked.

"Most people who travel below ground stay in the tunnels until they reach their final destination," Shimora answered. "It is usually safer than the streets for the travelers as well as some of the homeless."

At almost that instant two tough-looking young men came up to them. "Glad to see you made it back okay, old man," the teen who seemed to be in charge said with an evil smirk. "But you'll have to pay again since you went up top. Your friends too."

"I understand," Shimora replied, with no sign of resistance in his tone. "How much will it be now?" He was fumbling for the unobtrusive money belt he wore beneath his shirt and coat.

"Just a minute, doctor," Jeff stated abruptly.

At the tone of his voice one of the youths suddenly produced a small automatic pistol and pointed it directly at Jeff. At almost the same instant, Max's gun appeared in his hand. He pointed the lethal looking .50 caliber weapon at the youth and said, "I think you'd better reconsider."

With one look at the muzzle of the gun pointed at him, the youth lowered his weapon. But then, as if by signal, several more gun-wielding gang members appeared.

"Now give me your gun," the young thug demanded of Max.

"Not likely," Max replied gruffly as he cocked the hammer.

"You can't shoot us all," the amazed gang leader said in confusion. "We'll kill all of you."

"Maybe so," Max said with an intensity that said volumes, "but in the process you'll be very dead yourself."

"Nobody goes through without payin'," the furious gang leader bellowed. "It ain't worth you gettin' killed over, is it?"

"Stop!" Shimora said sharply. "Max! Jeff! This is the way it is now! I will pay!" Turning back to the thug, he asked, "How much is it?"

"It *was* fifty bucks," the agitated young man said through gritted teeth. "But now it's a hundred bucks—apiece!"

"I'll pay," Jeff commanded as he pushed his friend's hand away from his money supply. He reached into his pocket and pulled out a roll of bills, from which he peeled three one hundred dollar bills.

Taking the money while still holding the gun loosely, the leader said, "Thanks, old man. Hey, you'd better tell this dummy not to go walkin' around with that roll in sight. Some people ain't as *honest* as we are.

"We'll see *you* later, sucker," the leader said to Max, with courage born out of bravado.

"I'll be looking for you," Max replied, uncocking his weapon.

The young gang members walked away laughing and were quickly swallowed up in the maze of people.

"Jeff, I was so frightened," Karen said as she stepped close to him. "I believe that hoodlum would have shot you."

"Without a doubt," Shimora agreed. "That is the way of things today. But there is a code of ethics—even among the lawless. Once we have paid the toll to the gang controlling this area, they will leave us alone."

Max said nothing as he returned his gun to its holster. He suspected things were the way they were because people tolerated, no . . . feared, the would-be thugs.

"Why, that's extortion," Karen exclaimed as the realization occurred to her.

"Indeed it is," Shimora agreed, "but in reality it is only the tip of the iceberg. Just wait; you'll see. Jeff, you have not been to the city for a while. Do you not have these problems in Wyoming too?"

"Probably," Jeff agreed as he thought about what he'd seen on their trip, "but it just hasn't touched our lives yet."

"Then you are very fortunate. Perhaps we should all move to Wyoming?" Shimora remarked with a smile.

The thoughts racing through Jeff's mind made him wonder just how long it would be before the problems *would* reach the back lands of Wyoming. He couldn't have known just how soon that would be. If he had, he would have taken Karen and retreated even then.

The subway train system routed the trio under the most dilapidated and, thus, the most crime-controlled areas of the city.

"Our subway system was built as a government work project," Shimora said to Max, without his asking. "It was part of the EPA compromise plan for the cities. Unfortunately, the 800-billion-dollar contribution required of the city bankrupted us. Now many of the trains don't run because the city lacks the funds to operate them.

"Trains still run to the south side—what used to be called the ghettos," Shimora explained, "because if they didn't service those areas the rioters would simply bring the battle to the remaining patrolled areas. But," he said, "no one who is not heavily armed and a member of one of the controlling gangs would dare venture into the south side anymore."

"What about the police in those areas?" Karen asked in amazement.

"There are no police in those areas, my dear," Shimora explained. "The federal government pays gang members to control the streets. In exchange, they limit their fighting to the designated areas."

"Why, that's paying extortion too," Karen exclaimed in disbelief. "Surely the government wouldn't agree to that."

"They don't call it extortion, my dear. It is termed 'inner-city development funding.'"

"Un-be-liev-able," Jeff responded slowly, as he shook his head. "Is it this way all over the country?"

"One would assume so," Shimora acknowledged. "I personally haven't done any traveling for the last few years . . . the costs, you know. The university has stopped all nonessential travel. And about the only essential travel is to and from Washington to plead for more grant money. With the student population down seventy percent, it is difficult to operate the facilities."

"Seventy percent!" Jeff exclaimed in disbelief. "How in the world can enrollment be down seventy percent? Where are all the students going?"

"There really aren't that many, and with the government quota system in effect, we must accept those assigned to us. And confidentially, I must tell you that the quality of students we are assigned under the quota system is not very good. If my students took the tests you were given, none would be able to pass the course."

"Haven't you complained?" Jeff asked incredulously.

"One doesn't complain in our system," Shimora whispered quietly, "or one is unemployed."

Jeff looked at his friend in surprise. Shimora always had been a hero of sorts to Jeff since his days at Cal Tech. The older scientist had confronted his superiors to support what, at the time, seemed to be a young graduate student's wild idea on earthquake prediction. Jeff had never forgotten how Shimora helped during that time.

Now, as he looked at Shimora, he noticed that he seemed to have withered. Never a large man by any means, it seemed to Jeff that his friend had shrunk—not from age but from a system that sapped his vitality.

Shimora saw the look that Jeff was giving him and responded without any indication of offense. "Ah, my large young pupil, you think your old teacher is defeated by the system, and you are correct."

"No, I didn't . . . ," Jeff started to say.

"It is okay," Shimora commented as they shuffled through the debris lying all around. And you are correct. The system is in control now. You obey or you are cast aside."

"But any problems can be solved if enough people care," Jeff attempted to counter.

"Perhaps you are actually unaware of just how special you are, my gifted friend," Shimora interrupted. "You have many powerful friends in very high places. And those who would be your enemy are content to see you hide away in the wilds of Wyoming while they undo all you have accomplished."

"But we're not hiding away," Karen stammered defensively. Yet even as she said it and looked around at the decay around her, she knew Shimora was right.

"Hey, I never asked for any special treatment," Jeff protested.

"And I believe you, because I know you so well. But those who would destroy our country in order to rule its citizens are more than willing to keep you pacified," the old man whispered. "There are many eyes and ears listening for those who would rule. You can be certain that one as famous as you will be monitored. So be careful."

"Then you think we are in danger?" Karen asked. The fear she had felt many years earlier when she and Jeff were hiding from the Illuminati group resurfaced. She shuddered involuntarily as she remembered the feeling of being totally at the mercy of merciless people.

When Jeff had discovered the plot to use his Data-Net system against American citizens and he and Karen had fled for their lives, they had spent months hiding and running from their own government while Jeff was devising a way to shut down Data-Net.

Karen shuddered to think just how close she and Jeff had come to losing their own lives in that struggle. Even President Hunt had been murdered when he attempted to rein in the one-world advocates.

Shimora was right: Virtually all the gains that had been made in reining in the government seemed to have been lost. Perhaps the adage is correct which says, "A democracy will only succeed until the citizens find they can vote themselves largess from the Treasury. Then they will bankrupt it."

Responding to Karen's concern, Shimora replied, "I think you have little to fear while your friends still hold high positions. No one would be foolish enough to confront Mr. Galt and his allies."

"How does Galt figure into this?" Jeff asked defensively. He had the greatest of confidence that Galt was exactly what he always seemed to be: a slightly cantankerous multibillionaire, who also was a very good friend.

"I think Mr. Galt is being used by those who would like to see this once great country totally destroyed," Shimora replied softly. "He is very active in the environmental movement."

"So are a lot of others," Karen remarked, in defense of their longtime friend.

"Very true," Shimora agreed. "So am I, but you will find the movement has attracted a rather fanatical element."

"What do you mean?" Jeff asked. Somewhere inside his head an alarm went off. *Something is very wrong,* but he couldn't put words to what he was feeling. Perhaps it's just the defeat he sensed in a man who was very hard to defeat.

I have the same feeling I had when I first heard about the Illuminati, he thought darkly. *No, that's impossible,* he chided himself. *It's just the despair caused by the country's problems.* But inside, Jeff Wells knew that once again some force was tugging at him. What he felt was not fear. It was fury. And it frightened him.

The conversation had not been lost on Max Hilton. He knew the people who controlled the government would be watching them closely.

18

△

Maggie's Revelation

As they made their way through the subway system, a stench hit Karen's nostrils that almost made her gag. "What is that?" she exclaimed, placing her hand over her nose in a reflex action.

"It's human refuse," Dr. Shimora replied. "You get used to it if you use the subways very often."

"Whew! It smells like a backed-up sewer," Karen complained.

"Worse than that," Max countered. "Raw sewage is being deposited on the floors."

"Quite so," Shimora agreed. When they reached the bottom level where the trains arrived and departed, Karen could scarcely believe her eyes. There were literally hundreds of people of all ages milling around, many of them families camped out on the floors amidst some of the worse filth she had ever seen.

"Good heavens!" she exclaimed, "where did all these people come from, and how can they live in this filth?"

"Some are dope addicts who have had their brains fried on drugs," Max said sarcastically, "the result of our brilliant plan to legalize drugs and stop crime. Now they draw Social Security and live in this sewer."

"Yes," added Shimora, "but the majority are those who either would not go to the relocation camps or have escaped from one of the camps. The government now considers them to be nonpersons."

"Nonpersons?" Karen asked quizzically.

"You know, *persona non grata:* not acceptable," Max quipped.

"If they won't accept the government's conditions, they can't participate in the government's handouts. And since about seventy percent of all jobs are now government jobs, that means they can't work. No job and no welfare means they have to live in the subways."

Karen stared in unbelief at the sight of dozens of dirty small children dressed in rags. "What do they do to survive?" she asked quietly.

"Mostly they become lackeys for the gangs who give them a little food now and then. They prostitute, or pimp, as required."

"That's awful," Karen said angrily. "Someone should help these poor people. They're not criminals."

"All people are potential criminals if they're hungry enough," Max added sarcastically. "When you wipe out all the jobs through rules and regulations, this is what the cities become. Los Angeles is not unique, just bigger.

"Dr. Wells, one thing that thug said is very true. Almost anyone down here will kill you for that roll of money you're carrying. So keep it in your pocket if you don't mind.

"I know it sounds strange but, actually, things are a little better down here than they are up top," Max continued. "Up there, the killing goes on unabated. At least down here the gangs provide some semblance of order. Every once in a while a rival gang will try to expand its territory, and war will break out down here too. Then usually the government will call in the riot control units and wipe out everybody in sight. That calms things down for a while. You can imagine what a few concussion grenades or a flamethrower can do down here."

"Surely the government wouldn't use such weapons on innocent people," Karen exclaimed in horror.

"Oh, they give them adequate warning to evacuate, but these people fear the gangs more than they do the police, so most of them try to crawl into a hole somewhere during the cleanup operations. It really is war, and in war civilians usually get hurt the most."

Jeff was about to say something, but just then the subway train pulled in. There was a sudden surge of humanity as the doors swung open. Karen let out a little yelp as she thought she was going to be shoved off the platform. In response, Max shoved the person closest to Karen and he fell to the floor.

Max pulled out his gun and brandished it as he shouted, "Get back! If one more person shoves us I'll start shooting." At the sight of the gun, people began falling back, until there was a clear path to the open train door. Once inside, the doors closed, leaving the four of them in a virtually isolated car.

"You really wouldn't have shot those people, would you, Max?" Karen asked, trying to catch her breath again.

Max didn't say anything as he secured the safety on his gun and returned it to its holster.

Once the train reached the Cal Tech stop, Shimora led the way. The same scene awaited them at this terminal, including two young thugs who demanded payment in return for access to the street level. Without resistance this time, Jeff paid a negotiated $50 per person as Shimora looked on anxiously.

"Let me ask you something, Max. Why are all the gang members so young?"

"Because gang members don't have a chance to grow old," Max replied without further elaboration.

The subway exit had delivered them almost to the entrance of the Cal Tech campus. As they emerged from the tunnel, Jeff stopped and looked in disbelief at the school where he had spent several years. The walls of every building were covered with graffiti. The once-immaculate campus was littered to the point that it appeared to be abandoned. Tents of every shape and variety were scattered across the previously manicured lawns.

"These are student protest groups," Shimora offered without being asked, when he saw the look on Jeff's face.

"What are they protesting?" Jeff asked in disbelief.

"Almost everything," Shimora replied with a sigh. "The red tents are the animal rights protesters, even though all federally funded universities have ceased using animals for experimentation. This group is protesting the display of naked animals."

"You're kidding!" Karen said.

"I'm afraid not," Shimora replied with a shrug. "We have other students who believe it is inhumane to cut grass or to trim trees."

"Doctor, if you don't use animals for experimentation anymore, what do the medical students do for dissections and lab experiments?" Max asked.

"Sadly, they have ready access to aborted fetuses," Shimora replied with his head down. "The worst is that some of these fetuses are kept alive to grow vaccine cultures."

"No!" Karen cried out. "There's no way humans could do such things to other humans."

"You saw what humans are capable of doing to one another,"

Max growled, "and those are adults. What makes you think they would be any kinder to the helpless?"

Karen simply couldn't answer. Her mind was numb with the realization of what she had already seen during the last two days. "Are there no students protesting this inhumanity?" she asked Shimora.

"No," he replied. "It is a crime to protest against official government policies. The law allows the use of fetuses for medical research and the use of artificially maintained fetuses for experimentation and vaccine cultivation. Any protest is punishable by up to ten years in prison and confiscation of all property."

"Mercy! What have we come to?" Karen exclaimed. "Jeff, we have to do something."

"Be very careful what you say," Shimora warned. "You are not as safe here as you might be on your ranch in Wyoming."

"That's very true," Max agreed. "Dr. Wells, do what you came to do. Once you're safely back on your ranch you can tilt at windmills if you care to. Okay?"

"Agreed," Jeff said, looking at Karen. "We'll just look and listen for now. Okay, honey?"

Karen shook her head in agreement, although she was not at all certain she could keep quiet if anyone asked her opinion.

On the way to the faculty center they were met by a group of students carryings signs and shouting, "Save the Earth, Dr. Wells. Death to the polluters. Save the Earth, Dr. Wells. Death to the industrialists."

"I see that word of your arrival has preceded you," Max said. "You seem to be popular with the students."

"Indeed he is," Shimora concurred. "The Green supporters have been touting Jeff's ERTS program as the final proof that the Earth will die of pollution unless all useless industry is halted."

"I wonder what a 'useless industry' is," Max said sourly. "Where do these kids think they'll find jobs when they graduate?"

"These are all government grant students," Shimora explained. "They all have been promised positions with the government."

"With seventy percent of Americans on the government's payroll now, it'll be interesting to see how we'll pay their salaries," Max said disgustedly. "Stupid kids . . . and a government of idiots . . . maybe they deserve each other."

"Better to keep silent, my friend," Shimora whispered as he glanced around to see if anyone had heard the comment.

Once inside the building Jeff was astounded to see the rundown condition of the once superior facility. "Doctor, why have the buildings on campus been allowed to run down so? Doesn't the school have a sizeable maintenance endowment?"

"Perhaps you don't know," Shimora replied. "All endowments were absorbed and redistributed to help improve the inner cities nearly five years ago. It was part of the National Reconstruction Act. It is illegal to accumulate surpluses in academic institutions now."

"All in the name of equality," Max said sarcastically. "We wanted everyone to be equal in our country. Now we have it, nobody has anything."

"Incredible," Jeff stammered. "How did all this happen in such a short time?"

"All it takes is people who don't want to get involved," Max said in a somewhat accusatory tone.

"Touché," Jeff replied.

"No offense, doctor," Max said.

"None taken. I guess I've been sitting on the sidelines. But, I think we're about to get into the game."

Shimora hurried the group along as quickly as he could. He continually glanced around furtively to see if anyone was listening. Fortunately no one was.

"President Warrell said to offer you his apologies for not greeting you," Shimora said, "but he is involved with scheduling the IEF meeting. He said to assure you and Mrs. Wells that he will attend your discussion tomorrow."

"Tell him I appreciate his courtesy in allowing me to attend the conference," Jeff replied, "and I look forward to seeing him again."

Once they were settled in their room, with Max located in the room next to theirs, Jeff and Karen had a chance to talk with their old friend and colleague.

"Doctor, why do you stay under such horrible conditions?" Karen asked.

"There is no choice." Shimora shrugged and added, "Without government authorization, I cannot relocate to any other institution."

"But surely, with your credentials . . . ," she started to say.

"Credentials mean nothing where there are no jobs. You don't understand the way things are today. Over seventy percent of all the universities are closed, and only a few schools even offer classes in physics or mathematics."

"What?" Jeff exclaimed in disbelief. "Then what are they teaching?"

"Social integration, sensitivity training, cooperative discipline—these are the subjects required for accreditation today. Even in my physics classes I am not allowed to grade students who cannot comprehend. We are told that grading is classism and is not allowed by the human rights treaty."

"You mean that American schools are not teaching basic math and science anymore?" Karen asked incredulously.

"There is an underground element in the home schooling movement that still teaches basic science, but many of this group have been sent to prison for violating the law. Those involved have had their children removed by the Social Service."

Karen couldn't think of anything else to say. She simply shook her head.

"Doctor, do you have access to a computer terminal with a satellite modem?" Jeff asked.

"Yes, but you will need a federal access code to use the satellite uplink. Why do you ask?"

"I need some data from my computer in Wyoming. I have all the access codes. May I use your machine?"

"Certainly," Shimora replied. "We have been instructed to make available any facilities you need. Please come with me."

Jeff told Karen he was going to Shimora's office and then followed him to the computer lab.

"How old is this equipment?" Jeff asked his friend as he entered the lab.

"Quite out of date, I'm afraid," Shimora said apologetically. "Teaching labs are quite low on the priority status list. Only programs that are authorized by the government have access to new equipment. Science education is not high on the list of priorities today, I'm afraid."

Jeff had not seen the new ERTS computer center, but he was certain it was equipped with the latest in Asian computer technology, just as his own facility was. He couldn't help but feel a little guilty that his longtime friend was now considered nonessential to society.

Jeff sat down at Shimora's terminal while his friend went off to teach his only class of the day. Shimora would have been surprised to see a data scrambler connected to his system. Jeff was taking no chances that someone might be eavesdropping on Shimora's terminal.

He didn't have anything to hide, but he knew the wisdom of confidentiality where his computer system was concerned. He knew that once he had made the link to his computer Maggie would engage her own descrambler program to interpret his commands.

▲

In the ERTS control room, Dr. Ames was watching his terminal with great interest. *Aha,* he muttered to himself. *Just as I anticipated. Wells is logging on to Shimora's terminal.*

Jeff supplied the proper authorization codes and made the link between the CIT mainframe and his own mainframe in Wyoming. Having done so, he then enabled the scrambler.

"What the . . . ?" Ames grumbled as the data on his terminal turned into meaningless symbols and lines. *Wells is using some type of scrambler,* he realized. And try as he might, he could not descramble the data with any of the dozens of programs designed just for that purpose.

On the other end of the satellite link, Maggie had already picked up the scrambled code and initiated her own interpreting routine.

"Good afternoon, Dr. Wells," she signaled to his terminal.

"Good afternoon, Maggie," Jeff responded. "How are you doing?"

"Fine. Just a little lonely without you and Mrs. Wells."

With the formalities out of the way, Jeff got down to business. "Has all the data from ERTS been received, Maggie?"

"Affirmative," Maggie responded. "It has been received and processed. I have run comparisons of the historical data. The results are quite interesting. By the way, Dr. Wells, ERTS has tried unsuccessfully to retrieve the results several times. I have followed your instructions and sent them conflicting data. But they are quite persistent, so I simply terminated the communications link to the CPU the last time."

"Good for you, Maggie," Jeff typed in. "I don't want anyone else to see this data until I have a chance to review it thoroughly. They don't know about you, do they?"

"No," Maggie responded again. "As far as they know they are talking directly with the data base processor."

"Good!" Jeff responded. He was really impressed the way Maggie was able to correctly assess a changing situation and respond to it. "Please transmit the comparative data at this time."

"Affirmative," Maggie copied, initiating the download to Jeff's terminal.

The ancient printer in Shimora's office began clattering away as the data was received, decoded, and printed. After nearly twenty minutes, the printer was silent. Jeff was so totally engrossed in studying the first burst of data that had come in, he hardly noticed.

Unbelievable, he said under his breath as he sent Maggie instructions to shut down. He ripped off the printed summary and sat down to review the material more thoroughly.

He could tell at first glance that there was a fundamental discrepancy between the expected and the actual historical data. "Boy, do I wish I had my compugraph," Jeff said under his breath.

Without the compugraph, a digital-to-analog plotter that assimilates data and plots it in graph format, the best he could do was scan the data and convert it to chart format in his head. As he did so, he realized that the more data he reviewed, the more it refuted the notion of industrial pollution affecting the Earth's environment.

One of the more enlightening bursts of data was gathered from studies done over a period of three hundred years by several universities. It showed that according to fossilized tree ring data there had been at least three, and possibly four, major warming periods ranging from as far back as 6,000 years ago to as recently as 2,500 years ago. During each of these warming periods, the presence of increased carbon dioxide was evidenced by the increased growth rings in the trees.

What Jeff noted, with particular interest, was that each warming period was followed by massive plant growth and a general expansion of fossil activity. In other words, far from suffering from an increase in the so-called greenhouse gases, life on the Earth had greatly benefitted from them—allowing for rapid expansion of virtually all species.

He assumed this would have included the human beings living during these periods also. It was only during the cyclical cooling periods that fossil records were sparse and plant activity was diminished.

After spending nearly an hour digesting the data forwarded by Maggie, Jeff reached some conclusions: First, sizeable weather and climate cycles had occurred long before industrialization could have had any impact on them. And based on climate data, Maggie concluded that each major warming cycle had been preceded by significantly higher levels of greenhouse gases than were being reported currently.

Essentially, global warming was a natural planet cycle and not the result of industrialization. Even at previous twentieth century levels of industrial output, it would take ten thousand years to have any impact—if ever.

His second conclusion, and Maggie's too, was that increased carbon dioxide levels were greatly beneficial to life on Earth. If the current level of 360 parts per million could be increased to 600 or 700 PPM, the Earth would experience a growth cycle that would benefit the human race greatly.

Why not, Jeff thought. *Nursery owners used to pump high concentrations of carbon dioxide into their greenhouses to promote plant growth—at least until the Clean Air Act of 1998 made the use of greenhouse gases illegal,* he reminded himself.

Jeff gathered up all the data he had received from Maggie and started out the door of Shimora's office. Then, on impulse, he returned to the computer terminal and reestablished the link to his computer. Within a few seconds Maggie was back on line.

"Greetings again, Dr. Wells," Maggie responded via the computer screen. Jeff could envision her pleasant voice filling the room in his computer center. "How may I help you?"

"Maggie, tell me your analysis of the historical data provided by the ERTS team."

"Quite frankly, Dr. Wells," she replied, "I am puzzled."

"How so?"

"Well I can find no apparent link between the historical data and the current satellite data that would justify any degree of concern. In fact, just the opposite seems to be true."

"Explain," Jeff said through the terminal.

"Given the current levels of carbon dioxide and methane being reported, the Earth's atmosphere would seem to be in a cooling cycle. The thing that would apparently benefit humans the most would be an artificial increase in greenhouse gases. They might help to reduce the risk of another minor ice age."

"What about the ozone data?" Jeff asked.

"Inconclusive," Maggie responded. "But when the ultraviolet monitoring stations were active before they were shut down in 1993, the data shows a progressive decline in U.V. radiation."

"Your analysis?" Jeff asked.

"An increase in the ozone layer, rather than a decrease."

"Exactly my own conclusion as well," Jeff typed in. "Thanks, Maggie. You're the best!"

"You are welcome. Any further instructions?"

"Just one," Jeff responded. "Do *not* transfer any of this data to the ERTS headquarters, under any circumstances."

"Understood," Maggie replied.

"And one last thing, Maggie. If anyone attempts to violate any of my security codes, you are to wipe all the data files clean and shut down all data interface channels."

"Understood," Maggie said once again. "That will create some significant difficulties for them, don't you think?"

"Yes." Jeff chuckled as he shut down the link. Maggie's comment was a definite understatement. *That will cause Dr. Ames some sleepless nights if he attempts to force his way into my files.*

19

△

Kill
Wells

In the ERTS center, Brett Sterns concluded that Dr. Ames was a
paranoid schizophrenic, or at least something close. Ever since
Ames had learned that the ERTS data manager had transmitted all
the catalogued historical data to Wells, he had been stomping through
the center, swearing and yelling about traitors in "his camp."

When Ames had authorized the release of the data to Wells, he
hadn't bothered to verify the full extent to which his research teams
had done their jobs. He had intended that Wells have only the most
meager information and certainly not the in-depth studies they had
sent him.

Sterns learned that the teams had included data provided by
opposition scientists who did not support the EPA's position. Much
of it indicated a lack of global warming and even conflicting ozone
conclusions.

Now Sterns was the recipient of Ames' tirade: "I want all the
files in Wells' computer!" Ames commanded. "I don't care how
you do it; just do it! You worked with Wells for months; you must
know his codes by now."

"No, I really don't," Sterns replied with as much restraint as he
could muster. He didn't want to get Ames so angry that he would
remove him from the team. He had an idea that Jeff and Karen
might eventually need a friend on the inside.

"Dr. Wells always opened and closed his own files, and he
never shared the passwords."

"Surely a programmer as good as you are can break his codes," Ames growled sarcastically. "Remember, Sterns, you work for me, not for Wells."

"Dr. Wells is the best computer analyst I've ever known," Sterns said with more than a hint of irritation in his voice. "If he set the codes, you can be sure no one but him can unlock his system. If we try, he may have set traps to protect it."

"Nonsense," Ames snapped. "If someone can design a code, someone else can break it. You know more about Wells' system than anyone else here. I order you to unlock his files and retrieve that data!"

"Why don't you just call Dr. Wells at Cal Tech?" Sterns suggested, trying to keep his sarcasm within acceptable limits. "If it's information we need, I'm sure he'll be glad to help."

"You just mind your own business and do what you're told," Ames warned. "When I want your advice I'll ask for it. Now get on it!"

"I would appreciate it if you would put that in the form of a memo," Sterns said firmly. "I'm not at all certain Dr. Wells will take it kindly when he finds out we have tried to pirate his files."

Ames looked at Sterns with murder in his eyes. He had already guessed that the young whiz kid was more committed to Wells than to him, as were most of the others who had worked with Wells. *No matter though. Once Wells is done with his programming, he no longer will be necessary to the success of the project. I'll be in charge then, and there's nothing that Wells or Galt can do about it.*

Ames also knew that The Society needed a scapegoat to put their plan in motion. Thomas Galt would be "sacrificed" for the cause—and Wells too, if necessary, with all of his religious-right friends.

It's past time, Ames thought with a sinister grin. *The do-gooders are contrary to everything right. Subdue the Earth, and fill it with billions of useless kids; that's their mandate from God. They make me sick.*

Brett Sterns went back to his terminal and reestablished the satellite link to the Wyoming ranch.

"Access files: ERTS analysis," Sterns said through his computer's voice module.

"Access denied," the computer responded immediately. "Access codes required by order of Dr. Jeffrey Wells, system programmer."

"Just as I suspected," Brett muttered under his breath. "I sure hope you'll know I did this under protest, Jeff."

"Would you like to make that a part of the permanent log?" the computer responded.

"No," Sterns replied. "Run decode program identified as Burglar," he instructed the computer. Burglar was a routine he had written in college to gain access to the school's computer library. It would cycle through millions of possible codes until it found a match, or so it was intended. He was almost certain Jeff Wells would have developed a code that was uncrackable.

Almost instantly a computer alarm sounded in the room. Every programmer looked up as their collective screens went dead. "Computer access has been terminated," the computer reported in its monotone voice.

Within seconds, Ames was at Sterns' console. "What happened?" he shouted. "What have you done?"

"I did exactly what you told me to do," Sterns retorted. "I warned you Dr. Wells would have some kind of protection program. It has shut down our access to his computers."

Actually, it was Maggie who had terminated the data link to the ERTS lab. She monitored every input and output to and from the ranch computer system. When Sterns had initiated the code-breaking routine, she simply had followed a prearranged instruction that resulted in the disconnect. Had the illegal routine been initiated from within the building, she also would have wiped the entire memory bank clean.

Ames was fit to be tied. He knew they couldn't reestablish the link without Wells' help again. He placed a call to Dr. Cho in Washington, D.C.

"It is most unfortunate that this has happened at this particular time," Cho said calmly. "We need to know something of what Dr. Wells will report at the meeting tomorrow morning. Are you quite certain that he retrieved some information from the computer after your data was transmitted?"

"I'm sure," Ames replied angrily, trying to control his rage at Wells. *I'm sick and tired of being one-upped by Wells. Didn't The Society know Wells was a part of the religious right when they allowed him to start this project? It was Galt who brought Wells in. Yes, Galt has to be a part of Wells' conspiracy.*

"Most unfortunate," Cho repeated, "but it cannot be helped now. We will simply have to take the necessary precautions. In the meantime, doctor, we need to make plans for retrieving the data in Dr. Wells' computer."

"But I've already told you that he has locked us out of the sys—"

Cho interrupted, "It merely means that we must visit the ranch. I will arrange transportation for you and as many of your people as you will need to retrieve the data."

As soon as he hung up, Cho placed a call to the president and arranged to have a military transport plane pick up Ames and his team and fly them to the Wells ranch in Wyoming immediately.

"What will Wells present at the IEF conference?" the president asked of his mentor, Cho.

"Unfortunately, there is no way to know at this time," Cho replied, as expressionless as always. "We must assume that it will not be in our best interests. The other members of The Society believe it is best to prevent Dr. Wells from presenting his findings. He is known too well to risk having him undermine our efforts."

"What do you want me to do?" Rand asked. Anyone listening would have assumed Rand was the lackey and Cho the president.

"We have too many loose ends, with the THOR materials still missing, and there is still the threat from the Korean fanatics. We must tie up some of them. Arrange for one of your enforcement groups to silence Wells, but be sure it appears to be another case of random violence."

▲

After Jeff returned to his room, he spent the next half hour telling Karen what he had concluded from the historical data ERTS had supplied. "Basically there's no correlation between the EPA's assumptions and the historical records," he told Karen.

"That is remarkable," she replied. "What are you going to do?"

"Obviously, I'll tell the IEF and UNEEA committees that there simply is not enough evidence of any environmental crisis to warrant the current level of controls, much less more stringent regulations. I believe we need a thorough analysis of all the environmental regulations issued over the last twenty years to determine if they are warranted."

"Well, that certainly ought to cause quite a stir," Karen said.

Max, who had been listening at the door of their adjoining rooms rapped on the door and stepped in. "I apologize for listening in on your conversation," he said, "but snooping is a part of what I get paid to do."

Jeff started to say something when Max stopped him. "Listen, Jeff, you're a bright guy, but you don't know a lot about living in our modern society. I'm not too bright about some things, but I do know about politics and power. You're just going to have to trust me. Does anyone else know about this data you received?"

"They couldn't know the exact content, but it is possible they could know that I have some data the ERTS team doesn't have," Jeff said as he mentally sorted through the events of the last few hours. "Why?"

"Because if the people behind the environmental movement even suspect what you plan to do tomorrow, they'll try to stop you at all costs."

Karen could feel the old fear rising inside again. It had been years since she had felt real fear. *Lord, will this never end?* she asked silently.

"What can we do?" Jeff asked Max.

"First we need to know how much they already suspect of what I just heard," Max replied. "Is there any way you can find out what they know?"

"Maybe," Jeff replied. "I'll need access to a computer terminal again."

The trio made their way up three floors to Shimora's office again. Max and Karen stood by while Jeff reestablished the link to his computer system. It took him only a few seconds, and Maggie was back on line.

"Dr. Wells, I'm glad you called," Maggie said via the computer screen. "We have had an illegal entry. Someone at ERTS attempted to run a decoding routine to access your summary data files. Quite a good decoding routine, I might add, but a very clumsy effort. It was as if the intruder wanted to be caught. I had to terminate all inputs to abort the decoder. It is peculiar though. The intruder left a coded message."

"What message?" Jeff typed in.

"Loosely translated, it says, 'Life is real, games are for fun.'"

"Brett Sterns," Jeff said quickly. "Ames must have ordered him to do it and he wanted to be sure I knew."

"What is your current status?"

"All data links have been severed. I have transferred all data files to my main memory and am prepared to wipe all active memory clean upon your instructions."

"Excellent, Maggie," Jeff responded. "But keep this channel open so I can contact you if I need to."

"Ames ordered Brett to do what?" Karen asked, quite puzzled.

"Brett tried to access my files," Jeff said to Karen. "Maggie shut them out, but Brett left us a message. That means Ames must suspect something."

"Then we don't have a lot of time," Max said. He didn't want to alarm the Wellses, but time was of the essence. "These people don't mess around, and they have contacts everywhere, especially in L.A."

"You don't mean they might try to harm us?" Karen exclaimed, hoping his answer would differ from her intuition.

"I don't know for sure," Max lied, "but I'm not about to wait around and take any chances." He picked up the phone and placed a call to Galt's ranch in Montana. In less than five minutes he had briefed Galt's Montana security chief, Roy Sloan, on what he knew and had made arrangements for a plane to pick them up at the old Riverside airport in four hours.

"Let's gather up our things and get out of here," Max said in a no-nonsense tone that clearly conveyed his sense of urgency.

"You mean we have to leave now?" Karen asked in surprise. The reality of their situation was just beginning to sink in.

"*Right* now!" Max snapped. "Galt said to get you out of here in a hurry."

"But what about Dr. Shimora?" Jeff argued. "We can't leave our friend without telling him."

"He's a bright old guy," Max commented admiringly. "He'll understand."

What none of the three knew was that Shimora and his young graduate assistant, Laurie, had made their way to the Wellses room right after he completed his class. Laurie was a longtime admirer of Dr. Wells and was thrilled that Shimora had invited her to meet him.

Seeing the door slightly ajar and getting no response when he knocked, Shimora walked in. He and Laurie had just entered the room when outside on the grounds the CIO agent said to his companion, "Okay, they're back in the room. Let 'em have it." Having already targeted his weapon, the other agent fired the TAARS rocket at the window where the two figures, one a man and the other a woman, were clearly visible.

The first agent shouted, "Wait!" as soon as he realized the man inside was far too small to be Wells, but it was too late; the rocket was already on its way to the target.

The room exploded when the warhead hit the wall inside the room. Nothing could have survived that holocaust. Shimora and Laurie were killed without ever hearing or seeing the rocket.

Three floors above, Jeff, Karen, and Max were hurled to the floor by the impact of the exploding TAARS. Even as he hit the floor, Max instinctively drew his weapon and rolled to his feet in one swift motion. Outside the window he saw the fireball rolling up from below.

"Wh . . . what happened?" Karen stuttered.

"Bomb . . . , or a rocket," Max yelled. "Let's get out of here." He grabbed Karen's arm just as Jeff was doing the same thing, and they literally lifted her off the floor.

With fire alarms screaming, they made their way out of the building. By the time they emerged, there were hundreds of students and faculty streaming out of the buildings and onto the lawn. Shoving people out of the way, Max looked back at the building that was already ablaze.

"They hit your room with a rocket, I think," Max shouted as they hurried across the campus.

It was several minutes before they made their way to the subway that had brought them in earlier. There had been no time for talk or argument. Max had assumed control and was intent on just one thing: getting Jeff and Karen out of L.A. and to the safety of Galt's Montana ranch, as instructed.

Once they were inside the subway, Jeff paid the toll extracted by a gang member without discussion and they waited for the first northbound train.

"Oh Jeff, it's starting again," Karen cried as she caught her breath a little.

"I don't think it really ever ended," he replied, his eyes showing the anger he was feeling inside. "We naively thought we had won the war, Karen, while the other side assumed they had merely lost a battle."

You'll do, Dr. Wells, Max thought silently. *Glad to have you back on our side again.* Max knew from what Pastor John Elder had told him that Jeff Wells was a good man. "Once he knows the truth, he'll do what's right," Elder had told his followers. "And Jeff Wells can be a formidable opponent, as The Society already knows."

Max had been thoroughly trained in security and placed in Galt's employ specifically to watch over Jeff Wells. Elder knew the time would come when Jeff would become the Green movement's worst nightmare. *That time has come,* Max concluded. *Now all we have to do is stay alive.*

The next few hours would be a lifetime of learning for his two companions as they made their way through the biggest jungle in the world: Los Angeles, California.

20

△

The Wyoming Attack

When Dale Crawford crashed his car into the dry ravine, he was knocked unconscious for several minutes. After he came to, he looked around, trying to gather his senses. The sight of the old camper burning brought him back to reality. He knew it wouldn't be very long until someone would investigate the fire. In the dry Wyoming atmosphere, the smoke could be seen for miles.

He quickly checked to see if any of the passengers in the camper had made it; none had. So he gathered up his water bottle and the backpack containing the THOR records and headed away from the site of the wreck as fast as his wobbly legs would carry him. He had no idea where to go, but he knew that staying where he was wasn't a healthy option.

Crawford could not have known how providential his turn onto the side road had been. It was the back road into the Wells ranch. No one had used the road for years since it was no longer maintained. But for a man on foot or horseback, it was the fastest way in or out of the ranch.

As chance, or providence, would have it, Reno and little Jason were out riding fence that day. Reno saw the smoke and headed in that direction. In such dry country, no fire was to be ignored.

The government security team on guard at the main road also saw the smoke and hurried to investigate it. However, in the high desert, a man on a horse will always beat a man in a car, especially given the condition of the abandoned road. The security team had not even bothered to stake out the old road since it seemed totally impassable by car.

Long before the security team made the crash site, Reno was there with Jason by his side. The burning camper and wrecked car, as well as the skid marks leading to the wrecks, told a story to Reno's experienced eye. Someone in the camper had been trying to run the car off the road, he surmised, but instead had hit the old bridge and crashed. The loose fuel in the camper had exploded, killing all the passengers. However, the driver of the other car had walked away, toward the ranch according to the footprints.

"What happened, Uncle Reno?" Jason asked his friend and temporary guardian.

"Just an accident, little one," Reno replied, not wanting to alarm the boy. "We can't help those in the camper right now, but the driver of the other car is walking, so we'd better go find him. He may be hurt. Can you find his tracks?"

"You bet!" Jason squealed excitedly. "Look! Here they are," he said as he trotted off in the direction of the walking man. Even though Karen had told Jason before she left that he could only ride double with Reno, the old man had succumbed to the boy's pleadings and promises to be careful and had given him a pony to ride.

"Wait for me," Reno shouted, pretending to be following the boy's lead.

"Come on!" Jason yelled as he kicked his pony in the ribs. "Let's go!"

Crawford heard something behind him. He looked for a place to hide, but there was none. *It would be kind of futile to hide behind a sagebrush,* he told himself. So he sat down on a rock to await whatever his fate might be.

He was relieved to see a small boy, riding an Indian paint pony, come trotting around the bend in the road. But he was more than a little unnerved to also see a large white-haired Indian racing after the boy.

"Are you hurt, mister?" Jason asked, reining in his pony.

"Not too bad," Crawford answered as calmly as he could, considering the Indian had pulled a rifle from his saddle holster and was now pointing it at him.

"Just keep your hands where I can see them," Reno ordered in a manner that said much more than his words. He was not going to take any chances with Jason along. "Who are you, and what are you doing out here?"

Reno could see clearly that the man was a tenderfoot from the East. But there was something else about him that told Reno he was no threat to them—perhaps the way he looked directly at him with no shifting of eye contact. He always believed you could tell the character of a man by the way he made eye contact.

Crawford had a choice: lie, or tell the truth and take his chances. In reality his decision was made more out of fatigue than conscience. He told the truth.

"My name is Dale Crawford. I'm an EPA supervisor, or at least I was, and I've come all the way from Washington D.C. to see Dr. Jeff Wells. I don't know exactly where he lives, but I think it's in this general vicinity."

"And what do you want to see this Wells for?" Reno asked, without revealing that he knew Wells.

"I have some documents and a tape that were made by his father nearly fifty years ago. So far, at least one other man has lost his life trying to make them public. I think Dr. Wells would be very interested in them. Do you know him?"

"I might," Reno said cautiously. He was about to say something else when Jason spoke up.

"That's my dad!" Jason said in the typical manner of a six-year-old.

Crawford couldn't believe his good fortune, but he stood very still when he saw the grimace on Reno's face and saw that the old man had brought the rifle to a more menacing position.

"I just want to be certain this material gets to Dr. Wells," Crawford said, holding the package forward. "Can you do that for me? I've risked my life to bring it all this way."

Just then Reno caught the faint sound of a vehicle coming in their direction. He made a decision: "Get on," he commanded the stranger. With that he reached down and grabbed Crawford by the arm and literally swung him onto the horse he was riding while, at the same instant, he kicked the horse in the ribs and received a burst of speed in response. Jason's pony, startled by the sudden flurry of activity, responded with an equal burst of speed. It was all Crawford could do to hang on for his life as the two horses galloped away.

The two men in the car saw the wreck and correctly surmised that it had been Crawford in the car. They quickly surveyed the scene and knew that Crawford had survived the encounter, although no one in the other vehicle had.

When they saw the tracks of one man walking, intermingled with the horses' hoofprints, they sprinted back to their car and gingerly made their way across the dry ravine. Once on the road again, they accelerated as fast as they reasonably could in pursuit of their quarry.

The short delay by the two government agents had given Reno the edge he needed. He only glanced back a second to be certain Jason was behind him. Since Reno's horse was carrying double, Jason was easily able to keep up.

The smoke also had attracted two of Galt's ranch security men. They were approaching across the range in a four-wheel-drive vehicle, on an intercept course with Reno and the boy. When Reno first saw them, he bristled and raised his weapon menacingly. But when the men waved him on, he lowered the weapon and concentrated on his escape.

Reno and Jason were just entering the gate to the ranch when the car came into sight. Clearly the men intended to pursue the fleeing subjects onto the ranch, but Galt's security men had entirely different ideas. Once they saw the car was accelerating, they broke out their weapons. One brandished an automatic rifle, and the other hoisted a TAARS rocket launcher to his shoulder.

The sight of two armed men, one with a rocket launcher, standing in their path was more than sufficient to change their minds about pursuit. The driver slammed on the brakes, skidded the car to a stop, and with one quick motion, turned the wheel, gunned the engine, and slid the car around in the dusty road, heading away from the two armed security guards. Looking back, the driver saw one of the guards closing the ranch gate. He slowed the car to a safe speed and made his way back to their base station to call Washington.

Within minutes after the call from Wyoming, Henry Watts, acting chief of staff, was standing in the office of the president. In the adjacent office, Dr. Cho listened in on the conversation through the intercom.

"Mr. President, the missing EPA supervisor was seen entering the Wells ranch by two of our agents. When they tried to stop him, they were accosted by two armed security guards."

"Are they sure it was Crawford?" President Rand asked with as much control as he could muster. *After all this time, to lose him now,* he thought sourly. *And to allow him to reach the Wells ranch too!*

"As sure as they can be." Watts went on to describe the crash site and how Crawford had escaped.

"Okay, Henry," the president said angrily, "tell your people to stand by." As soon as he had dismissed him, Cho entered the room.

"We've lost him," Rand growled. "Now Wells will have the THOR records."

"Not yet," Cho replied. "Remember that Wells is in Los Angeles to attend the IEF conference. We can still recover the documents. You need to have the attorney general issue a search-and-seizure authorization for Crawford. We will recover our property."

"Consider it done!" Rand responded with some relief. With Wells away from the ranch, the politics of the search would be a lot easier to explain.

▲

When Reno got Crawford to the ranch, Maria treated his wounds from the crash and fed him. As soon as he had eaten he told Reno: "I need to get this information to Dr. Wells. Is he here?"

"No," Reno replied, "He and Mrs. Wells are traveling." He refused to share more than was absolutely necessary.

"Then is there anyone else who can help? The longer I stay here with this information, the more danger all of you are in. The men who are after me will not hesitate to come in here to get me."

"They may try," Reno growled. "Perhaps I know of someone who can help," he said. "Wait here until I return." Then he looked at Jason and said, "Little one, you stay here also."

"Aw," Jason complained, "why do I have to?"

"Reno has some urgent business," Maria answered. "When he is done, you can go with him again. Would you like some pie? I made it fresh this morning."

Trying to make the best of a bad deal, Jason replied, "Can I have two pieces?"

"If you eat all your vegetables first," Maria responded in typical motherly fashion.

Reno was already out the door and headed toward his horse. He mounted and rode in the direction of what he knew to be the Galt security team's headquarters.

Once Reno had described as much as he knew about Crawford and the documents, Paul Weir, the agent in charge, placed a call to the Galt ranch.

"It all fits what we heard about some EPA employee with top secret files," Galt told his security chief. "You need to stay alert. Crawford may well be right. If the government has gone to all this trouble and expense to find him, they won't hesitate to come after him.

"I'll contact some friends in Washington, but in the meantime, Paul, don't allow anyone on the ranch—no matter what! Use all necessary force to keep them off. I'll have General Sharp send a helicopter from the Air National Guard in Cheyenne to pick up Crawford and his package. I want that ranch locked up tight."

"Done, sir." As he hung up the phone, Weir explained the gist of the call to Reno, who didn't protest the additional security measures. Then he conveyed Galt's message to his security men at the ranch.

Reno had a nagging feeling that the heat was about to be turned up, and he wanted to get back to Jason as soon as possible.

It was nearly four hours later when two government-issue cars, carrying five FBI agents and Deputy Attorney General Marjorie Franklin approached the ranch entrance. They were greeted by no less than ten armed security guards from Galt's team.

"We're here to arrest a fugitive by the name of Dale Crawford," attorney Franklin said firmly. "We have a court order allowing us to search the ranch."

"I can't permit you to do that," the guard replied.

"You have no choice in the matter," Franklin spat back. "I have a warrant and a search order, so stand aside." With that she signaled the driver of her vehicle to proceed. She instructed him to crash the fence gate, if necessary.

Suddenly the Galt team moved as if they were part of a well-choreographed stage act—each taking a defensive position and brandishing weapons of all types and sizes, including at least two anti-tank rocket launchers.

The driver of Franklin's car stopped as if he'd been struck by lightning. "Go on, you coward!" Franklin shouted at him. "They're bluffing."

"Not on your life," he countered, "or my life either. We're out-manned and outgunned."

Franklin was enraged, and she screamed at the driver again to crash the gate. Looking into the arsenal pointed in their direction, no amount of cursing or threats would make him move forward. "You're more than welcome to drive this thing yourself," he said, much to the relief of the other agents in his car, "but I'm getting out before you do."

She was still screaming obscenities as the driver and two other agents piled into the other car and backed away from the gate.

"We'll be back," Franklin screamed at the Galt team as she slid behind the wheel. "We'll be back!"

"We'll be here," was Weir's response. He had no doubt that she would make her threat good. He immediately repositioned his men to take maximum advantage of the terrain. Knowing that Franklin would return with significant reinforcements, he made a second call to the Galt ranch to inform them of the situation.

During the next twelve hours or so, more than one hundred government agents were diverted to the Wells ranch. Two armored personnel carriers were secured from the armory at Casper and moved into position. It was clear the government meant to have Crawford, one way or the other.

As details were fed to Galt at his ranch, he made numerous calls to friends in Washington, only to find most of those he called were away from their offices. He began to get the idea that he had been placed on the don't-call-me list in the capitol. Finally, deciding that he would get no help from the political wimps in Washington, he called General Sharp with the Wyoming National Guard, and asked for help.

"What do you need, Thomas?" Sharp asked.

"I need something that will stop a determined assault from our government. Can you help?"

"Well, I just happen to have two very well-armed Cobras that need some checkout, Tom. I'll have them escort a Huey on maneuvers near the Wells ranch."

"Thanks, my good friend," Galt said with a sigh.

"No problem" the general replied. "I think we have mutual adversaries."

The government's assault on the ranch began at three o'clock in the afternoon. The personnel carriers led the way, intending to smash the gates and roll into the ranch, followed by several truckloads of armed EPA regulators. Weir shook his head in amazement at the stupidity of the assault.

Just before the carriers would have reached the gates, Weir pressed a button, and hidden explosive charges hurled two ten-foot-diameter blocks from beneath the roadbed into the path of the vehicles. It was something he had learned from his army tour in Switzerland, where virtually every major roadway was similarly guarded. The blocks stopped the carriers in their tracks, totally exposing the occupants to his team's defensive fire. Galt's security team could defend this position against a vastly superior force, which Weir did not consider his opposition to be.

The EPA regulators hit the ground running when the carriers crashed into the defenses, with men spreading out in all directions.

Weir knew it would be only a matter of time until the government moved more troops into the area, but in the meantime his job was to hold them off for as long as possible.

At the ranch the sounds of battle were evident. When the first loud explosions went off, Reno gathered up Jason and made his way to the reinforced ranch house, with Maria and Crawford close behind.

They hid inside the sprawling house, expecting an invading army to appear at any time. Reno had his ancient Winchester ready to defend his ward with his life, if necessary. Jason kept insisting that he be allowed to go and see what was happening, and only the constant grip of Reno on his arm kept him from charging down to the front gate. Crawford was content to sit and await his own fate. He had done everything he could to deliver his message; now all he could do was wait.

It was Reno who first heard the thump of the helicopter rotors as they approached the ranch house. Still clutching Jason, he stepped to the window to see if they were friends or foes. He was relieved to see Galt's security men signaling to the pilot of the first chopper to land in the open area between the ranch house and the Sanchez cottage.

The chopper that was landing was a big Vietnam-era Huey. The other two were very lethal-looking Cobra assault helicopters. As the Huey sat down, the other two tilted forward and flew away, toward the sounds of battle.

The regulators, under the control of Marjorie Franklin, were totally unprepared for what they saw: two high-speed attack helicopters, guns protruding from every crevice, bearing down on their position.

At first Franklin thought they might be part of her support team. That thought was dispelled quickly when the first chopper sent a burst of 20mm cannon fire across the firing zone separating the two groups. The second chopper hovered in a menacing position, facing the regulators.

The effect was immediate and predictable: The EPA forces broke and ran toward their vehicles. In less than two minutes they, along with a white-faced Marjorie Franklin, were racing away from the ranch as fast as the road would allow. On either side of the fleeing band were the two gunships skewing sideways so that their cannons and rockets remained aimed at the caravan.

Back at the ranch entrance, Galt's security team let out a loud cheer. Weir directed them toward the Huey's landing area. Once the civilians were transported safely, the security team would be airlifted out. Eventually Franklin and her little army would be back and probably with a lot more firepower.

Reno pushed a protesting Jason into the helicopter. He was still intent on watching the action. It was only when one of the helicopter crew suggested that he might want to help fly the aircraft that he changed his attention and headed toward the pilot.

Even as Reno helped Maria onto the helicopter he knew something was wrong. He was having a difficult time breathing, and his arm felt like it weighed a hundred pounds. By the time it was his turn to climb aboard he couldn't get his legs to respond. He pulled himself up on the skid to climb inside, but never made it. He dropped back to the ground in a heap. Maria screamed above the churning rotor blades and tried to get out to help her husband, but one of the crew restrained her.

On the ground, one of the security men had already reached Reno and was taking his pulse. He looked up at the crewman on board and shook his head. Quickly he signaled to three other security men and, together, they lifted the inert Reno on board the helicopter.

Maria knew when she looked into the face of her husband, he was already dead. She sat down on the floor of the aircraft with her husband's head in her lap as the big machine lifted off and hurried them toward the waiting plane in Cheyenne.

21

△

Survival

At his ranch in Montana, Thomas Galt was awaiting word of Jeff and Karen. Most of his crew from Wyoming had arrived shortly after Jason, Maria, and Dale Crawford had gotten there. He'd arranged for Reno's burial and was trying to comfort Maria and Jason. Jason was having more difficulty adjusting than Maria; he just couldn't accept that his best friend wouldn't be around anymore.

Galt's anger was rising by the minute. Reno was dead as a result of the government's actions. His security director also informed him that Jeff's friend, Dr. Shimora, and a graduate assistant had been killed in Jeff and Karen's room at Cal Tech.

Galt knew the attack had actually been an attempt to get rid of Jeff and Karen, and he was enraged. In his younger days, he probably would have done something stupid—like attack Washington. Older and wiser, he realized that he would have to wait and pick his own battlefield. His time would come.

When Galt finally was able to meet with Crawford he asked, "Just what is it you have that is of such interest to our government?"

Crawford gave him a thumbnail sketch of what he knew and what was in the backpack he had carried all the way from Washington, D.C. It seemed to Crawford that his adventures had started two years ago and yet, in reality, it had been less than two weeks since he'd last sat at his desk in the EPA center. Now here he was, sitting in the study of the world's wealthiest man, having witnessed what could be the start of the next American Revolution.

Galt had a difficult time believing what Crawford was telling him. *If what he says is true,* Galt reasoned, *everything I've been doing is a fraud. I've been helping the very same group of fanatics that nearly took over the country a decade ago.*

But thinking back over the events of the last few days, Galt knew there could be no other explanation. At the highest levels of government there was a conspiracy to take away the freedoms of its citizens, and he had been aiding the takeover.

The more he thought about the near-fatal attacks on Jeff and Karen and the assault on their ranch, the madder he got. He excused Crawford and sat down to listen to the tapes he had brought with him.

▲

At the White House, Rand was equally furious. "What do you mean, 'they got away,'" he shouted at Henry Watts. "Didn't you have enough regulators there to do the job?"

"Yes we did," Watts said defensively. "But when you're dealing with someone like Galt, he has virtually unlimited resources and a lot of friends in high places. He actually called in assault helicopters on our people. If they had resisted they would have been annihilated. By the time we got back to the ranch with more people, the place had been cleaned out and everyone was gone. The CIO tells me they have all relocated to Galt's ranch in Montana."

"What about Wells?"

"No word yet. We have to assume that Galt has arranged for his escape too."

"I want them found and arrested, even if you have to tear down Galt's ranch piece by piece. Do you hear?"

"I don't think that would be wise, Mr. President," Watts argued. "Our intelligence people think Galt has turned his ranch into a fortress. He may have ground-to-air missiles, maybe even his own defensive aircraft. It would be a bloodbath. Our people calculate it would take a full division of troops to rout them out."

Rand was in a rage. He could see everything he'd worked for falling apart just because of two men. *I know Watts is probably right. Thomas Galt is one of the best known men in the world. Even the American media wouldn't lay off that story if we assaulted Galt's ranch. No, there has to be a better way. After all, both Wells and the THOR documents eventually will be in one place.*

"I want you to clamp a total security lid on this thing," Rand said calmly as he reverted to his less manic personality. "And I want all satellite communications into and out of the ranch jammed. We'll just cut them off from the world and let them rot on that ranch."

Yeah, he thought ecstatically, *we'll let Mr. Galt and his wonder boy rot in their own little prison.*

Henry Watts scurried out of the Oval Office before Rand could change his mind. *I have to admit though, the president has a good idea. Just cut the ranch off from the world. As reclusive as Galt and Wells are, no one will ever know or care.*

▲

Jeff and Karen, led by the ever-vigilant Max, had made their way across L.A. by subway to the most northern station at Riverside. There they exited the tunnel system and surfaced into what looked like a Watts ghetto of the twentieth century. Many of the buildings were burnt-out hulks, testimony to the many homeless who had occupied them and used open fires to heat and cook by. The streets were reasonably clean though. Karen remarked about the contrast, considering the run-down conditions of the whole area.

"There is precious little to waste for most of these people," Max explained. "In general, these people are not thugs and murderers," he said. "They're just ordinary people with families who have seen their jobs and their hopes dry up. With almost no infrastructure left in L.A., the businesses simply pulled out and moved somewhere else—usually out of the country.

"If you want to see prosperity, just go down to Mexico. They have most of the jobs we lost. In fact, the Mexican government has a big problem with illegal gringos. If you get caught in Mexico without a legal work permit, you go to prison. And I've seen their prisons; you don't want to go there!"

"Un-be-liev-able!" Jeff said for about the tenth time since he'd left his ranch oasis. "We need to hurry, Max. I have to get to a computer as soon as possible."

"I'll do what I can. In the meantime, we need to find our ride." As he spoke, a drab gray car pulled around the corner. Instinctively Max placed his hand on the gun in his shoulder holster, but then he saw the driver and knew it was one of Galt's security men he had seen at the ranch previously.

"That's it!" he said, motioning toward the car.

"But this is a government limo," Karen exclaimed.

"Right you are, ma'am," the driver agreed. "Mr. Galt has friends in high places. This thing is armor plated. It's what the president uses if he comes to L.A."

"Where are we going?" Jeff asked as he dropped his big frame into the plush limo seat with a grunt. Looking at the driver, he asked, "And how did you get through the gangs?"

"The gangs won't mess with this car. They know that if they did Rand would have thirty thousand troops in here tomorrow to teach them some manners. Nope, we'll be safe as long as the government doesn't know we have the president's personal limo—and they won't. We're going to the old Riverside Airport. There's a plane waiting for you now," the driver explained.

"How in the world did . . . never mind," Jeff said. "I know. Friends in high places. Right?"

"Right you are. Not everybody in the country is stupid. They've just been waiting for Mr. Galt to wake up too."

"Yes, and us too," Karen added. "Welcome to the real world, Mr. and Mrs. Wells," she said with a sigh.

At the airport they were met by a contingent of armed National Guard personnel. "All ex-regular army," the driver who never identified himself offered. "Rand has emasculated the military, but there are still some old hats who remember what it was like when the government worked for the people, rather than against them.

"Your chariot awaits, madam," he said with a sweep of his arm.

Before them was a sleek passenger jet, bearing the Wyoming governor's seal, with its nose pointed down the runway. Parked beside it was another smaller plane, with Wyoming National Guard emblems, which Jeff recognized as a late twentieth century fighter.

"Why the fighter?" he asked.

"Just in case," the driver replied without further comment. "He'll see you through to your destination."

"Which is?" Jeff asked.

"Mr. Galt's ranch."

"But I want to go home and see my son," Karen started to protest.

"Your son is already at the ranch," he replied. "I'm sure Mr. Galt will explain everything when you get there."

"Is Jason all right?" Karen asked. There was a hint of alarm in her voice.

"He's fine. There was some trouble at your ranch, and Mr. Galt had your son and your staff moved to his ranch."

"What kind of trouble?" Jeff asked, concern clearly visible on his face.

"Mr. Galt will explain," the other man repeated as he started for the door of the plane. Turning to face them, he said, "Remember what Pastor Elder taught you: 'He who is in you is greater than he who is in the world.'"

Before Jeff could respond, the door was shut and the pilot began to slowly wind up the engines for takeoff.

"Who was that?" Jeff asked Max as the plane accelerated down the runway.

"That is a two-star general who is concerned about our freedoms. I understand he is a good friend of someone you know—Pastor John Elder?"

"Why, we're part of Pastor Elder's church satellite network," Karen explained. "He organized a large number of families to move to Wyoming a few years ago."

"And we can all be grateful he did. We'll need all the help we can get," Max said as the plane took off.

Two hours later the plane touched down on the runway at Galt's ranch. Karen could see Jason standing with Galt at the entrance to the makeshift terminal building. She was so excited that she didn't notice his lack of emotion. Usually Jason would have been struggling to break free and reach her. *I wonder where Reno is. Why is Jason with Mr. Galt?* she thought.

Max also had noticed the scorched area in the adjacent field. He knew the only thing that could have caused that much damage was a burning aircraft. Many of the pieces still lay strewn around the crash site.

Karen was scarcely to the door of the terminal before Jason bounded out to meet her, his little eyes still red from crying. "Oh, Mommy," he cried out, "Uncle Reno is dead!"

"What? Oh, honey, I'm so sorry," she exclaimed. "What happened? How did he die?" She directed her question toward Galt, who had just reached them.

Galt spent the next several minutes trying to explain what had happened at their ranch and how Reno had died.

"Where is Maria?" Karen asked through her tears.

"She's in the house," Galt answered. "I brought her and Jason here. She seems to be okay, but she's taking Reno's death pretty hard."

"I need to go to her," Karen told Jeff. "Jason, would you like to stay with Daddy?"

"I guess," was his reply. Jason didn't like seeing Maria cry. He kept thinking that maybe Reno would show up again. But then he remembered all the times he and Reno had talked about death—like the time when Jason's dog had died after a snakebite.

"All things die, little one, even your friends and family. Don't be sad when I die. I'll just go to heaven ahead of you so you won't be lonely when you get there."

Jason had argued that Reno wouldn't die, but now he knew he had, and it hurt a lot. He ran to his dad, who reached down and lifted him into his big arms.

"Daddy, Uncle Reno is dead," Jason said as the tears rolled down his face.

"I know, son. I know . . . ," was about all Jeff could manage to say.

Jason clung tightly to his father. "Daddy, can you make Reno come back?" he asked through his sniffles.

"No, I can't, son," Jeff replied, choking back his own tears. "Reno went to be with Jesus. Remember? I don't think he would want to come back now."

"But I miss him," Jason sobbed.

"Me too," Jeff said. "You know, son, I've known Reno since I was your age, and I loved him too."

Galt vowed that he would make Rand and his group pay if it took every cent he had. After listening to the THOR tapes, he knew how stupid he'd been to be taken in by the radicals who believed trees and animals were more important than humans.

"I need to get to a computer terminal as quickly as possible," Jeff told Galt as the urgency of the situation struck him. "I need to make contact with my computer in Wyoming."

"That won't be possible," Galt said angrily. "We've been cut off. Apparently the government is jamming our satellite feed."

"You have an identical system to mine don't you?"

"Yes, our people duplicated everything just like you asked when we began the ERTS project."

"Good," Jeff responded with a smile. "I think I can contact Maggie then."

"Maggie?" Galt questioned.

"Maggie is my latest attempt at artificial intelligence," Jeff explained. "I just hope they haven't turned the whole system off. I suspect Dr. Ames already has a team trying to recover my data files."

"Ames!" Galt growled. "I should have fired him when I first suspected something."

Once inside the computer center, Jeff instructed one of the technicians on duty to call up his LASA program.

"LASA? I'm not familiar with that program, sir," she replied.

"It stands for Laser Assisted Satellite Acquisition," Jeff explained. "You can access it through code name CRISIS. I put it there just in case of this eventuality."

When the technician initiated the retrieval of LASA, the computer paused. "Access code," the voice module requested. "Crisis," the technician responded.

"Code file name required for access to this file," the computer announced. "Code file name must be supplied within thirty seconds or a total system shutdown will be initiated," the voice warned.

"Dr. Wells," the startled technician said, "the computer wants a code file name—whatever that is."

"The code file name is ACCESS," Jeff instructed her.

Once the code file name was supplied, the program was loaded for operation.

"What was that code file name?" the technician asked Wells.

"If you had not supplied the proper second file name, the system-protect program would have executed a shutdown routine that would have wiped out all the data in the entire system. It's a safeguard I built into my decoder to prevent the use of random decoding routines to break into my files."

"Wow!" the technician exclaimed. "I sure wouldn't want to tap into your stuff without knowing that second code."

Once the LASA program was loaded, Jeff went to work. Under computer direction, a small laser transceiver on the roof was raised from its concealment and aimed at one of Galt's jammed telecommunications satellites. The acquisition light indicated the link was positive. Jeff sent his commands via the laser transmission system and linked the telecommunication satellite to one of the ERTS satellites used between Wyoming and California.

Although the frequency jamming had quite effectively stopped all radio transmissions to and from the ranch, because the laser was an optical transmitter, the jamming was ineffective. Jeff had installed the laser transmission system after designing Galt's latest communications satellite with a matching unit. Nothing but heavy cloud cover could block the transmission—which was not a problem in Montana or Wyoming.

Once the link to Wells' computer was made, the screen responded: "Good afternoon, Dr. Wells."

With a smile Jeff switched to voice mode: "Good afternoon, Maggie. How are things there?"

"Not too well, I'm afraid. It seems we have unauthorized personnel in the building trying to access your files."

"Did you execute the instructions I gave you?"

"Yes I did," Maggie said in a cheerful voice. "I have wiped all data files from resident memory and installed a virus in the stored data files. When they attempt to retrieve the data they will receive a great surprise."

"Good for you, Maggie. Now I want you to transmit all data files within your memory to my location. Once you have completed the transfer, transmit your resident program to my location as well."

"Am I to assume that you wish for me to move to your location and cease to exist here, Dr. Wells?"

"Exactly," Jeff replied. "We're going to beam you over—in a manner of speaking."

"Affirmative," Maggie replied. Instantly the data began streaming into the computer at Galt's ranch. It took nearly three minutes for the transfer to be completed. The machine paused for a moment, as additional data was transferred, and then the data link went dead.

"Here goes nothing," Jeff muttered, terminating the LASA program. He then called Maggie again.

"Greetings," Maggie said in a cheerful voice.

"You made it," Jeff said with a sigh of relief. "Welcome!" He hadn't realized that he had come to think of his program as a person until now.

▲

At the Wyoming ranch, Ames was furious with his team of scientists. "What do you mean the system has been wiped clean?" he screamed. "That can't be. Wells isn't here and there is no way he could have made contact with his computer. We have all of the data links jammed."

Your problem is, you don't know who you're matching wits with, Brett Sterns thought to himself. *In a battle of wits, the whole bunch of us are unarmed compared to Jeff Wells.*

"Well, nonetheless, the system is wiped clean," Brett said calmly. "We have the data files on laser disc, but I would recommend that

we not attempt to use them. It's quite possible they've been pro-
tected. Dr. Wells is the best computer specialist . . ."

"I'm sick and tired of hearing about Wells," Ames shouted at
Sterns. "He's just another programmer. We'll run the files through
a debugging routine. Whatever he can bug, we can debug!"

Sterns started to say something else but decided it wouldn't do
any good, so he simply dropped the disc into the storage container
and handed it to Ames. "Then you do it," Sterns said. "I'm
through."

"You sure are," the red-faced Ames shrieked at the top of his
voice. "And I'll see to it that you don't ever work on another government program."

"Oh really," Sterns said calmly. "I thought this was a privately
funded program."

Ames gave him a threatening stare but said nothing else. He
realized he had said too much already.

▲

At Galt's ranch, Jeff had initiated the program to assimilate all
the data and present it in graph format. That process would take the
better part of two hours. In the meantime he picked up Jason, who
had been with Galt's housekeeper, and headed out to find Karen.

He found her in the suite of rooms Galt had provided for them.
"How is Maria?" he asked with concern.

"As well as could be expected, I guess. The reality of Reno's
death is just now beginning to set in. Do you know she wanted to
go help in the kitchen?"

"That's Maria, for sure," Jeff said compassionately. "Maybe
that isn't a bad idea. She probably needs something to occupy her
mind. To tell you the truth, I do too. If I stop and think about it, I
can't believe Reno's gone."

"Me too," Jason said as he transferred from Jeff's arms to
Karen's.

"We all will miss Reno, son, but we both know he would want
us to be strong. Right?"

"I guess so," Jason answered. "Can I go see Maria?"

"I bet she'd like that," Karen agreed. "I'll go with you."

There was a knock on the door. Jeff opened it to find Thomas
Galt standing there.

"Mr. Galt, come in, please," Karen said warmly.

"No thank you, Karen," Galt replied while reaching out to pat
Jason's head.

"I just wanted to give you some news about Reno. The doctor said he died of a massive heart attack. He assured me that Reno didn't suffer at all. In fact, the doctor said it was amazing that Reno was able to do what he did. Apparently he'd had this condition for some years now, though he probably didn't tell anyone."

"No doubt," Jeff agreed. "Reno was not one to complain or baby himself. But I still blame the government. The assault on my ranch caused his heart attack."

"You're right!" Galt said through clenched teeth.

"I need to share something with you, Jeff. It's what the government was looking for when they attacked your ranch. Can you come with me to my office?"

Jeff looked at Karen. "Go ahead," she said. "I'll take Jason to see Maria. I'll be along when we get a little more settled."

"What about the ERTS data?" Jeff asked.

"I think you need to see this stuff first. A man by the name of Crawford was willing to risk his life to bring it to you," Galt replied. "I think you'll have a hard time believing anything about the environmental movement after listening to what he brought."

Part Two

Project THOR

22

△

Project
THOR
Cape Canaveral, 1961

Outside the Galt ranch, preparations were being made for whatever the government's next step might be. Galt's security, which now numbered more than five hundred, were deployed in military fashion. It would take a full-scale military assault to penetrate the ranch's security now, and even then, those who might attempt it would suffer severe casualties in the process.

Thomas Galt had spared no expense, monetarily or politically, in fortifying the ranch. His security teams were armed with the latest military hardware available, including Hawk ground-to-air missiles, capable of downing virtually any aircraft operated by the military. Galt had effectively declared war on the forces of President Rand and was daring him to do anything about it. The next step was up to the government.

As they were walking toward Galt's office, he asked Jeff, "How's Maria doing?"

"As well as can be expected," Jeff replied with a hint of weariness in his voice. "I'm glad she's here; I don't think she could take living at our ranch right now, with all its memories."

"I understand. Please let her know that my home is her home."

"I appreciate that," Jeff replied, "and I know Maria does too. I just wish we were here under better circumstances."

"Yeah. Me too," Galt replied, opening his office door. "It's like old times though, in many ways—you and I taking on the government again. This time, let's drop a rock on this one-world-government bunch. I'm getting a little tired of having to fight them every time we turn around."

"I agree," Jeff replied as he entered the room. "I just don't understand why the government is trying to have us killed. Surely not just to suppress the ERTS data!"

"That's only a part of it. I think I know the rest," Galt said as he recovered a package from his desk drawer—the package delivered by Dale Crawford.

What Galt didn't tell Jeff was that he had another larger file on the THOR—one provided by Dr. Alan Shoer.

Shoer had been monitoring the events in L.A. and Wyoming closely. He had discovered the original file on THOR dating back to 1960, when the idea was born. Every cover-up and every murder had been carefully documented and then filed away in the top secret CIA/CIO data bank.

After the failed assassination attempt on Dr. Wells and his wife, an order had come down to destroy all records and references to project THOR, which he had done—right after he copied it to his own secret files. Shoer was smart enough to know, when the leaders panic, it's time to pull out.

He had offered the material, including digitized videos of the actual THOR launch, to Galt for $25 million after he monitored the internal CIO memos describing the attack on the Wells ranch in Wyoming. He correctly assessed that Galt might be interested in more data on the THOR project.

The data was transmitted to Galt's ranch prior to the jamming, and immediately thereafter Shoer was on his way to Argentina under a new identity. With Galt's $25 million safely tucked away in a variety of bank accounts, Shoer assumed he would be able to live in style.

As Galt handed Jeff the first package, he said, "I want you to listen to these tapes," referring to Crawford's package of materials. "This will be pretty difficult to believe at first. I know it was for me. But you can take my word for it; it's all been verified."

Jeff looked down at the package and then at Galt. "What is it, exactly?"

"You'll have to hear it for yourself; but it involves your father."

"My father!" Jeff exclaimed. "My father's been dead for fifty years."

"You just need to listen to the tapes." Galt walked to the door, then stopped. "This is the most incredible thing I've ever heard. It's been a half century of lies."

After Galt left, Jeff settled back in his chair and laid out the material from the THOR project on the oversized desk before him.

Galt had secured a reel-to-reel tape player so he could hear the original tapes.

Jeff just sat staring at the tapes for several minutes. *My father,* he thought. *How could that be?* Finally, he threaded the tape machine and flipped the forward switch.

"My name is R.S. Moss," the voice began. "Most people call me Pappy. The story I'm gonna tell you really happened. Since you have this tape, then you prob'ly have some documents. The documents are part of a secret project, code-named THOR.

"You'll hear the story about the THOR project from a friend of mine shortly; but first, let me say that this project has been the biggest gol-darned blunder of the century. Stupid is as stupid does, and this was stupid with a capital *S*.

"I've violated federal security laws to swipe documents of this event, 'cause we both believe that the government will try'n cover up project THOR, but prob'ly put my life and Colonel Wells' in danger. Future generations have a right to know what's been goin' on, 'cause otherwise, it's more'n likely our government will do somethin' even dumber next time."

Jeff clicked the player off to process his thoughts so far. *Colonel Bob Wells,* he thought. *That has to be my father. Pappy Moss and my father collaborated to preserve information from project THOR and make it public.* Jeff had the feeling of being a time traveler—returning to the twentieth century to meet a father he had never known. A rush of adrenaline went through him as he turned the player back on. Suddenly the fatigue of the last few days was gone.

Another voice spoke from the tape, and although he had never heard it before, he knew it was his father.

▲

"This is Colonel Robert Wells, chief security officer on project THOR," the voice from fifty years earlier said. "If I'm still alive while you are listening to this recording, I am ready to testify under oath to all the events described here.

"Both Pappy and I have been placed under the Military Secrecy Act regarding this project. I have been a member of the U.S. Military Intelligence for more than twenty years now, and I have never revealed any national security information—until now.

"However, this debacle has the potential to alter the world as we know it. I want to tell the true story about the THOR, from the start, to ensure that this lesson will not be forgotten by the American people or the world.

"Several other personnel associated with project THOR have suffered mysterious deaths over the last year. There is reason to believe that Pappy and I are in danger too. If, in fact, either or both of us die *accidentally,* you should assume that we were targeted by those in the government who will do anything to conceal the truth."

Jeff turned off the player again. He knew his father had been killed in an accident at Alamogordo, New Mexico, in 1963. He sorted through the documents on his desk and stopped when he found the two he had glanced at earlier. Both were copies of death certificates: his father's and Pappy's. They had been copied from the government's records by Andy Moss during his initial search. His name and departmental account number were embossed on both copies.

Andy Moss? Who is that? Jeff wondered as he stared at the death certificates. *Moss . . . I wonder what the connection is between Andy Moss and Pappy Moss.*

The death certificates confirmed the obvious: *My father and Pappy Moss were killed in the same accident! They were both murdered, just as my father warned they might be.* His hand was unsteady as he turned the player back on.

"Project THOR was born as an effort to defend the U.S. against a possible nuclear attack by the Russians. In principle, the concept was simple: to position U.S. rockets armed with nuclear warheads throughout the Arctic perimeter. In the event of a Russian ICBM attack, the U.S. would launch a salvo of its own rockets and explode the warheads directly in the path of the oncoming Russian missiles. Theoretically, the incoming warheads would be vaporized by the nuclear blasts.

"Since this type of defense system had never been tested, a team of German and American rocket scientists were assembled to demonstrate the concept. The site selected for this demonstration was the Pacific Ocean Testing Center near the Anawetok Islands.

"Since at least a dozen hydrogen bombs already had been detonated by the U.S. in the Pacific Islands region, it was felt this location would attract the least attention for the test.

"From the earliest days that I heard about project THOR, I opposed it. I have always felt that a nuclear war is *not* inevitable, unless one side acquires a decided advantage, which neither has, thus far. But even if such a nuclear war does erupt, I voiced the opinion that project THOR would only exacerbate the dangers.

"The Arctic and Antarctic regions are the weather engines for the entire planet. Deliberate nuclear pollution at either pole would almost certainly be spread throughout the entire globe. So, from the first time I heard about this project, I argued that it should be scrapped.

"But, as with most government programs, the powers that be steadfastly refused to acknowledge the risks of their brainchild. Once I was assigned as security chief of project THOR by General Marshall, I committed myself to making the project as risk free for the launch teams as possible. I had the approval of General Marshall to recruit the best people for the job at hand.

"If we were bound and determined to do this thing, at least I wanted the best nuclear weapons specialist available to monitor the test; and that was Pappy Moss.

"I'll pick up the discussion of project THOR at the point where I recruited Pappy to head the Sandia nuclear weapons team. Pappy had just finished up the Mace program and was awaiting another assignment when I called him."

▲

The story on the tape started nearly fifty years earlier, when Colonel Wells and Pappy had sat in Wells' quarters dictating the description of the THOR saga. They both knew they never could convey fully the drama of those few months. As the old saying goes: *You just had to be there.*

But even as Wells was dictating the abbreviated version for his unseen listeners, his mind was recapturing the real-life drama that had become his worst nightmare: project THOR.

▲

April 1962

"*Pappy, I need you to head a Sandia team for a top secret project.*" Wells said. "But I need you to volunteer."

Pappy responded with an air of sarcasm, "Colonel, I've heard that one before. I volunteered once to go fight in World War II. You know what? I ended up disarmin' live bombs on a carrier deck in the Pacific. So why should I volunteer again?"

"Because I need you," Wells answered honestly.

"That's good enough for me, as long as it ain't carrier duty."

"Don't worry, Pappy. There won't be any carriers. It'll be soft breezes and warm nights on a beautiful island."

"What island and where?" Pappy asked.

"Can't tell you that right now. It's a highly classified project, and everybody assigned to it has to have a crypto clearance. Is yours still up to date?"

"Sure! But what are you guys doin' that everybody has to be cleared to crypto level? You ain't plannin' a sneak attack on Russia or somethin', are you?"

"Can't tell you any details, Pappy. But I can assure you, we're not attacking Russia. This is a test team—not an operational unit."

"Well, colonel, if you're sure I won't have to pull carrier duty, I'm in."

"Thanks, Pap. I knew I could count on you. But just one more thing. Don't say anything about our conversation to anyone."

"You don't have to worry about that! I don't know what we jist talked about myself."

Once Wells left, Pappy started thinking. He figured the project would involve his recent training on atomic warheads. For nearly three years he had worked on the Sandia arming system used on the Mace pilotless cruise bomber. The Mace had been designed to carry an atomic warhead and had recently been refitted to carry a hydrogen bomb.

How did I ever get into this business? Pappy asked himself. His thoughts went back to the Pacific Theater, 1943. He had joined the Navy under an assumed name because he was too old to enlist. But when his only son, Paul, had been killed flying his F4F off the decks of the *Enterprise,* he knew he had to get in the war and fight.

He volunteered for ordnance and quickly became the best student in his class of fifty. And why not? He was a widower. His only son was dead; he had nothing to lose. He wanted to fight "Japs," and the big aircraft carriers were his country's best weapons. So, he volunteered to handle ordnance on a carrier. Once on board, Pappy learned quickly. Each bomb he armed was intended to punish the killers of his only son, who died early in the war. Pappy was decorated six times for bravery while defusing Japanese bombs stuck in the carrier he served on.

After the war he had migrated to the Cape, where he headed an ordnance team to arm and disarm missiles. It was on the Redstone Project that he had met Lieutenant Colonel Bob Wells, the head of project security. They developed an instant respect for each other. Wells was a tough and thorough security chief, but he was also fair and flexible, unlike most of the other Army brass.

Pappy was known as the best ordnance boss at the Cape. In an accident-prone business, he had a flawless record. Two standards made his team the best: First, Pappy tolerated no "hotshots" on his team; second, he personally supervised all live ordnance loading.

Two days after the meeting with Colonel Wells, Pappy was sitting by the pool at the Sea Missile Motel in Cocoa Beach when a hard-faced sergeant, wearing an official Army crew cut, approached him. "Are you R.S. Moss?"

"Only to my dear old mother," Pappy replied. "To everyone else, I'm Pappy."

"I'm instructed to escort you to Patrick Air Force Base," the younger man said curtly.

Pappy felt sure that if this kid smiled his whole face would crack. *This is gonna be a long assignment,* Pappy decided as he headed back to his room to get dressed.

At Patrick, they boarded a military transport already loaded with other passengers. Pappy recognized many of them from projects he'd been involved with at the Cape. From what he knew about several of them, he realized they'd been handpicked from among the best of the launch crews.

The flight to Alamogordo, New Mexico, the first stop on their long journey, was uncomfortable and uneventful. Pappy stepped out of the plane into the morning desert heat that was approaching 100 degrees by eleven o'clock. By three o'clock it would rise to 115 degrees, and all outdoor work would cease until at least an hour after the sun had set.

As they entered the big hangar, the temperature change was abrupt. It wasn't that it was cool—only less hot out of the direct rays of the sun. The sky was cloudless and ocean blue, as it was nearly 300 days a year.

"Make yourselves comfortable, gentlemen," said the Air Force officer who greeted them. "This will be your home for the next few days, while you're getting familiar with project THOR. You men have been selected because you're the best at what you do."

Uh, oh, Pappy thought. *Any time the Army starts a session with praise, you can be sure somebody's in for it.*

"You're going to train on the most sophisticated weapons system ever created. This system has the capability to deliver a warhead with more destructive ability than all of the bombs dropped in World War II.

"From this point on, you're all under military security and committed to this project to the end. You will be confined to this base until further notice; and all mail will be screened, coming and going. All telephone lines are monitored and recorded, and access to any outside line must be approved by Colonel Wells, our chief of security."

"May-jor," Pappy said in his best Southern drawl. "Are you sayin' we're stuck out here in the middla nowhere and cain't even make a call to the 'real' world?"

"That's exactly what I'm saying. You've signed on for the duration. This project is top secret, and as of now, you gentlemen are too."

"What if I want to check out of this *op-por-tun-ity* right now?" Pappy quipped.

"Well then, Pappy, you'll find yourself confined to quarters until project THOR is completed," replied Colonel Wells, rising from his chair to stand beside the major.

"You mean I'll be arrested and thrown in the brig?" Pappy exclaimed.

"Exactly," Wells replied. "We need and appreciate your special abilities, and it would be most inconvenient to lock you up for the next few months," said Wells through a half grin.

"Okay," Pappy replied. "I just wanted to be sure I was loved." That filled the whole room with laughter.

As soon as the orientation meeting broke up, Colonel Wells went to his quarters, tossed his suitcase and duffel bag on the bed, and headed out to meet with the military project manager, General George Armstrong Reed.

Wells knew Reed only by reputation, but what he knew disturbed him. Reed was a bootlicker and a back stabber. He had been the project manager on the Air Force's Navajo project. When that ill-fated project had collapsed, Reed had blamed it on his chief of security, and Reed's friends in Congress had gotten him this assignment.

Wells knew Reed had fought to limit the THOR project to an all-German launch team under his absolute control. General Groves, Army chief of staff, had disagreed and prevailed, which was why Wells and the American team were involved.

Wells found the general in his temporary billet at the base commander's post. He entered and told the orderly at the desk who he was and that he would like to see the general.

Wells saw the sergeant disappear through the door marked TEMPORARY HEADQUARTERS, U.S. BALLISTIC MISSILE TEST FACILITY. Through the open door he could hear the conversation. Without any attempt to cover his booming voice, he heard the general say, "Tell the colonel that I don't have time to see him right now. I'll call him when I need his input. Have him go see Deitz."

When the sergeant returned to the orderly room, he found it empty. If he had looked out the window, he could have tracked Bob Wells by the smoke trail he was leaving as he floored his Army-issue Jeep.

23

△

General George Armstrong Reed

Furious would not have adequately described Bob Wells' attitude as he roared away from the command post. He reminded himself what General Groves had told him: "Don't expect any help from Reed. He was a blathering idiot at the Point, and time has not improved him."

Meanwhile, General Reed was silently congratulating himself for having dispatched General Groves' lackey so successfully. Reed was a man who reveled in bullying and generally demoralizing any and all subordinates. Groves had embarrassed him in his Navajo report when he had identified Reed as incompetent. But Reed had friends in Washington who quashed the report. Reed was not about to give Groves another shot at him if he could help it.

Major General George Armstrong Reed was named after his distant relative, General George Armstrong Custer, who was immortalized after the Little Big Horn debacle in South Dakota. Like Custer, he was more politician than soldier.

Reed stood six feet, two inches in his custom-made uniform. He had large protruding ears and red hair that covered his hands, head, and neck. It was well known that he was a man who would not tolerate a comment about his looks or any reflection on his intelligence.

The general was a career officer who had won his first star by chauffeuring congressmen around the Pentagon during the fiercest battles of the war: the battles to see whose district got the biggest defense contracts.

In fairness to Reed, it wasn't that he was a coward and didn't want to go to war; he had tried to get assigned to a combat unit, but nobody wanted him. He was a known incompetent who had graduated from the Academy at the very bottom of his class. He probably would have been a great tight end at the Academy, except that he could never remember the plays. After ten weeks of cramming with two assistants, he finally was dropped from the team.

He passed the Academy by perfecting his many skills of deceit and cunning: He cheated. The Academy leaders were so certain that a cadet would never stoop to cheating, they operated totally by the honor system. This obviously suited cadet Reed perfectly. Later these same skills would be very useful when dealing with the many politicians who oversaw the military's spending.

When the war ended, the Army was left with a one-star general they couldn't use, so General Reed was transferred to the newly formed Ballistic Missile Systems Command, where he inherited the German scientific team from the Peenemunde rocket facility. With anti-German sentiment running high in the country, the Germans were relegated to an information-only role, while American teams dissected and reassembled the confiscated V2s from the Nordhausen launch site.

The first Russian launch of a Russian satellite changed everything. The military, as well as the politicians, awoke to the space age and began a desperate effort to match the Russians.

Suddenly the German launch team, with over 3,000 rocket launches to their credit, became America's first team. An all-out effort to develop a U.S. rocket program commenced. This race was heightened by the disasters of the Navy's Vanguard rocket. Russia could put satellites in orbit; the U.S. couldn't.

This was the golden opportunity that General George Armstrong Reed had long awaited. Since his whole future rode on the success of his German wards, they became the benefactors of his cunning and contacts.

When Van Braun and his Redstone team launched the first successful U.S. satellite into orbit, Reed's career was launched with it. He received his second star from President Eisenhower himself.

As fate would have it, General Reed's career took a left turn when the next president, John Kennedy, placed the primary emphasis on manned space flight and established a new civilian agency, NASA, to control and direct it. General Reed languished in relative obscurity on the pilotless bomber project, Navajo, nicknamed "Nevergo" by the range support teams. The Navajo failed, and with it went millions of taxpayers' dollars. Reed would have been demoted for his incompetency in managing the project if Groves had had his way. But Reed had made powerful allies in Washington.

Then along came the THOR project—born out of the necessity to counter Russia's growing nuclear ICBM threat. It was the military's bold leap to overtake and pass the Russians where it really counted: a nuclear defense system.

Reed was furious when General Groves called to tell him that Wells and the American team would be coming to project THOR. And worst of all, that they would be operating under the security directorate and outside of his direct command.

I'll have Wells shipped back to Florida just as soon as Groves is out of my hair, he assured himself. He felt he had taken the first step in that direction by snubbing Wells in his office.

Wells began to calm down as he drove down the desert road toward the other end of the base. *It won't do any good to let Reed get me riled,* Wells told himself. *That's just what he wants. He'll use any excuse to ship me back to Florida. I need to keep my cool and remember what I'm here to do. The stakes are too high on this one to screw it up just because my pride's hurt.*

By the time he arrived at Deitz's office, he had calmed down. *After all,* he thought, *if you have to have a two-star general hating your guts, it might as well be this one.*

"Dr. Deitz will see you now, Colonel Wells," said the well-groomed middle-aged secretary.

"Come in, colonel, and have a seat," Deitz said as Wells entered the room. Wells thought to himself, *This looks like a scientist's office. Everything is in stacks, and each stack is laid crosswise to the others. I'm sure Deitz can locate anything he wants in this mess and probably has issued orders that nothing is to be touched by the cleaning people. Obviously they have followed orders: It looks as if nothing has been cleaned for at least a year.*

Dr. Kurt Deitz was tall and distinguished looking but he had the haggard look of someone under constant stress.

"Doctor," said Wells, "I'm here at the request of General Groves, to head security as a part of the American launch team."

"Colonel, I must be honest and tell you that I don't see the need. My team has developed the THOR. We have been working on this project now for nearly two years. We simply don't need your launch team. In fact, I'm concerned that they will delay our progress."

"Doctor," Wells replied, a little irritated with his second snub of the day, "if I had my way, I would stop this entire project until more studies could be done. I question not only its validity but its safety."

"But you don't have that authority, colonel; only the president does."

"Duly noted," replied Wells. "But I do have authority over security . . . and personnel safety. This is not Peenemunde, doctor."

"Colonel, you obviously have a preconceived bias about all Germans. I cannot help the fact that I was born a German or that I lived in a country run by a madman. I am a scientist committed to furthering the use of rocketry. The THOR will put America decades ahead of the Russians in nuclear defense."

"Or in radiation pollution," Wells countered.

"Your concerns are groundless, colonel. Every element of this project has been thoroughly evaluated by very qualified scientists. If you find a security problem, please let me know. Otherwise, I would suggest that you limit your concerns to your duties at hand. We do not require a layman's evaluation of nuclear physics. These are better left to my scientists."

"Be assured, doctor, you will be the first to know if I see any problems—within my area of expertise, of course."

"Fine!" snapped Deitz with obvious exasperation in his voice. "Now please go about your business and let me get back to mine."

Before Wells could respond, Deitz had redirected his attention to the papers on his desk. As he was leaving, Wells said sarcastically, "Don't bother to show me out, doctor. I know the way." Deitz never looked up from the test reports he was studying.

Later that day, Wells addressed the assembled American launch team. Stepping up to the platform, he introduced himself.

"Gentlemen, I'm Colonel Bob Wells, chief of security for project THOR. I know most of you are still in the dark about what THOR is all about. Once you understand, I think you'll have a better appreciation for the extraordinary security we'll have on this project. Each of you is a handpicked specialist with experience in missile systems. You will be working alongside a German counterpart on the THOR project.

"Our mission is to equip a rocket with a ten-megaton hydrogen warhead, launch it into the projected path of another missile, and test the capabilities of using a thermonuclear explosion as a ballistic missile defense system."

Al Gates, one of the propulsion engineers, spoke up. "Colonel, with the reliability of rockets being what they are, aren't a lot of people going to have their day ruined if one of these rockets explodes prematurely?"

"These are a new generation of rocket engines that have been tested extensively by the Germans out here in the desert," replied

Wells. "It's really the first stage of a multistage rocket they have been working on for several years.

"But you do bring up a valid point about launching live ten-megaton bombs. Dr. Deitz's team believes they have a fully tested and reliable arming system for the warhead that will prevent premature detonation. However, just the residue from the plutonium core would contaminate a ten-mile area in a rocket explosion. So, it has been decided that we will take our show on the road and launch the THOR from an island in the Pacific Ocean, about 3,000 miles from the nearest American city."

Just then General George Armstrong Reed, wearing fresh Army gabardines with knife-like creases, stepped onto the platform. "I'll take over from here, colonel," he said in a demeaning manner, clearly meant to undercut Wells' authority. Wells felt his face flush, but he said nothing and stepped off the platform.

General Reed began, "Gentlemen, as you will see for yourselves, we do not have a fully integrated model of the THOR here at the Alamogordo test facility. The first complete vehicle is being assembled at the Pacific test range launch facility. However, I can assure you that this test complex will provide you with all the experience you'll need on your individual systems."

Another of the American scientists spoke up. "General, where are our German colleagues?"

"I'm not at liberty to discuss that right now. All you need to know is that they already have undergone their initial training and are developing the next element of the launch program."

"Which, in government gobbledygook, means they're already out in the Pacific working on the real thing, while we're stuck out here in the desert," shouted Pappy.

The general turned red from the tip of his hairy ears to the line of his red-haired neck, where it disappeared into his tailored gabardine shirt. But he struggled to control his temper and replied through gritted teeth, "When you gentlemen are certified as launch-ready, you will be integrated into Dr. Deitz's THOR team—not before. Failure to meet our launch team standards on this test will disqualify you from project THOR."

With that, Reed stepped down from the platform and exited the building, giving Pappy a threatening look as he parted. Pappy responded with a mock salute.

Luckily for Wells, the general wasn't looking his way to see the smirk on his face.

The rest of the briefing went pretty smoothly, considering. At the conclusion of the session, the members of the launch team were given their assignments for the upcoming launch countdown simulation.

Wells returned to his hut to prepare his report for General Groves on the American launch team's arrival at Alamogordo. He was just getting started when there was a knock at his door.

"Colonel Wells, sir," the young corporal said when Wells opened the door. "You're wanted in General Reed's office. I was told to wait and escort you, sir."

This morning he was too busy to see me, Wells thought to himself while trying to keep a straight face, *and now he can't wait to see me. I'll bet I can guess what he's got on his mind. It's a good thing flogging is out, or I'd say Pappy's in real trouble.*

"Corporal, tell the general I'll be right there as soon as I clear up some security matters."

"But sir, I was told to wait and escort you," said the soldier, obviously nervous about his situation.

"Am I under arrest, corporal?" asked Wells.

"No sir, not that I know of. I was only instructed to escort you to the general's office."

"Well then corporal, sit down and wait. I'll be done in a few minutes." He started writing notes in his daily logbook—a detail that he normally would have left until evening, but he felt it would be an opportune time to alter his routine.

Wells wrote in his logbook for over an hour while the increasingly nervous corporal fidgeted and paced around the room. "Colonel, sir, couldn't we go now?" the corporal asked in a pleading voice that sounded like a man about to face execution. "The general will be mad enough to put me on permanent KP now, if he doesn't court-martial me."

"I'm about ready to go, corporal," replied Wells. "But don't you worry about General Reed. I'll be sure to let him know you did your job. He didn't tell you to bring me right back, did he?"

"No sir, colonel, not in so many words, but he made it clear that I was not to leave here without you," replied the frustrated corporal.

"And leave with me you shall, corporal. Let's go."

Wells thought to himself, *You know this started out as a rotten day, but it's turning out better all the time.*

When Wells arrived at the general's office, the sergeant at the desk was just putting the phone down. He shouted at the corporal, "Where have you been? The general is in a rage."

Wells stopped him. "Sergeant, the corporal did just as he was instructed; he escorted me back here. I had some urgent security work to complete and couldn't leave until it was done. You be sure to tell the general that I take full responsibility for any delay."

"Colonel Wells, where have you been?" shouted General Reed as Wells entered his office. Wells gave him his best salute and stood there until the red-faced general returned it.

"I've been briefing the American launch crew, sir, and preparing my report for General Groves," Wells replied, standing as stiffly as a marble statue. "You did say that I was to proceed with my security duties, didn't you, sir?"

"Colonel, I personally sent an orderly to locate and escort you to my office," said the general.

"Yes, sir, and he did, sir." Wells was still standing at attention, which visibly irritated Reed.

"Mister," boomed Reed, "when a general summons a junior officer, he expects him to drop everything and come running. Do you understand that? I know what you're trying to pull, mister, and let me tell you that you're playing with fire."

"Sir," replied Wells with an unnatural formality, "I explained to your orderly that I had a security summary to do, as ordered by General Groves when I was assigned to the THOR project. I merely thought that the performance of my official duty was first priority, especially since your orderly didn't indicate that your *request* was of an urgent or critical nature. If you will instruct your men to apprise me of the criticality of your situation, I will most certainly drop any other project I may be working on that is a lower priority."

Reed stifled the urge to reach across the table and grab Wells by his neck. It was probably good that he didn't. Bob Wells was two inches taller than Reed, at six feet four inches, and in significantly better physical condition. Plus, Reed had the flaw of all bullies: cowardice.

Instead, he just looked at Wells with pure hatred in his eyes and with the sure knowledge that in this man's Army it would only be a matter of time until he would have his revenge. With great effort, he forced himself to speak calmly.

"Colonel, I believe you have a civilian by the name of R.S. Moss who is a part of the trainee team." It was really more of an announcement than a question from Reed.

"Yes, sir, although most of the time he goes by the name of Pappy." *Now,* thought Wells, *we'll get down to the real purpose of this command performance. Pappy twisted his tail, and now he wants to skin him.*

"I want that man off of my complex today, colonel."

"But general," replied Wells, allowing his body to relax without awaiting permission. "Mr. Moss is our most experienced ordnance man and our only technical expert trained in the Sandia nuclear arming system."

"I don't care if he's the only man on this base who can read," Reed roared, turning red around his hair-lined collar. "I want him out of here today. Do you read me, mister?"

"Yes sir, General Reed," replied Wells in a little less contrite voice. "But sir, may I respectfully remind you that I am under special orders from *Lieutenant* General Groves and cannot make any changes in personnel without his direct instructions. May I make a call to Ballistic Missile Systems Command and relay your instructions to General Groves?"

With a sinking feeling, Reed knew what the outcome of that phone call would be. Groves was the one who pushed for these ragtag "experts" to be assigned to project THOR in the first place. He knew Leslie Groves was no man to be trifled with. He was as tough as they come, and he had friends at the highest levels of the government and military.

"No, Colonel Wells, that won't be necessary," replied the more subdued general. "I'm going to give Moss another chance since you think his abilities are necessary to the success of THOR; and the success of the program *is* the most important task we have before us. But, colonel," snarled Reed, "from this point on I will hold you personally responsible for the discipline of the American team."

"Yes, sir," Wells agreed. "And I appreciate your confidence. I'll be sure to tell General Groves that I have your full support."

For the first time in a long while, Major General G.A. Reed was totally speechless.

As Wells strode out the door, the general was collapsing in his overstuffed chair on the raised platform that allowed him to look down on those seated across from his desk.

The desk sergeant quickly replaced the intercom phone connecting his office to General Reed's. The open speaker phone on the general's desk, which allowed him to summon the sergeant without expending the effort to lift a phone, also allowed the sergeant access to a very entertaining conversation. But as Wells left, he saw the sergeant flash his corporal a thumbs-up sign.

24

△

Countdown Simulation

G entlemen, you're about to enter a very critical phase of your training," Dr. Deitz told the American launch team. "The purpose of this test is to simulate the countdown and launch of the THOR as closely as possible. Each of you has been briefed fully on the systems for which you will be responsible during the countdown.

"The fuel and oxidizer tanks will be fully pressure tested just prior to loading. Once the tanks are loaded, extreme caution must be exercised at all times. As you are aware, the fuels used on the THOR are extremely toxic. In the event of a problem, all personnel will evacuate to the control center."

Next it was Wells' turn to explain the procedures the American team would follow during the countdown simulation.

"Gentlemen, obviously I don't need to explain your jobs to you, but we will be observing some extraordinary security measures for this program. The first is that no one will be allowed on the test site alone once the countdown commences, and that means *no one.*

"The second is that once the propellant tanks are loaded, the entire complex will be under a level-two security watch. That means no changes can be made to a system that has been verified in the countdown without the approval of security. Also, each step of the launch simulation will be verified by a minimum of two people if it involves a potentially hazardous system. These same safety procedures will be enforced once the American team is relocated to the Pacific test range to participate in the actual THOR launch."

"Colonel, are you expecting some trouble on this test?" Pappy asked.

"No, I'm not," replied Wells. "And I'm not going to take a chance on anything happening either. The two-man rule is firm."

Dr. Deitz called to Wells just as the last of the launch team was leaving the ready room. "Colonel, I need to talk with you for a moment."

"Do you have a problem with my security plan, doctor?" Wells snapped.

"Not while your team is in New Mexico," Deitz countered. "But remember, the THOR project is under my direction, and I will decide who has access to the rocket once we reach the Pacific test station. Is that clear?"

"Doctor," Wells replied while returning the German's icy stare, "I thought the THOR was under the control of General Reed, who is under the authority of the U.S. military. Since this is an American military project, that would seem to be the logical chain of command. If you disagree with my decisions, you can appeal to General Reed, who then can appeal to General Groves, to whom I report. Is *that* clear?"

Deitz's reaction to the challenge was totally unexpected. "Perhaps you are correct, colonel," he replied as he turned and walked away, leaving Wells completely puzzled.

The next day was spent in verifying all the systems in preparation of fuel loading. Both Deitz and Reed left the American team to do their tasks without interference.

At T-minus-two hours, the fuel and oxidizer had been transferred to the rocket engine's tanks without incident. Once the volatile fuels were loaded, the teams at the site were in constant jeopardy, and tensions were running high.

"Well, how are you doing, Pappy?" Wells asked the ordnance chief, who was seated at the Sandia console in the control center.

"How could I be, colonel?" grumbled Pappy. "There's no bomb or ordnance on this test, so I'm sittin' here playin' nursemaid to a black box that wouldn't go POP if it was struck by lightnin'."

"You just hang in there," replied Wells. "You'll get your chance at the real thing soon enough. Do you think you can check out the arming system on the THOR's warhead when the time comes?"

"In my sleep, colonel. If the schematics you've given me are right, it's not really all that diff'rent from the warheads we saw down at the Cape."

"The schematics are accurate, Pappy. General Groves had them sent by special courier from Oakridge."

"T-minus-one hour and counting," reported the countdown director.

At the test site, preparations were under way, hot and heavy, for the test firing. At T-minus-one hour in the countdown, the final check of the propulsion system was being made. The leak detection team was carefully scouring every square inch of piping and tanks for any signs of leaks.

At T-minus-thirty minutes, all personnel were evacuated from the test site. The countdown progressed to T-minus-five minutes, at which time the fuel and oxidizer tank safety seals were ruptured remotely. This allowed the propellants to flow down the feed lines to the main engine valves.

This was the most critical step in the countdown of a static engine firing. If either a fuel or oxidizer valve leaked, the test would have to be canceled and it would take several days to drain the tanks, purge the system, and change out the main tank seals and engine valves.

"Main tank seals ruptured," reported the engineer on the propellants console.

"Affirmative," responded the engine control console operator. "We show liquid on both valves."

"Propulsion, do you detect any leaks?" the test controller asked at T-minus-thirty seconds.

"Negative, control. We show the engine is still clean. Request permission to commence engine start sequence."

"Hold one," replied the controller. "Range safety, we are about to commence firing sequence. Are we clear?"

The range safety console was where Wells sat monitoring the progress of the countdown. His console was linked to every other console in the control room, and the summation of their consoles, if everything was okay, was a green "go" light.

Since most of the other normal rocket systems, such as guidance, destruct, hydraulics, and the warhead, were nonexistent for this test firing, they were being simulated through black boxes attached to the consoles. The affirmation was really a formality to satisfy the launch countdown procedure.

The range safety operator responded, "That's affirmative, sir. We are go for firing at this time."

"T-minus-thirty seconds," the controller announced. "Rocket systems cycling to internal power."

Dutifully, the simulators imitated the sequence when the THOR would cycle over to internal batteries.

"T-minus-fifteen seconds," the controller announced.

The simulator attached to Pappy's console began the sequence that in the real warhead would first verify the firing circuits were grounded and then would initiate the arming sequence. After liftoff, the plutonium core would be remotely inserted into the firing chamber. From that point on, it would be a live hydrogen bomb awaiting the signal to explode.

"Sandia?" the controller asked, in response to the countdown instructions.

Pappy responded from the Sandia console, "Mr. Disney, this is the bomb squad. Mickey Mouse is ready."

Snickers went through the entire control room, except for General Reed and Dr. Deitz.

"T-minus-ten seconds . . . nine . . . eight . . . seven . . . six . . . five . . . four . . . three . . . two . . ."

At T-minus-two seconds, the main engine fuel valve opened, flooding the chamber with a fine mist of fuel. At the same instant, the launch site's fire control system cycled on, and the exhaust tunnel was flooded with thousands of gallons of water a second to keep the rocket exhaust from melting down the entire test site.

"T-minus-one second . . ."

The oxidizer valve opened, allowing the nitric acid to flow into the spinning turbine chamber. The combination of the fuel and oxidizer resulted in a controlled explosion that rivaled any conventional bomb ever dropped.

The ignition was audible to everyone in the control room. The almost invisible plume from the engine shot out from the flame deflector for nearly three hundred feet as the engine strained to tear itself away from the metal tower restraining it.

After what seemed like an eternity since the ignition, the controller announced, "T-plus-five seconds."

The propulsion engineer reported, "Engine shutdown commencing on my mark: three . . . two . . . one . . . mark."

Suddenly the room was filled with a deafening silence as the rocket engine shut down.

"Safety, I have an abnormal shutdown on the engine," reported the propulsion engineer.

"Please report the nature of your problem," the controller commanded.

"It would appear that the main engine oxidizer valve didn't cycle completely shut. I still show a flow through the turbine sensor."

"Control, this is instrumentation," the engineer on the console to Wells' left reported. "I show a steady drop in pressure on tank number two. Tank number one is stabilized."

"Do we have a visual?" Deitz asked.

"Affirmative," said Wells, peering out at the test site through the periscope mounted on top of the control room roof. "There's a big red cloud beginning to form around the test stand."

"Pad safety, this is control. Can you cycle the water system back on to dilute the acid spray?"

"Negative," replied the safety engineer. "Pressure is down in the system. It will be at least thirty minutes before we can even get the flame bucket spray to operate."

"That'll be too late," Tom Speers, the lead engineer on the propulsion console said with some alarm. "By then that acid will have eaten through the fuel tubes in the engine housing and we'll have a bad mix."

The bad mix he was describing meant that the fuel would be mixed with the oxidizer. The result would be an explosion in the engine compartment and, likely, a rupture of the large fuel holding tanks.

"How long would you estimate before a rupture?" Deitz asked in his stoic German fashion.

"Ten minutes . . . fifteen at the outside," Speers replied.

"Can we drain the tanks in time?"

"Negative, sir," was the reply. "It would take at least an hour and we would need a crew at the test site to handle the valves."

"Can the oxidizer valve be closed manually?" Pappy asked from his console.

"It's possible," Speers replied. "But it would mean someone working in that acid cloud. And who knows when the acid will eat through the tubes and the whole thing will go up? I can't send anybody down there."

"You won't have to," replied Pappy. "I'm goin' myself. You boys just find me one of those purty little splash suits and a backpack."

"I can't allow that," replied Deitz. "It's too risky."

Pappy laughed. "I used to defuse dented bombs on a flight deck with kamikazes all around us, and nobody had to tell me it was dangerous. You get me a wrench and the suit. I'm goin'."

"Mr. Moss, this is General Reed. You stay on your console. No one is going to the site area. We'll wait this thing out."

"Put a cork in it, general!" Pappy was glaring back at the scowling, red-faced general. "If I remember right, I work for the colonel on this program. Whatcha say, colonel?"

Wells knew if it went wrong, he would be digging his own grave and Reed would gladly throw him in it. "I say, let's do it, Pappy," replied Wells. "Time's wasting."

"What do you mean, let's," gruffed Pappy. "You ain't goin'."

"If I don't go, then you don't go," replied Wells in a very official tone. "Remember, we have a two-man policy on this project."

"Okay, colonel. If you want to get killed, I guess you have the right. I figger that tin-star soldier would prob'ly skin you and hang you out to dry anyway if I went and got myself killed without his approval."

In fact, General Reed had already assessed the possibilities of Wells and Moss getting themselves killed and had decided that wouldn't be all bad. So he agreed. "Colonel Wells, this is your responsibility. I wash my hands of the whole thing."

Bob Wells knew the official line real well. It meant, "If you get yourselves killed, don't blame me."

"Acknowledged," Wells responded as he and Pappy headed for the splash suit storage room.

Within a minute they were suited up and waiting while the big steel blast doors were opened to allow them outside. Once they were outside, the huge doors swung shut and locked behind them. Wells felt a momentary twinge of panic, just as he had many times before during the war. At first he had been concerned that he might really panic in the midst of a mission, but later, after each mission was over and he had kept his nerve, he realized that a little fear is both normal and healthy. He had seen men in war who became immune to fear. Most of them got killed because they got careless.

"Pappy, are you nervous?" asked Wells, wondering about this man who lived with danger.

"Nope, not a bit," replied Pappy. "I'm just scared like I always am when I'm about to do somethin' stupid. But I figger somebody's got to do it, and I've lived longer than most."

"Good!" replied Wells. "At least I won't need to watch you." He saw Pappy give him a big thumbs-up in response.

Pappy led the way up the ramp to the engine compartment. The signs of acid erosion were already evidenced at the test site. Some of the acid had mixed with standing water to form little pools that would have stripped human skin from bones in seconds. If it hadn't been for the protective suits they were wearing, the red vapors surrounding them would have quickly dissolved both men to mush.

"Colonel, this stuff has already pitted the metal around the top of the engine," Pappy shouted. "If we don't hurry, it'll eat right through those engine tubes."

"Pappy, I can't see a thing up here," said Wells as loudly as he could through the breathing mask. His voice sounded tinny and artificial behind the glass faceplate.

"Neither can I, colonel," yelled Pappy. "And I can't find that valve. If you got any ideas, I'd suggest you try 'em now."

"I need to talk to the control room. See if you can locate an intercom stand," yelled Wells.

Groping around in the red acid fog, Pappy tried to recall where the communications stands were located. "Here's one, colonel," he yelled as he bumped into the communications receptacle.

"Great," yelled Wells. "Plug me in, will you?"

"Sure. No sweat." yelled Pappy. He brushed the red cloud back a little to get a look at the intercom panel and yelled again, "Okay, colonel. You're on."

"Speers, are you there?" Wells yelled to the control room engineer. "Speers, come in." Wells shouted even louder, "Can you hear me?"

"Sure, colonel. I'll bet they can hear you in Alaska. I'll have to have my eardrums replaced."

"Sorry," Wells said. "Pappy and I have been yelling back and forth. I forgot I was on the intercom. Speers, we can't see a thing down here. This acid cloud is everywhere and it's already pitted the upper engine parts."

"Then you and Pappy had better get out of there. There's no telling when those tubes will rupture."

"No, I've got an idea that may work," Wells replied, half yelling so Pappy could hear too. "Do you guys have any pressure on the water system yet?"

"Hang on, colonel. I'll see." Five seconds later he answered, "Site safety says they've got about forty pounds, but that won't last thirty seconds in the exhaust bucket."

"Listen, we're going to try to close the main valves to the exhaust bucket and leave the engine spray on. That should give us enough water to clear out the valve area so we can see. You tell safety to turn the water on when I yell."

Pappy was already moving back down the ramp toward the main water valves when Wells turned around. Grabbing the flame bucket water control valve handle with both hands, Pappy began the slow process of closing off the six-inch pipe. In less than a minute he signaled to Wells that it was closed.

"Okay, Speers," Wells shouted into the mike. "Turn the water on."

When Wells looked up, the engine spray sprinklers were billowing clouds of fine mist above the engine.

"It worked, colonel," yelled Pappy, heading toward the engine compartment again. "I can see the valves now."

In less than thirty seconds, using the two-foot wrench he had brought with him, Pappy had cycled the oxidizer valve shut. Within a few seconds, the red cloud was beginning to thin out and Wells heard the instrumentation engineer in the control room report, "The pressure on number two tank has stabilized. The leak has stopped."

A shout went up from the control room crew, which then broke out in applause. Even General Reed found himself clapping. He didn't like Wells or Moss, but he had to admire their courage. He had hoped the simulation test would fail and he could send the American launch team packing, but he knew there was nothing he or Deitz could do to keep Wells and his misfits off the THOR now.

25

△

The Pacific Test Range

Not exactly a tropical paradise, is it?" commented the engineer sitting across from Pappy as the plane approached the Anawetok launch site in the Pacific.

"I'll be satisfied if it just has a few native dancin' girls," quipped Pappy.

"Sorry, Pappy," Wells responded in mock remorse. "They've evacuated all the dancing girls for several hundred miles around. Something about launching a live H-bomb that discourages dancing girls."

"Just my luck!" sighed Pappy. But as relaxed as Pappy appeared to be outside, inside a thousand memories about the Pacific were nagging at his brain.

He often had heard others say he had a sixth sense; maybe he did. He just knew that he had a knack for staying alive. More than once, this "sense" had saved his life while disarming bombs during the war. He had outlived smarter, more skilled men because he had learned to trust his instincts.

One time on the *Saratoga* a Japanese bomb had plowed through the upper deck and lodged in the flight deck A-lift. As he had approached the bomb, which looked to be a dud, he'd felt the tingling inside his head. Without even checking the bomb, he'd headed for the flight deck and told the OIC to clear the lift area in a hurry. Ten minutes later, the bomb exploded. It was a delayed-fuse, anti-personnel bomb designed by the clever Japanese to wipe out curious sailors like him.

Pappy had learned to listen when his warning alarm went off— as it was doing now.

"Colonel, there's something about this place I don't like," Pappy whispered as the plane touched down on the runway.

"I can't say that I blame you, Pappy," Wells replied. "This is a bad place and a bad project; but we're here, so let's do the best we can."

"Right you are," Pappy agreed as he unsnapped his seat harness. "But if I remember correctly, the old *Sara [Saratoga]* went down not too far from here, didn't she?"

"You served on the *Sara-Maru* didn't you, Pap?"

"I sure did . . . though I haven't heard anybody call her that for a long time. Why do ya ask?"

"Because the *Sara* was one of the target ships used during the A-bomb tests out here. She was sunk not fifty miles away."

"It's a sad way for a grand ol' lady to die, colonel. She served her country well and deserved to rest easier."

"At least it's better than being cut up for scrap iron and made into some politician's limousine," responded Wells.

"True enough, colonel. True enough," Pappy replied, his thoughts drifting back to 1945. The Japs were launching their final, desperate assault on the American fleet. With their own carrier fleet laying on the bottom of the Pacific Ocean, they had turned to suicide attacks on the American carriers.

Young pilots flying zeros loaded with explosives launched themselves as flying bombs. Most never reached the carriers, shot out of the sky by the seasoned carrier pilots and gun crews. But some made it, and the results were devastating.

A kamikaze struck the bow of the *Sara* just below the flight deck. Instead of exploding, the plane rocketed into the upper hangar. The crushed hull of the aircraft, containing 1,000 pounds of explosives, skidded to a halt just short of the ordnance storage locker. The terrified flight deck crews scrambled to escape what would become a holocaust if the plane exploded. The charred wreck just sat there, as if in suspended animation.

"Ordnance disarming crew to hangar level one!" the P.A. blared over the Klaxon. "On the double!"

Pappy dropped the ammo box he was carrying to the aft gun crew and literally vaulted over the wreckage on the deck. The rest of his ordnance crew quickly found their way to the hangar just as Pappy was approaching the fuselage of the kamikaze.

"Stay back," he commanded. "I'll take a look. You guys get

everybody off the forward flight deck. If this thing goes, it'll take half the bow with it."

The wreck was still so hot that Pappy could feel the skin on his hands burning, even though he wore thick leather gloves. Using the fire axe he had grabbed off the wall, he swung at the remainder of the Plexiglas canopy. *I hope you're all prayed up, Pappy,* he thought to himself. The tingling in his neck had all but disappeared, as it usually did once he was in the thick of the action.

The axe struck the already shattered canopy, and it burst into a thousand pieces. Peering inside, Pappy could see the Japanese pilot, who appeared to be hardly more than a teenager, slumped over the control stick. *They must be hurtin' for volunteers,* he noted. *This is just a kid.* His head had nearly been severed by the impact when his plane had struck the carrier.

"He's as dead as he'll ever be," Pappy said aloud as he cut the restraining straps away. Then he dropped the body over the side of the fuselage. Squirming into the compressed cockpit, he dropped the seat back out of the plane so he could access the explosives packed in behind the pilot's seat.

Just then, one of his team returned and stuck his head in the opening. "What's it look like, Pap?"

"Get outta here," Pappy ordered. "There's no point in both us gettin' killed."

"I'll stay, Pap. If this thing goes, there'll be a lot of widows tomorrow."

"Okay then," Pappy said without further argument. "It looks like the impact fuse failed. But the charge is intact, and anything might set it off."

"Can you get at it?" the young seaman shouted over the clanging Klaxon.

"Yeah, but I'll need a pair of sidecutters. I'm gonna cut the main buss wire to the fuse," Pappy shouted back. "Hand me your cutters."

"What if that thing is booby-trapped, Pap?"

"Then I guess we'll see our Maker a little sooner," Pappy shouted. "I can't wait. This thing's hot as a firecracker, and who knows when that fuse'll trigger. Now you get outta here! That's an order!"

As the young sailor handed Pappy the pliers, he shouted, "How old are you, Pappy—really?" The whole crew often had argued about Pappy's age. Nobody knew for sure, but some covert spying had revealed a driver's license that showed him as thirty-eight.

Everyone knew the license had to be a clever forgery to allow Pappy to sign up for the Navy. He had been an Army ordnance sergeant in the last months of World War I. If he were really thirty-eight, he would have been three years old when he joined the Army.

"I'm really thirty-nine," Pappy shouted back. "Now get outta here."

How old am I? Pappy asked himself, wincing as he touched the side frame with his knee. The heat from the metal seared his flesh and melted fabric and skin together.

I guess I've lied about my age so long I don't really know anymore. I told 'em I was eighteen back in the first war, and I musta been about fifteen. That's been more'n thirty years, so I must be nearly fifty. No wonder I feel old. I am!

Grasping the cutters firmly, he looked down at the wire bundle attached to the sidewall. "Well, I just hope the Japs use red for the buss wire too," he said aloud.

Praying silently, he squeezed the handles. He felt the pliers cut through the tough wire with a click.

Well, it's done and I'm not dead, so I guess red was the right color, he said to himself as he wiped the sweat off his brow.

Standing up in the cockpit, he saw his ordnance crew waiting just inside the hangar door. "Let's get a crew in here and shove this mess out the hole," Pappy shouted. "The war won't wait!"

Pappy sighed as he made his way down the C-135's ladder and onto the tarmac of the Pacific testing station. *I still think it was a rotten end for a grand ol' ship,* he told himself silently.

▲

"Gentlemen, this session is to introduce you to the THOR launch vehicle," Deitz announced. "Each of you has successfully completed the training phase at Alamogordo, so you understand the basic concepts. However, from this point on, you will be working with a fully operational rocket.

"This will be a fully integrated launch, carrying a ten-megaton hydrogen device. An Atlas rocket carrying test instruments will be launched from Vandenberg Air Force base in California—to test the feasibility of using THOR as an anti-ballistic missile defense system."

"At what altitude will the THOR be detonated, doctor?" one of the radiation specialists asked.

"At approximately twelve kilometers. This will put the blast area well above any targeted area and will provide the maximum shield for any incoming missiles."

"What about the potential for upper level atmospheric combustion?" the American scientist pressed.

"This has all been thoroughly analyzed," Deitz said irritatedly, "long before the American team was involved. There is no need for concern."

"Now that makes me feel a whole lot better," Pappy whispered sarcastically to Wells who was sitting next to him. Wells nodded in agreement.

The THOR launch complex consisted of an instrumentation and countdown control center, known as the blockhouse, and a vertical assembly area, known as the pad, where the THOR would be assembled and launched. The two areas were a quarter of a mile apart and linked together by an underground cable tunnel that was just large enough for a man to walk between the cable trays and the concrete walls.

Few of the launch team actually used the tunnel to reach the launch pad even in the most inclement weather because it was inhabited by very large wharf rats brought onto the island by the supply ships. With almost no natural enemies, they quickly multiplied in number and size.

It was pretty unnerving to look down the tunnel and see five hundred sets of beady eyes peering back from every crevice. But they were not aggressive and had never, to anyone's knowledge, attacked a human.

However, they did play havoc with the cables running between the blockhouse and the pad. Being typical rodents, they chewed on just about everything, including power cables, and more than one rat had gone up in a blaze of burning fur and skin. It left a horrible smell in the cable tunnel for a day or so after being incinerated. The cable repair crews worked in shifts with one crew throwing up while the other worked on the damaged cables.

The sea gulls were another problem. Nobody knew who the first wise guy was to offer a part of his lunch to the ever-circling gulls, but once he did the word was passed quickly within the gull community. From that point on, nobody's lunch was safe from gull attacks.

The gulls would often work in teams to swipe food from distracted humans. One would swoop down squawking while another approached quietly from another angle. When the unsuspecting worker attempted to protect the sandwich he was eating, the second gull would grab something from his lunch bag and be gone before he could defend it. Needless to say, gull hunting became a favorite off-time activity.

The integrated launch crews completed several simulated countdowns on the THOR over the next several weeks. Wells noted with satisfaction that, although they experienced the normal problems associated with any verification of complicated rocket systems, there was nothing out of the ordinary.

The next phase was to be a wet test of the rocket's fueling system. This involved a simulated countdown, including loading the rocket with propellants.

The countdown would be identical to an actual launch in all aspects except for three critical areas. First, although live ordnance would be installed, all firing circuits would remain grounded. Second, the bottom seals in the propellant tanks would remain closed so that no fuels could reach the main engine valves. And third, the plutonium core would not be loaded in the warhead.

The simulated countdown went without incident. The propellants were transferred from the storage tanks into the rocket. Then Pappy and his team installed the destruct ordnance simulators and rechecked the arming system carefully—to ensure that there would be no surprises during the eventual live countdown. All of the warhead systems were simulated by inert "black boxes."

At T-minus-two seconds, the engine valves were cycled open to simulate ignition of the rocket engines.

At T-minus-zero, liftoff was simulated by mechanically disconnecting the liftoff switch.

The remainder of the simulation consisted of verifying the in-flight functions of guidance and the nuclear warhead arming sequences. A barometric pressure simulator duplicated the in-flight altitudes necessary for the warhead arming system.

At exactly 12.001 kilometers above sea level on the descent phase, the warhead arming system initiated the destruct signal and the imaginary ten-megaton warhead detonated. Deitz declared the final simulation a success, and the de-tanking process was begun.

Once de-tanking was completed, the THOR's tanks were purged, cleaned, and refitted with new seals for the actual launch countdown that would commence in one week. For the teams it meant seven days of around-the-clock work to get the rocket ready for launch.

Two days later, the THOR team was ready for the next phase: transporting the complete missile and warhead to the launch site.

26

△

The Lightning Strike

The THOR was transported from the test bay to the launch pad without incident, and preparations were under way to load it onto the erector. There was an air of excitement about the whole project that Pappy couldn't deny. He just hoped that future generations would appreciate the history that was being made.

The more he learned about the THOR project, the more he questioned the sanity of the whole thing. They were about to launch an untried hydrogen bomb 500 miles downrange, on an untested missile, and then blow it up at the precise point projected to intercept the incoming missile from Vandenberg. *Pretty iffy stuff,* he concluded.

But Pappy had long since determined that it was best to stick to the job at hand and leave the ifs to those who called themselves rocket scientists. He was going to make very sure the bomb didn't explode while it was in his possession.

His team checked over the warhead carefully after its journey from the test bay. The erector would make two trips: The first would be to set the rocket in place; and after it was securely bolted to the launch pad, it would be lowered again to hoist the warhead and set it atop the THOR.

The warhead, even without the plutonium core, carried enough explosives to make a very nasty hole in the ground, so Pappy was leaving nothing to chance. Once the access door to the bomb was uncovered, he verified that all the grounding plugs were in place.

When the erector was in position, he would run a grounding cable from the warhead to the erector. If properly grounded, there was virtually no way the charges could detonate accidentally.

The rocket itself was securely fastened inside the erector with an elaborate mesh of cables stretching from the erector's beams to metal eyes fitted into the struts transversing the THOR. Once it was secure, the signal was given to raise the erector. Deep inside the pad's concrete walls, massive relays clacked shut. The huge electrical motors hummed to life, and hydraulic pressure began to build in the lifting pistons.

Slowly the whole metal structure housing the eighty-ton rocket began to creak and groan as it inched its way up. The first twenty feet of the lift were the most critical as the entire mass of the erector and its load had to be overcome by the hydraulic pumps.

Just as the erector cleared the thirty-foot mark, a brisk wind picked up. It was one of those Pacific squalls that commonly attacked the island. However, the erector was only rated for a thirty-mile-per-hour wind when lifting the THOR. The loading engineer, Jack Sims, called THOR control in the blockhouse for an estimate on the wind conditions.

"We're showing a small squall area approaching the island from the south," reported the range safety officer. "It is possible we will have winds of twenty to twenty-five miles an hour, with gusts up to forty. We also show some lightning and possible hail as the squall approaches."

"That's great," Sims growled. "We've got 250,000 pounds of erector and rocket thirty feet in the air, and now you tell me we may have forty-mile-per-hour winds. Where's your brains, safety? I can't lay this bird back down. If we don't get that erector vertical before those winds hit, it'll end up lookin' like a pretzel."

"Mr. Sims, this is Deitz. What are our options at this point?"

"I recommend that we continue with the lift, doctor," said the exasperated engineer. "The chances of the wind severely damaging the erector are too great to risk lowering it. At least we have better odds if the erector is all the way up. Once it's locked in place, it'll withstand 100-mile-per-hour winds."

"What if the wind load is too great for the erector while it's lifting?" asked Deitz.

"Who knows?" Sims shouted over the rising wind. "The whole thing may come crashing down."

As the squall approached, the wind picked up abruptly and the erector began to sway and moan in the gusts. Sims had stopped the lift long enough for two men to climb the tilted erector and roll up the side curtains, which tended to act like sails in the wind.

Pappy was busy with his crew too, stretching a heavy canvas covering over the nose cone and tying it to eyebolts on the ramp. He was shouting orders between outbursts of highly salted Navy profanity. The newer men on his team, who had never seen Pappy react to a critical situation, were shocked at the change in his normally placid manner. The result was highly effective though. They jumped into action, stretching the heavy tarp over the nose cone to protect its fragile ablative coating.

Meanwhile, Pappy had grabbed the grounding cable and headed for one of the structural "I" beams supporting the umbilical tower. "Get this cable grounded to that beam," he shouted over the rising fury of the squall. "A lightnin' strike could set off the ordnance. There won't be nothin' left but a smokin' hole out here!"

"Let's get out of here, Pappy," the technician shouted. "That lightning storm is headed right for us."

"You get that cable grounded or I'll kill you myself," Pappy said menacingly. "We're not losing this bomb now. Forgit the lightnin'. If it hits anything, it'll prob'ly be the tower," he lied.

The two men on the erector had finished securing the curtains and slid down the escape rails provided for emergencies during the rocket's testing. For now, they made excellent escape routes for the highly motivated technicians.

Pappy yelled to Sims and his crew, "If that bomb goes off, there won't be anything left where we're standing."

"I'm not leaving that rocket hanging out in the air like this," Sims shouted above the howling wind. "I'll stay with it and take my chances. The erector has to be vertical or it will twist itself to pieces. You take off, Pappy," he shouted between bursts of lightning. "There's no sense in you staying. It's not your job."

"Guess I'll stick around too," Pappy yelled back. "Let me know what I can do to help."

Meanwhile the erector was continuing its slow but steady pull to raise the rocket. Below, in the engine room, the operator wondered how long the big electric motors driving the hydraulic pumps could stand the strain. Every time a violent wind blew against the erector, the motors would wail in complaint.

It was only a matter of time until a bearing burned out and the pumps stopped. The rocket was doomed if that happened. If the wind didn't tear it apart, the sudden fall to the pad would. The hydraulic fail-safes were never made to support such a load for more than a few minutes.

Up top, Pappy looked out at the storm rapidly approaching from the ocean. The wind was whistling through the metal erector; some of the canvas covers had come loose and were flailing the structure with a constant flap, flap, flap; and the frequent lightning bursts made the storm cloud look like a big, angry giant coming to run the intruders off of his island. As the squall approached the beach, he saw a huge lightning bolt strike the shoreline. But instead of evaporating, it appeared to ball up.

Pappy blinked to be sure he wasn't seeing things. He had heard of balled lightning, but few people had ever seen it and lived to tell about it. And this ball was rolling toward them in what looked like slow motion as his heightened senses slowed the action down. It rolled like an enormous wheel being turned by the invisible giant.

No sense in tryin' to run, he decided. *Besides, where would I run anyway?* He didn't even try to yell to Sims and his crew. *What the heck,* Pappy thought to himself, *they already have their hands full. Why bother 'em more?*

It's like watching a movie, Pappy mused. *Only this one ain't gonna have a happy ending. Maybe the Lord don't want this thing to fly. When that ball of energy hits this warhead, they won't have to worry about burying us. But it sure will make a mess.*

He was struck by the beauty of the whole scene: The huge black cloud belching out tongues of fire was outlined against a light blue sky, sprinkled with small, lighter clouds. And highlighting the whole show was this bouncing wheel of pure energy. *I wish I had a camera. Nobody will ever believe this.*

Lightning is no respecter of persons or things and this bolt, or rather ball, was merely looking for the best source of a ground it could find. Just before it would have reached the pad, it veered off sharply and struck the power substation feeding electricity to the pad area. The big transformers exploded with a fury only an ordnance man could appreciate.

The coolant oil inside the main transformer went up like a 500-pound bomb, scattering sparks and flaming debris hundreds of feet in every direction. An enormous ball of fire burst into the cloud-darkened sky, showering the men on the pad with small fragments of the exploded transformer. Fortunately, the demolition was nearly perfect and the largest fragment was less than the size of a quarter.

The erector was just dropping into the vertical alignment slots in the launch pad when the power failed. At first Sims thought the explosion was the bomb going off. But looking around, he saw the huge fireball nearly 500 feet away. By reflex action from two years in the war, he fell to the ground and covered his head. The other three team members, seeing Sims fall, quickly followed suit, even though they had not yet seen the source of the explosion.

The erector dropped its load in the exact spot that it should have. The THOR sat squarely over the hold-down studs used to keep it in place.

When Sims realized they weren't dead, he shouted to his crew to get up and put the retaining nuts on the bolts. They reacted quickly and had the rocket secured in less than a minute.

Pappy peeled himself off the wet concrete and came walking over to Sims. "Man, wasn't that somethin'?" he said as if he had been watching a fireworks display. "Nobody's better at pyrotechnics than the good Lord. I just wish I'd had my camera. Nobody's gonna believe this."

"I don't know what happened," Sims said. "But I'll be a witness to whatever you say, Pappy. You couldn't tell a lie big enough to top this."

Pappy filled him in on what he had seen when the lightning struck the beach. *The squall's approaching rapidly but seems to have lost some of its ferociousness,* Pappy thought. Then he remembered all the times he nearly had been killed before.

It always seems calmer right after you come face to face with death and survive. It's as if everything pales in comparison. That's the time when alotta guys get themselves killed. They're so busy pattin' themselves on the back for survivin' they stop looking for the present danger.

Pappy asked, "Is that thing secure?"

"Yes," Sims shouted over the wind, which was gusting at what he calculated to be at least sixty miles per hour.

"Then let's get out of here," Pappy yelled again. "I figger we've 'bout used up our luck for one day." He headed toward the truck he'd left at the entrance to the pad area.

Sims waited long enough to be sure his men were following. Then he headed out too. With the power out at the pad area, there was nothing more they could do. And he agreed with Pappy: Their luck was probably running a little thin right now.

The storm continued its path over the complex with the fury that only a Pacific Ocean thunderstorm can generate. The lightning continued to crackle as the storm passed overhead. But as lightning is prone to do, the strikes were aimed at targets like power poles, which actually presented far less appealing targets than the erector and gantry standing at least a hundred feet taller than the surrounding structures. Fortunately, within ten minutes the worst was over and the squall had passed over the island and was headed out to sea again.

Pappy and Sims returned to the pad to survey the damage and found that, other than the power substation that was struck by the lightning ball, the rest of the complex, including THOR and its warhead, were intact.

It was clear that the erector would be out of service for at least a full day until power could be restored. Pappy decided to return the warhead to the bunker until the erector was back in service. He didn't want to take the chance of another storm passing that way again before it was mated with the rocket.

Once the warhead was safely tucked away in its bunker, Pappy and his team ran a total systems check to ensure it was still functioning properly. The initial systems test on the THOR would have to wait until power was reinstated at the pad. In the meantime, Dr. Deitz ordered a complete visual inspection of the rocket to ensure there was no mechanical damage.

27

△

The Dignitaries

Scarcely eighteen hours later, the launch team returned to the pad area to complete their earlier mission.

"Power's restored," reported the pad engineer. "We're ready to throw the switch on your command, control."

"Okay," said Sims as he took a deep breath. "We're ready here. Give it a try."

Almost immediately the big motors hummed to life, and hydraulic pressure began to build in the erector lift system.

It's hard to believe the lightning didn't burn out any of the electrical system, Pappy thought as he watched the erector begin its slow descent.

But lightning has a mind of its own, and this particular bolt decided it wanted to obliterate the substation. With a little rigging, they had been able to reroute power from another substation. It looked like a B-47 had unloaded its bombs directly onto the substation. Even the concrete pad was cracked and powdered. It would have to be chipped out and replaced.

Pappy and his team were already in place with the warhead, waiting for the erector to reach its horizontal position. After the chewing out that General Reed had given the range safety officer, he was sure somebody would be keeping a sharp eye on the weather radar this time. But it was a crystal clear day with few clouds in the sky, so there was little chance of more unnoticed squalls.

"Pappy, are you ready to position the warhead?" asked Sims as the erector clanked to the concrete pad.

"That's a roger," replied Pappy. "We'll push the nose cone into position at your command." Pappy knew that the warhead needed to be handled with the greatest of care. Even the smallest scratch in the ablative coating could cause the warhead to burn up on reentry. Since they didn't have a spare hydrogen bomb laying around, any damage could take days or even weeks to repair. He would allow no one else to oversee this project.

The warhead was positioned in the erector precisely as directed by Pappy. When it was lifted to the top of the rocket, it would be exactly three inches above the mating ring. From there it would take only a few minutes to connect the instrumentation cables used to monitor the bomb's internal systems. The plutonium core would be loaded through the access door located just behind the ablative nose covering when the time came.

It took ten minutes for the erector to lift the warhead into position and to get the work platforms extended. Pappy was there and waiting when the erector locked into position. He had climbed the steel escape ladder on the side of the gantry. The rest of the crew arrived in the erector elevator.

It took another ten minutes for the crew to connect the wiring harness to the warhead. Pappy called to one of his crew, stationed at the Sandia console in the blockhouse, and told him to verify the electrical hookups. When he was totally satisfied that everything was working properly, Pappy gave the okay to lower the warhead.

It slid down perfectly over the alignment pins and onto the rocket. To ensure the warhead and rocket were locked together, one of the smaller crew members crawled through the access door in the bulkhead and installed some temporary bolts.

During the final countdown, Pappy would crawl into the cramped space and install the explosive bolts used to separate the warhead from the rocket during the targeting phase of reentry.

In preparation for the launch countdown that would start in less than a week, each team was doing its own verifications. The launch pad was literally crawling with crew members performing final inspections of the thousands of components that made up the THOR rocket. In addition, the numerous outside facilities that would be necessary to monitor an H-bomb explosion were being readied.

The Air Force would provide two specially equipped B-47s to track the launch and observe the detonation of the bomb. The newly formed NASA agency would provide high-powered telescope coverage of the launch and detonation. The telescopic camera operators were warned to shield their lenses with sun filters from three-and-one-half minutes into the launch until detonation. The explosion of a ten-megaton hydrogen bomb would fuse the retinal tissue of anyone foolish enough to stare into its intense energy at the moment of fusion.

In addition, Ballistic Missile Systems Command wanted to do extensive tests on the effects of the electrical magnetic pulse (EMP) released by the detonation of a hydrogen bomb. This information would be vital if the THOR were ever to become operational. The EMP itself might be useful in the destruction of an enemy's defensive radar system.

The Air Force was to supply two drone jet planes to circle the detonation zone, one at five miles out and the other at twenty miles. Both carried sensitive equipment to measure the pulse effects on radar and navigational equipment.

The Navy cleared a fifty-mile-wide corridor between Anawetok and the target area. No vessels were allowed in that corridor.

By T-minus-one day before the start of the launch countdown, every system had been checked and double-checked. The teams probably would have been better off to relax a few hours before the countdown started. But with nerves on edge, the team leaders felt they needed to keep them busy. They could rest in three days if the launch was successful.

Even Pappy had a case of pre-launch nerves. He made his team recheck the bomb's systems so often he was concerned they might wear out the circuits. The bomb was ready to go.

He secretly hoped that the rocket would tumble into the ocean about a hundred miles out or so. But he knew if it did, they would just roll out another one and start all over again. *When men are bound to kill each other, they are very persistent,* Pappy reflected.

General Reed issued orders that the launch would be operated under military jurisdiction. To most of the civilians that didn't mean much, because it was a military program anyway. But to Colonel Wells, it meant that the general was the final authority on all issues once the countdown started.

The launch director controlled the countdown, but the general controlled the director. He wasn't sure what the end result would be, but he was certain the general would take every opportunity to demonstrate his authority in front of the Washington dignitaries who would be there to observe.

Dr. Deitz was in his office again, going over the launch countdown procedures. He already had reviewed them at least two dozen times, but as he often told his launch team, "Thoroughness is the element that often separates success from failure."

Later that afternoon Wells sat in on the briefing for the launch countdown. He was impressed with the way Dr. Deitz handled his team of American and German scientists. They were a complex group of individualists. Singularly, most of them detested rules and regulations. But once they were committed to the project, their individual interests were laid aside. They would still bend the rules from time to time—but always to the benefit of the project.

The pre-launch briefing was concluded by 14:00 and the teams broke up to go over their individual assignments again. The most critical, and the least practiced, was the actual loading of the nuclear material in the warhead.

Pappy's team had practiced using dummy materials, but that was never like loading the real thing. Of course, that limitation was a necessary one. It was best to limit the handling of plutonium to as few times as possible.

Pappy was briefing his team on the step-by-step procedure they would follow in reverifying the system during the countdown.

"At T-minus-one hour, I'll load the core into the warhead," Pappy explained as he had twenty times previously. "The core will be secured outside the firing chamber by the arming system until insertion during the actual flight. But once that core is on the pad, I want every one of you to think: thermonuclear explosion. The 'oops' you hear from the guy next to you may be the last sound you'll ever hear, and this island will become a monument to man's stupidity for the next two thousand years."

The countdown commenced right on time. The first phase was a complete verification of the ground-based equipment, using specially designed fault boxes attached to the rocket's interface connectors.

With a hundred possible configurations to be verified, this procedure took all of the scheduled twelve hours. The only hitch in the ground system verification came when another of those unpredictable Pacific squalls roared in from the ocean and sent the pad crew scrambling to cover the rocket's access covers and clear the pad until it passed. Only Pappy stayed with the warhead, and no amount of threats from either General Reed or Dr. Deitz could persuade him to leave.

The observers from Washington were arriving just as the weather front passed the island. The pilot was obviously not much concerned with the comfort of his passengers and barreled his way right through the weather, dodging in and out of the many thunderstorms.

By the time he had the island in sight, he was delighted to see his passengers heaving their lunches in the brown plastic air bags. Being an ex-bomber pilot from World War II, he had his twenty-plus years in and was retiring in a few weeks anyway.

"Compared to dodging flak, these storm cells are kid stuff," he said to his copilot. "And it gives these stuffed shirts a feel for what it's like to be scared," he added with a chuckle.

The range safety weather tower called the DC-6 pilot. "Do not attempt to land until the storm has passed," he said several times. "We have strong crosswinds and gusts to thirty knots."

He heard the pilot respond, "Roger that, control. I copy that we are clear to land."

Try as he might, the duty sergeant could not raise the pilot again, so he turned on the landing lights. The big plane barreled toward the runway, crabbing nearly fifteen degrees in the vicious crosswind.

Finally, the landing field was in sight, and the plane careened through the air like a hawk caught in a whirlwind; just before touchdown the pilot cut the power and dropped the final three feet to the runway. The plane bounced several times before it rolled to a stop in front of the tower.

The passengers were so glad to be safe on the ground, they didn't pause to say anything as they deplaned. By the time they were inside the corrugated steel building that served as a control center, the storm was passing over the far side of the island and out to sea again.

The pilot requested clearance to take off, believing that a quick exit to the NASA tracking station, almost a hundred miles away, would be very prudent once the politicians recovered from their exciting ride—especially when they learned that standard procedure was to circle at sea until such storms passed the island.

In the group of observers was Congressman Melvin Hines from Michigan; his aide, Lester Harvey; and staff advisor to the president, Dr. Lisa Feldstein.

Project THOR was so secret that no one outside of the direct personnel involved, the Pentagon, the president, the vice president, and the congressional National Security Council knew anything about it. The president's instructions were simple and direct: Keep it that way!

As soon as the incoming plane had been identified, a call had been made to General Reed. He was already on his way to the airfield as the pilot was making his approach. Knowing how bad a Pacific squall could be, the general assumed the pilot had some kind of an emergency. The staff car was just rolling to a stop at the field when he heard the plane's engines revving again and saw it take off. He made a mental note to find out why.

Reed stormed into the terminal, shouting at the duty sergeant, "Why did you allow that plane to land in a storm like that, you idiot?"

"But I didn't, sir," the sergeant replied. "I tried to reach the pilot, but I guess he had radio interference from the storm. I assumed he had a mechanical problem and was forced to land."

"Then shut up about this," the general said in a low voice. "Not one word to the passengers."

"Yes, sir," the sergeant agreed as he hurried back to the tower.

Reed quickly made his way over to the new arrivals. "I'm General Reed," he said, extending his hand.

"And I'm Congressman Hines. Give me a few minutes to catch my breath, and then I'd like to talk with you privately. That was absolutely the worst flight I've ever been on. It seemed like the pilot went out of his way to hunt for bad weather."

"I'm sure he didn't, congressman," the general lied. "The storms out here are particularly bad this time of the year and hard to track on radar." He hoped the congressman didn't know anything about weather radar.

"Well, general, I hope this launch is a good one because I, for one, will not be coming back to this death trap. I also hope your team is on the ball. We have a Security Council hearing in two weeks, and we'll need a success here to keep the program on track. This is an extremely expensive project; it takes the majority of our discretionary military budget."

"We're all set, congressman," Reed said enthusiastically. "The countdown has begun and we're scheduled to launch in two and a half days, if we don't have any major problems."

"I sincerely hope you don't. There are a lot of rumors around the Capitol that opposition is mounting to the development of strategic defense weapons. The latest idea is that development of multiple ICBMs is the key to a national defense. The brass at S.A.C. call it Mutually Assured Defensive Destruction (MADD). The concept is, if nobody can win a nuclear war, nobody will start one."

"And besides, general, we have no evidence that the THOR concept will even work," said Lisa Feldstein, the president's advisor. "I favor a more traditional approach. But the president is open to alternatives. That's why he sent me to observe the launch of the THOR."

Reed looked toward Lisa, whom he had hardly noticed in the rush to meet the Washington dignitaries. "Miss . . . ?"

"Lisa Feldstein," she replied. "Doctor Lisa Feldstein."

"General, Doctor Feldstein is the president's technical advisor on the Armed Services Committee and holds a doctorate in nuclear physics from CIT. She's the first woman in the country to hold that degree," said the congressman.

"I'm impressed," the general said, trying to retrieve his air of authority. "All those brains in such a pretty package! I trust you'll be as enthralled with the THOR as we are before you leave, Dr. Feldstein."

"I'll withhold my judgment until after the launch, general," she replied with an icy stare. It was clear that General Reed had not impressed Lisa Feldstein.

Reed said, "I would suggest that we proceed to your quarters. The countdown started at fifteen hundred hours today, and the teams are beginning their final systems' verifications. By tomorrow morning the ground support systems will be verified, and we'll be ready to start testing the rocket's systems. I think you'll find that very interesting. As you know, this is the first actual launch of a hydrogen bomb. We're making history here that will change the way wars are fought for the next thousand years."

"General, I hope there will *be* a next thousand years after the world is armed with weapons of this magnitude," Lisa commented as they headed toward the drab green staff car. She caught the glare in the general's eyes as he looked her way. She could tell he was a man who liked to talk without being questioned and probably felt a woman's place was behind a typewriter. She decided she really did not like this General George Armstrong Reed very much.

The general dropped the three visitors off at the bachelor officers' quarters on the base. They were the best accommodations available, which didn't say very much unless they were compared to a standard Army tent.

The congressman complained steadily about everything from the plane ride to the lack of shocks in the staff car. The sergeant driving the car decided the congressman would be a royal pain for as long as he would be there.

But at least, while the congressman's busy complaining, the general isn't on my back. In fact, it seems they're hitting it off real good. Probably have common interests, he decided. *They both like to complain about everything.*

28

△

Lisa
Feldstein

isa decided she wasn't tired enough to sleep yet, especially
after looking at her room. *I'm sure this place was never
intended for human habitation,* she mused. *And the general
said this is their best accommodation. I know I won't sleep, so I
guess I'll walk over to the control center and observe some of the
system checks.*

Making her way to the blockhouse entrance, she was met by a
guard who asked for her access badge. "I don't have one yet. I just
arrived today. I'm a part of the civilian observation team," she
explained.

"I'm sorry, ma'am, but you'll have to get clearance from
either Colonel Wells, the head of security, or Doctor Deitz, the
program director, before I can allow you to enter," the young corporal said.

"Could you tell me if either the colonel or the doctor are in the
control center?" she asked.

"Yes, ma'am," the husky guard replied. "They're both inside.
I'd be happy to call the colonel for you."

The guard called Wells on the intercom. "Colonel Wells, there's
a lady out here by the name of Feldstein who says she's a part of the
observation team and would like permission to enter the control
room."

"Tell her to contact General Reed for permission," Wells
replied curtly. "The guests are his problem."

The guard had carelessly left the intercom speaker on when he called, so Lisa was able to hear the conversation. Her face turned red, as it always did when she was either embarrassed or irritated; and right now she was both. It always frustrated her when she became flushed.

"Colonel Wells," she said brusquely. "This is Doctor Lisa Feldstein. I would greatly appreciate it if you would allow me thirty seconds of your precious time. I promise you I won't disrupt your schedule."

Bob Wells clearly detected the irritation in her voice, but he also recognized something else. Perhaps it was the quality of the person behind the voice. For whatever the reason, he stopped listening in on the countdown and made his way to the blockhouse entrance. By the guard shack, standing with her back to him, was the woman he'd heard over the intercom.

As Lisa turned to face him, the first thing that caught Wells' attention were her piercing blue eyes—almost magnetic in their clarity. But more shocking was the fact that he knew this woman! At first he thought his mind was playing tricks on him.

"Erika?" he shouted so loudly that it startled the young woman.

Wells felt a rush of emotions he thought were long dead. Her eyes were exactly as he remembered them. Lisa started to say something just as Wells reached out and grabbed her. Before she even realized what was happening, she found herself being kissed.

Shoving him away, she swung her open hand and caught Wells squarely on his cheek. At the sound of the slap, the guard, who was watching with his mouth agape, turned in embarrassment and hurried into the guard shack. The slap on his face also snapped Wells back to reality.

"I . . . I'm very sorry," Wells stammered as his face flushed, covering the mark her hand had left on his cheek. "It's just . . . I thought you were someone I knew a long time ago. I really am sorry."

"I should hope so," replied the still flustered Lisa. "Is this standard procedure for all of your visitors, colonel?"

"I swear it never happened before, and it won't happen again," replied Wells, sputtering like a schoolboy. As he looked at her, he was still shaken by the resemblance between this woman and the German Waffen lieutenant he had known at Peenemunde.

Then it suddenly struck him. He'd always heard that everyone had a double somewhere in the world. This woman before him was the perfect copy of Erika, the woman he'd once loved so desperately, except that she was twenty years younger than Erika.

"Who was this person you knew, colonel? Why did you think I might be her?" Lisa asked more compassionately.

"It really doesn't matter," replied Wells, withdrawing into his professional shell. Long ago he had developed the ability to hide his real feelings, as many sensitive people do. He had loved once and had lost her. After that experience, he decided he would never love again.

"Will you at least allow me to enter the control room, colonel?" she asked with just a touch of humor in her voice. *That's just like a man,* she thought to herself. *I get assaulted and he gets his feelings hurt.*

"Of course." He turned to the guard shack to sign the authorization, catching the eye of the guard who was smiling sheepishly. "Don't you say one word, Stony!" Wells said to the guard he had come to know as a friend. "Not unless you really like the climate in Greenland."

"Don't you worry, colonel. I won't tell anyone about our security chief being socked by a girl he assaulted outside my guard shack," he said with a toothy grin.

"Okay, just be sure you don't," Wells said, smiling back at Stony. He started to sign the entry log and realized that in the confusion of the last few minutes he didn't remember her name. Embarrassed again, he leaned outside the guardhouse and asked, "Sorry. What was your name again?"

Amused by his obvious embarrassment, she replied, "Why, colonel. You can't remember the name of the woman you kissed— and on government property too?"

Inside the shack Stony hooted with laughter. Pointing to his two stripes, Wells made a comment about him returning to the rank of private for the next fifty years while he was shoveling snow in Greenland. Then he heard the young woman reply, "It's Lisa Feldstein, colonel." He quickly wrote down the name and signed her authorization to enter the launch control room.

Inside the room the activity was slow, except at the propulsion system console where the tank pressurization tests were in progress. Wells escorted Lisa around the control room, pointing out the various systems and what they did.

When he made his way over to the launch director's console, Dr. Deitz stood to meet the visitor and, in German-accented English said, "Good evening. I'm Kurt Deitz, launch director."

"I know a great deal about you, doctor. I'm truly honored to meet you. I've admired your work for many years. I'm Lisa Feldstein."

"Doctor Lisa Feldstein from CIT?" asked the launch director.

"Yes," she replied, flattered that he remembered her.

"I am truly pleased to meet you, doctor," said Deitz with an air of respect that Wells knew was reserved for people the doctor genuinely held in high esteem. "I read your article in the *Science Journal* several months ago on the potential of nuclear fusion reactors for space flight. It was brilliant! It was like reading my own thoughts."

"Thank you," Lisa said. "Coming from you, I consider that a compliment." Even as she spoke, her cheeks turned a beautiful rosy red. She wished she could put a bag over her head to hide from the two men in front of her. She imagined that they would think her some kind of silly female as she flushed even more at the realization that she was blushing. Had she been able to read Wells' mind, she might have blushed even more. Colonel Robert Wells was captivated by the beautiful woman in front of him.

Trying to get over her embarrassment, Lisa said, "Actually, it was your letter in response to my article that brought me here, doctor. When the president was looking for a scientific observer, your letter tipped the scales in my favor. Thank you!"

"You don't have to thank me, doctor," Deitz replied. "Your work in this field puts you years ahead of your colleagues. I am pleased to have you as an observer and would be pleased to have you as a colleague, if you ever choose to join the project."

"Thank you, doctor, but I believe I'll stay in the laboratory instead. At least I can sleep in a real bed at night and not have to fight off hordes of insects like you do here," she replied with a smile.

"I certainly can't argue with that," Deitz agreed. Before turning back to the console, he said, "Please make yourself as comfortable as the conditions will allow, Dr. Feldstein. If I can be of any assistance, let me know."

"Thank you, doctor," she replied. But he was already absorbed in the activities taking place around him. As she turned to walk away, she noticed Wells staring at her. He turned away quickly, and she gave no indication that she had noticed, but she felt a strange attraction for this intriguing man.

That's utterly stupid, she chided herself silently. *You don't even know the man. And besides, you're here to do a job: one that will demand all of your attention! You just remind him of someone he knew a long time ago. It happens to people all the time. It'll pass!*

"I guess I really made a fool of myself twice tonight, didn't I?" asked Wells.

"It doesn't matter, colonel. Let's forget it. But what do you mean twice?"

"Well, here I've been, describing the events and systems on the THOR, when you probably know more about them than I do," he said sheepishly.

"No, that's not necessarily so. I'm a theoretical scientist looking for new ideas. All I know about the THOR is what I could glean from a few brief reports, which is really precious little. I am familiar with the concept of the THOR and the mission of this particular rocket, but I don't know about the actual systems, so I'd appreciate all the help you can give. I'm here to observe and learn. On this project, colonel, you're the teacher and I'm the student."

"Please call me Bob," Wells said.

"Only if you'll agree to call me Lisa. Dropping the formalities will do a great deal to make this visit more enjoyable and informative for me. I'm here because the president has some concerns about project THOR. I don't want to be an adversary, but I do want to do my job."

Wells decided he was going to like this young woman, who quite obviously was not intimidated by anyone. He considered mentioning the concerns he had about project THOR, but old habits restrained him from saying anything. Instead he replied, "I'll help all I can, but you probably should try to get some sleep. The time change will begin to take its toll in a few hours and you'll find yourself wishing you had rested when you had the chance.

"We're at T-minus-forty-six hours in the countdown now. We'll enter a built-in hold at T-minus-forty hours for about twelve hours while the fuel loading systems are leak checked. Then we'll begin the final launch countdown. From that time on, life will get real hectic around here, and you won't want to miss the show."

"I'll bow to your wisdom on that, colonel . . . uh, I mean Bob," she replied. "I would like to see the warhead control system since that is my particular specialty. Could you arrange that?"

"I don't see why not," he replied. "We use a two-man . . . I mean a two-person system at the pad area once the countdown begins, so you'll have to stay with me, if that's all right."

"That will be fine," she replied a little too enthusiastically, suddenly realizing she would be disappointed if she weren't with him. *That's childish!* she reminded herself again. *You're not a high school girl looking for a date for the prom.* Then she remembered that she never had a date to the proms. She had always intimidated the boys in her peer group.

She had both beauty and brains—a fatal combination for a high school or college student. She lived in a self-imposed isolation, created by a fluke of nature that gave her parents who were both intelligent and handsome. From one she had gotten the looks and from the other she had gotten the brains. She had often thought, *How nice it would be if I had inherited only one or the other—looks or intelligence—or maybe neither.* Having both made for a lonely life.

"I'll walk you to your quarters," Wells offered.

"That's really not necessary," she replied more brusquely than she intended. She always bristled when she thought someone was patronizing her. Then she realized he was only trying to be friendly, and her tone changed abruptly. "I'm sorry, Bob. I get defensive too easily."

"I understand. A professional woman has to fight for respect in this business."

Lisa was taken aback by that remark. Bob Wells had accurately summarized her professional career. She suddenly decided, *Yes, I am going to like Robert Wells.*

"Okay, colonel," she said with mock seriousness. "But you just keep your distance. I'm a black belt in karate, and my hands are lethal weapons."

"Are you really a black belt?" asked Wells with a look of surprise.

"No, not really. I broke my little finger the first time out and never went back."

"Good," Wells said. "I never escort a woman who can beat me in a fair fight." They headed toward the door, laughing together.

Outside it was a perfect Pacific night. The moon was a mellow crescent and the night breeze blew across the island in unison with the swells on the ocean. Without the man-made buildings, it would have been as it was when Captain Cook sailed these waters nearly two hundred years earlier and had described the isles as a paradise in the great ocean. He speculated that the original garden of Eden had been preserved here so that man might see what nature could be like without sin.

Thinking about this paradox brought a scowl to Wells' face. When he thought about the cargo they were launching in less than two days, he had a terrible feeling of dread—no, helplessness.

"Why the frown?" Lisa asked.

"Oh, nothing," he replied. "This really is a beautiful part of the world. I hadn't realized it until now, walking with you. Before, it was just a launching site for a missile I'm here to protect. But we're about to launch a ten-megaton hydrogen bomb into this blue sky and blow it up. Who knows what will happen if this thing goes astray."

"Is there really a chance the THOR could go astray?" she asked quickly. "Everything I have read on the project indicates there is little risk."

"There's always the chance that something can go wrong, regardless of the assurances," Wells replied. "No one has ever mated a hydrogen bomb to a rocket. We're dealing with the fabric of the universe, and I'm not at all sure we understand how it's put together."

As they approached the entrance to the Quonset hut, Wells said, "Lisa, I apologize for my earlier attitude. I know you have a job to do too, and I guess I lumped you in with the politicians who came with you. I'm glad you're here, and I'll try to do anything I can to help. I sincerely hope we will become good friends while you're here."

"Thank you. I appreciate your vote of confidence. I think maybe we're already friends. After all, we have kissed." She opened the screen door and stepped into the hut, amused to see Wells' face turn red. She closed the door before he could say anything else.

Bob Wells walked back toward his own quarters, thinking that he was looking forward to the next day more than any other since Erika had been killed at Peenemunde. He felt really alive for first time in a long time.

As Lisa entered the small, drab hut, she also experienced a feeling she hadn't known for a long time: loneliness. She had shut other people out of her life for so long, she thought she was immune to emotions. She knew her associates at the institute called her a snob, but it hadn't bothered her. At least she hadn't let them know when it did.

The feelings she was having were unfamiliar, and she didn't especially like them. She wasn't sure it if was the isolation she felt on the small island in the middle of the Pacific, the uncertainty of the THOR test, or Wells himself. She had heard of love at first sight but had always believed it was the by-product of overactive hormones. But now? She wasn't so sure.

29

△

The Roach Coach

At 05:00 a staff car pulled up in front of Lisa Feldstein's quarters. She was already waiting and stepped out of the Quonset hut door even before the private driving the vehicle could get out. She slid into the backseat, the driver shifted the car into gear, and he headed directly for the base chow hall as instructed. Colonel Wells was just arriving as they pulled up.

"You aren't really going to eat breakfast here, are you?" he asked in mock sincerity.

"I had planned to," she replied. "Why? Is there something I should know?"

"I'd really rather delay this conversation until after you've eaten," Wells said seriously. "If you survive the experience, you'll be inducted into the Army's valor corps and given a silver star."

"Don't you listen to him, miss," Pappy said as he approached. "He's just a sissy college boy who doesn't know when he's well off. I swear I don't know how we ever won the war with ninety-day wonders like him. It's the best chow you'll find west of California—nectar of the gods."

"Lisa, meet Pappy Moss, head of the Sandia team. You'll be spending some time with Pappy, so it's best you know something about him. In the first place, this is the *only* chow you'll find west of California, as Pappy well knows. Second, he has a cast iron stomach that will be donated to medical science when he dies. Why, I've seen him eat two helpings of creamed chipped beef for breakfast, with a side order of boiled possum. Right, Pappy?" Lisa pretended she didn't see the wink that passed between the two men.

"Right!"

"Suddenly I don't feel very hungry," she said, joining in the camaraderie of the moment. "Maybe I'll just get a cup of coffee."

"Good choice," said Pappy. "I happen to know the cook threw in some nearly new grounds just yesterday in honor of our guests. But don't drink it on an empty stomach. It's been known to eat a hole in the linin' of a tenderfoot's stomach before they can make the latrine. And, by the way, I'm glad to meecha, Miss," Pappy said, sticking out his hand, which Lisa grasped warmly.

They entered the chow hall and the ever-present odor of creamed chipped beef struck her like the aroma of singed chicken feathers. "What is that awful odor?" she exclaimed, wrinkling her brow. *Maybe they weren't joking about the opossum.*

"That's what Pappy calls the nectar of the gods," Wells said, holding his nose.

"Amen!" Pappy said. "That's the staff of life for us ole Navy guys. It's known as 'the soldier's delight' in polite circles."

"But it has other names in not-so-polite circles," responded Wells as he drew off a cup of the usual black draught called coffee.

"Ugh . . . What's that? Printer's ink?" asked Lisa.

"That, my dear, is what keeps us goin' on the cold winter nights here in the Pacific. It's called java. To you tenderfeet, it's coffee," quipped Pappy.

"I think I have just started a prolonged fast," Lisa said as she watched the cook dishing out an assortment of greasy eggs and bacon, over which Pappy poured creamed chipped beef.

"Don't worry yourself, honey," Pappy said. "They have sissy coffee in the control room, and the roach coach has those dainty little sandwiches for the unenlightened."

"The roach coach? Now that really sounds appetizing. What's that?" Lisa asked with a wrinkled brow.

"It's a motorized chow wagon run by the permanent base staff here. They service the launch area during the countdowns. It's only a nickname the men have affectionately attached to the traveling food service. Really, there are hardly ever any roaches found in most of the food," Wells said with a big grin.

"Now I think you're pulling my leg," Lisa responded. "But, all the same, I think I'll skip breakfast."

By 06:00 they were approaching the blockhouse area. A thirty-minute overlap in shifts gave the teams time to interface with each other. The schedule throughout the launch countdown would consist of two twelve-hour shifts, operating around the clock.

"Bob, I would really like to see the rocket itself before I get caught up in the control room," Lisa said. "Would that be possible?"

"I think so. The loading areas are running leak checks right now, so the rocket is in the standby mode. I'll take you down to the pad area for a quick look." Wells started toward the pad area with Lisa by his side, but he had gone only a few feet when the guard called to him.

"Colonel, may I speak to you?" Wells walked back toward the guard shack where the guard was standing with clipboard. "What's the problem?" he asked.

The embarrassed guard said, "Sir, I don't know how to tell you . . ."

"Just say it, corporal," Wells snapped. "What's the problem?"

"Well, this morning at 04:00, General Reed sent down orders controlling access to the pad area during the launch countdown."

"So?" Wells said.

"Sir, your name isn't on the list of authorized people."

"What?" Wells exclaimed. "There has to be some kind of mistake. I'm project security. He can't limit my access to the launch pad area. Did you double-check the list?"

"Yes, sir, I did. The general said the orders came down from Ballistics Systems, and he was sure it was an oversight on their part. He said he would check it out and get the error cleared up."

I'll just bet it was an error, thought Wells. *The general is getting back at me by barring me from the project I'm assigned to protect.* "Where's the general now?"

"He's in the control room with Congressman Hines and his aide," the nervous guard replied.

"Lisa, why don't you go on to the pad with Pappy since I see that your name is on the authorized access list. I'll just go have a discussion with the general," Wells said, fighting to control his temper.

"If you don't mind, Bob, I'd like to go with you. I'm interested to see what the general has to say."

"Suit yourself," replied Wells, getting angrier by the minute. "But stand back if I decide to take my chances on Leavenworth and smash a two-star general in his ugly nose."

Wells stormed off toward the control room with Lisa hurrying to keep up. He found Reed standing by the director's console, red-faced, the veins sticking out on his neck. Wells overheard the conversation as he approached.

"Doctor, if you don't get this countdown started, I'll have you removed from the control room for the duration of the launch," the general was shouting.

Deitz replied calmly, "General, if you do that, you'll find yourself launching this rocket by yourself. The men do not respect you, nor will they take your directions. You truly are a pompous peacock, general. Usually I don't mind, but now you've threatened the safety of the project and the teams for whom I am responsible. You will either clear Colonel Wells for access to the entire complex, or we'll sit right here until that rocket rusts on the pad."

Wells stopped in his tracks as he heard Deitz' comments. Apparently the director already had seen the access list and was supporting his position. The others around the general were obviously embarrassed. It was the congressman who spoke first.

"Doctor Deitz, you are going against the orders of the military. The general is responsible for this project, as I understand it."

"Then I would suggest that he reevaluate his decision to deny the colonel access; otherwise this will be the longest countdown in history. I have seen too many military blunders to believe that generals know what they are doing," Deitz said with finality.

General Reed stammered and stuttered while his slow brain tried to decide what he should do. Finally he said, "I'll have to call Washington for further instructions."

"You do that, general," Deitz said with authority. "In the meantime we'll sit and wait for your answer."

"You can't do that!" Reed shouted. "It may take me days to get this order rescinded. The countdown has to continue."

Wells and Lisa had come up behind the general during the conversation. Wells' temper had calmed greatly when he heard Deitz defending his position.

Wells said, "General, you didn't seem to have any difficulty in getting me banned from the launch pad area. I wouldn't think you'd have any problem getting the ban lifted."

Reed wheeled around as Wells spoke. He was just about to cut loose with his usual profanity when he noticed Lisa standing there. She spoke first. "General, it's obvious that this order inadvertently omitted the colonel's name. Certainly no one in their right mind would bar the head of security from the launch site. Think of what would happen if there were a malfunction and the mission were a failure. I can assure you it would be you who would be blamed." Her implied threat was painfully clear.

That was too much for the general's simple brain to assimilate. He knew he was defeated on the issue of Wells. All he wanted to do now was retreat and save face. "I certainly don't want anything to endanger the project," he said in a huffy tone. "I'll get a message off to headquarters requesting that Colonel Wells be added to the pad access list. But, because of the time change, it may take a few hours before I can get a reply. Doctor, will you agree to resume the countdown, awaiting the reply?"

"Agreed," replied Deitz, "provided the colonel doesn't object."

"No objection here," replied Wells. "But I want to double the pad security until the approval is given."

The general hurried off to send his telegram. He wanted to salvage as much of his dignity as possible under the circumstances. He knew he had erred in making his move to oust Wells too soon, but he never expected Deitz to oppose him like he did. He'd always been able to control him before. *I just don't understand it,* he thought to himself, his head pounding from the toil of thinking.

In the control center, Deitz called a meeting of the systems leaders to inform them that the countdown would resume in one hour at T-minus-forty hours. The loading depots had been thoroughly leak-checked and the fuel was being pre-cooled for transfer to the rocket's tanks. Once the propellants were loaded, the countdown would take on an entirely different atmosphere.

Caution would dictate every move. Any accident with fuels aboard could mean the obliteration of the pad crew and the launch team. The next critical juncture would be the loading of the warhead. After that, it would be a matter of expediting the departure of the rocket and its lethal package.

Pappy escorted Lisa to the pad area to have a look at the rocket before the propellant loading began. He had assumed she was some bigwig's daughter until he found out that she had a doctorate in physics. Then he figured she was some kind of child genius. Lisa could do nothing to convince him otherwise. Finally, when she broke down and told him that she was twenty-five years old, he flatly refused to believe it.

"You look sixteen," he said incredulously. "And I don't care how old you say you are, I'm gonna keep an eye on this crew to be sure no one takes advantage of you—including a certain colonel," he said as he winked.

Lisa shrugged her shoulders. Her petite size and youthful appearance fooled nearly everyone she met, including many erstwhile suitors. Secretly she hoped Bob Wells would not think of her as a child too.

As they approached the pad area, Pappy said, "Let's start with the business end of this thing." He punched the erector elevator button and the solenoid engaged with a loud clank, sending the elevator to their location. They stepped in and Pappy pressed the "up" button. The elevator climbed the erector slowly and stopped at the sixth level—the warhead platform.

"Inside that purty white nose cone is the armin' system for a ten-megaton hydrogen bomb," Pappy said. "That one bomb has the destructive power of all the conventional bombs dropped during World War II. It's a hunnerd times more destructive than the bomb dropped on Hiroshima. And yet, it's only one-fourth the size and weight of Fat Man."

"Fat Man?" Lisa questioned.

"Fat Man was the name of the second atom bomb dropped. It got its name because it was big and fat-lookin.' It took up nearly the whole bomb bay of the B-29 that carried it."

"We named this li'l' sweetheart Skinny Girl cause it looks slimmer and is much more sophisticated. If we're lucky, it may be able to breed a generation of bombs that will kill a hunnerd million people."

"Why do I get the feeling you're not totally in favor of this project, Pappy?"

"I'll do my job," he replied. "But I don't have to like it. Just think about this weapon in the hands of numskulls like Reed. That ought to ruin your day, sweetie." Lisa started to scold Pappy for the nickname but then decided she didn't mind his calling her sweetie; somehow, coming from him it seemed okay.

They continued the tour of the rocket and pad area for nearly an hour. In the meantime, the launch team was preparing to resume the countdown. They heard the public address announcement: "The launch countdown will resume at T-minus-forty hours on my mark: three . . . two . . . one . . . mark. All unnecessary personnel must clear the pad area, propellant loading will commence immediately."

"We need to get back to the blockhouse. We're about to start the fuel loading tests. It looks like they're really serious about launchin' this thing," Pappy said, exiting onto the approach ramp.

"Thanks, Pappy. I know it's just a rocket, but it seems to have a grace and beauty all its own."

"Remember," Pappy said, "the defensive weapons of today can quickly become the offensive weapons of tomorrow. I saw a lot of war firsthand during the forties and we didn't have anything to match this beauty then."

Pappy chatted all the way back to the blockhouse. Lisa quickly realized that underneath his rough exterior and poor use of English grammar Pappy was a thoroughly professional ordnance engineer. When she questioned him about plutonium grades and firing circuits, he knew every detail flawlessly.

As they reentered the control room, the pad engineer was receiving his last-minute instructions regarding the propellant loading and leak tests. Just as in all the previous tests, the fuel would be loaded first. The rocket's tanks would be leak-tested and then filled to the level required for launch.

Then, following the same procedures, the oxidizer would be loaded. Once the propellants were loaded and the cooling system connected to the tanks, the final systems verifications would begin. The last function would be loading the plutonium core into the warhead.

30
△

Preparing
the Bomb

Lisa was fascinated by the coordinated efforts of the launch
team. To her it seemed they worked as a single unit, much as
bees do in providing for the needs of their hive. Each step was
coordinated between all the systems' leaders, with each team passing control to the next system smoothly.

There were a few tense moments when a sensor in the fuel tank
showed a persistent rise in the tank temperature. If the propellant's
temperature rose above the nominal seventy-two degrees calculated to maintain the correct temperature until launch time, it
would be necessary to off-load and recool the hydrazine. No one
really had a desire to handle the fuel more than was absolutely necessary to get the job done.

After several tests, which included attaching a thermometer to
the exterior skin of the tank, it was determined that the problem
was a bad indicator in the control room console. The unit was
exchanged and the temperatures quickly returned to the normal
zone. But by the time the problem was isolated and corrected, the
countdown was down to T-minus-twenty-four hours.

Since it had been more than twelve hours since she had eaten
anything, Wells asked Lisa if she would like to get something.

"To tell you the truth, Bob," she responded warmly, "I'm starving, but I'm not sure I'm up to eating the food in your mess hall."

"Well, it's either learn to eat it or go hungry for the next few
days," Wells said, only half in jest. "You'll find that it tastes better

when your ribs start to stick out. And you don't have any too much on your bones now," he added. Then he realized that she might take his comment the wrong way and hastened to add, "But what you have is more than adequate."

"More than adequate? Are you saying I weigh too much? Or was that your attempt at a compliment, colonel, or maybe a scientific evaluation?" she asked in a serious tone. She noticed that his face turned red at her comment and decided that she definitely liked this man; just how much she liked him, she wasn't sure. *Any man who blushes when he puts his foot in his mouth is a real rarity,* she decided.

Before Wells could respond, Lisa said, "I'm willing to try some food, Bob. But I may just decide to go on an extended fast if dinner is anything like breakfast was."

"The countdown is at T-minus-twenty-four hours on my mark," Deitz announced to the launch team. "Three . . . two . . . one . . . mark. T-minus-twenty-four hours and counting. Systems' status report:"

"Propulsion?"

"Go!"

"Guidance?"

"Go!"

"Instrumentation?"

"Go!"

"Sandia?"

"Go!"

"Range safety?"

"Go!"

"All systems are go for launch countdown at T-minus-twenty-four hours."

During the next ten hours, the rocket was loaded with propellants and made ready for systems' flight verification. The next critical phase was a total launch and flight simulation prior to loading the ordnance and arming the warhead.

Lisa tried the food in the mess hall and, to her surprise, found it very palatable. Her dinner consisted of a small but delicious steak, a baked potato, and a fresh salad. She was about to comment on Wells' greasy hamburger when the cook walked up.

"Is that food okay, ma'am?" he asked, rubbing his hands on the well-used apron he wore.

"It's delicious, sergeant."

Wells was trying to catch the sergeant's eye, who was still looking straight at Lisa, when he said, "I took it from the general's private stock—just like the colonel ordered."

"Oh, I see," Lisa responded with a quick glance at Wells, who was giving the cut-throat sign to the cook.

"Thanks, Bob," she said. "You are a lifesaver. I really was starving."

Once back in the control room, Lisa sensed the mood change. There was an air of anticipation, generated by the fact that the countdown had passed the critical propellant loading phase.

"Knowin' there's a loaded rocket sittin' on the launch pad less than a half mile away sure raises a body's adrenal output," Pappy explained. "That's why wars are fought even though they're so goldarn stupid. You can get hooked on excitement."

Wells could sense, more than see, Lisa's anxiety rise as the countdown progressed hour by hour. She tried to conceal it but with very little success. He didn't realize he was staring until he noticed Lisa looking his way. Then he quickly looked away.

He's embarrassed about something again, she concluded. *He really is a nice guy. I just hope we can find some time after this project is ended to see if we have common interests. I suspect there's a lot more to this man than just another colonel putting in his thirty years.*

"T-minus-two hours and counting," the launch director announced. "The systems verification is complete. Ordnance loading will commence in thirty minutes. All personnel must clear the pad area immediately. Repeat: All unauthorized personnel must clear the pad area immediately."

Wells' pad authorization had long since come via telex from General Groves, so he made his way to the pad area and was standing on the approach ramp waiting for Pappy to arrive with the destruct system ordnance. Lisa had argued, and even threatened, to be allowed to observe the ordnance loading, but Wells had been adamant.

"It isn't just the risk to your own life," he had told her. "That's yours to risk. But the distraction to Pappy might just cause him to lose concentration at a critical moment."

Pappy and his team had rehearsed the loading routine many times, and Wells was not about to allow any changes that could prove disastrous. Finally, Lisa had acquiesced because she knew he was right. But her ego was a little bruised.

Pappy pulled up in the paddy wagon—a converted armored car used to transport the destruct explosives. For this launch, Pappy personally would load all of the explosives. It wasn't that he didn't have confidence in his team, and they knew it; it was just that he became nervous if he wasn't busy.

During this time, he reminded them of an old bear that had been roused out of its den a month too early. So half of the team acted as gofers for Pappy at the pad, while the other half sat around in the control room playing cards and pretending to be calm.

Even General Reed knew better than to say anything about their card game during this time. They needed a diversion to maintain their sanity. As the loading progressed, the game degraded until, by the time the final primacord was installed, the most complicated game they could concentrate on was Go Fish.

"Well, colonel, ya ready to meet your Maker today?" Pappy quipped as he climbed down from the truck carrying a box marked "High Explosives."

"I guess I'm as ready as I'll ever be, Pappy," replied Wells in their normal Laurel and Hardy routine. "How about you?"

"Maybe the good Lord don't want to be bothered with me jist yet. He's missed some purty good opportunities to cancel my ticket in the past. Besides, I haven't had my three score and ten yet."

"Pappy, you'd better stop and pray before we begin," Wells said, "and the first thing you need to do is ask forgiveness for lying." To his amazement, for the first time in their extended friendship, Pappy did actually stop and ask God to forgive their sins, keep the thunderstorms away, and forgive their stupidity for being a part of this project.

"Colonel, I've got a bad feelin' about this rocket and the package it's carryin'," Pappy said as he looked up again. "I jist hope we're not about to open Pandora's box 'n' discover it's fulla demons."

Wells grunted his agreement, even though he wished Pappy hadn't said anything. Somehow, he'd hoped the feeling of dread he had was just his cautious nature coming out. He knew Pappy was saying what he already was thinking. Then he shook his head to clear his mind and tried to concentrate on the task before them.

They began at the top level installing the explosive bolts that would separate the warhead from the rocket just before targeting. Pappy also installed the ignitors that would start the warhead's tiny solid rockets used for final targeting during the descent phase.

They moved as rapidly as safety would permit, installing the primacord in the tubes running the entire length of the rocket's tanks. Wells was fascinated by Pappy's efficiency and calmness. Despite his age, Wells knew the ancient mariner could work circles around most men half his age, or less.

Pappy crawled between tanks to install and arm a variety of explosive devices with the same detachment a skilled surgeon would use in performing exploratory surgery. He first checked the firing circuits for any stray voltages. Then he called the range safety officer in the control room to verify that the destruct switch was in the "disable" position.

The safety officer knew the risks Pappy was taking at the pad and gladly opted for the snug and secure blockhouse. The huge blast doors were closed and the slide bolts in place. The control room was receiving its air supply from the ventilators on the opposite end of the island. Even so, no one really knew what an explosion on the pad would do to the blockhouse; and no one had the slightest desire to find out.

Finally, they made their way to the bottom of the erector and the last ordnance installation: the hold-down bolts. Wells was drenched in his own sweat from the intensity he always felt during these operations.

Pappy laughed. "Colonel, you need to carry a towel with ya. Ya look like ya got caught in a gullywasher."

"Don't even say that word, Pappy," Wells grunted through his clenched teeth. "That's all I need right now to really make my day: another thunderstorm."

"Well, it would make the day go by a lot faster," Pappy chuckled. He unscrewed the dummy bolt head, holding the rocket to the launch pad. "You know, colonel, I knew a Navy aviator once who had a fear of flying. He sweated like that before every mission."

"Why in the world did he become a pilot then?" Wells asked.

"He was a lot like you. He wouldn't let anything git the best of him—not even his own fears."

"What happened to him?" Wells questioned. The conversation usually helped to settle his jangled nerves. He knew it helped Pappy, and he usually carried on a constant chatter while he was working.

"Why, he got killed on a mission two days before he was to rotate stateside," Pappy said soulfully.

"Thanks a lot, Pap!" Wells said with a grimace.

"You're welcome, colonel," Pappy responded as they both laughed.

Pappy installed the explosive bolt and connected the firing circuit. He repeated the process for the other three remaining bolts and then called the control room. "Launch control, this is ordnance one. We have completed the ordnance installation and are ready to return to the control room."

"Affirmative, ordnance one. We copy that ordnance installation is complete. You are cleared to return to the control room."

"Attention all launch countdown personnel," Deitz announced. "The ordnance installation is complete. We will commence phase three, final systems verification, in thirty minutes. At T-minus one hour, the warhead will be armed. All systems tests must be completed by that time."

"General, what will be the effect of the bomb when it explodes?" Congressman Hines asked while they waited for the ordnance team to return.

"Perhaps that question can be answered better by Dr. Kile," the general replied. "He is the manufacturer's representative for the nuclear warhead."

"Are you the same Dr. Kile who worked on the hydrogen bomb development?" Lisa asked.

"I am," replied Kile. "Dr. Teller and I worked together on the theory of hydrogen fusion."

"What is the expected effect of this weapon, doctor?" the congressman asked again.

"It is difficult to say exactly. The previous hydrogen devices have been detonated at ground level. This device will be detonated at an altitude of twelve kilometers. Therefore, the effects of the blast are more difficult to predict precisely. This is a relatively small device yielding the equivalent of about ten million tons of TNT."

"And you call that small?" Hines exclaimed.

"Everything is relative—compared to bombs that will yield one hundred megatons of energy, it is," replied Kile.

"And you can build such bombs, doctor?" the congressman asked.

Lisa interrupted: "Perhaps we should limit the discussion to the project at hand, doctor. Not everyone here has a need to know about future projects."

"Of course you are absolutely right, Doctor Feldstein," agreed Kile.

"This bomb is capable of obliterating a ten-square-mile island when detonated at an altitude of 100 feet above sea level. Theoretically, at twelve kilometers, it will cause little or no surface level damage."

"What about the effects from the fallout, doctor?" Lisa asked. "How far will the radiation spread after the explosion?"

"Based on the other tests we have run in the Pacific, we believe the radiation fallout will be dissipated by the time it reaches the United States," the scientist said, trying to evade the question.

"But what about the effects on other countries and sea life? What about the effects on those people living on other islands in the Pacific?" she pressed.

"We don't have sufficient data to evaluate that presently, doctor," replied Kile. "This test will help us better evaluate the effects of high altitude hydrogen detonations on the climate and world population."

"Then what you're saying is, you're willing to subject millions of innocent people to radiation fallout for the sake of research?"

"Doctor, that is a risk we must take to protect our freedom," Hines said authoritatively. "We obviously need to know the effects of hydrogen bomb explosions on the world's ecological system, in the event of a nuclear war."

"That's easy for you to say, congressman," Lisa retorted. "Your family is safely tucked away back in Vermont. But what about all those human beings who will be guinea pigs for our bombs? Why don't you and your family move out to one of these islands for a few months to see what effects the radiation has on you?"

Hines muttered under his breath to the general, "That's why a woman will never be president. They're too emotional."

Lisa got up and stormed away toward the Sandia console, where Wells and Pappy were just arriving.

Wells had caught the last part of the conversation. "You'll never win that argument. The question is not whether we will build bigger bombs; it's how many and who will control them."

"I know that, Bob," she said tersely. "But it still galls me that innocent people will be subjected to radiation poisoning needlessly if the winds change from their calculations."

"Easy, Lisa. I'm on your side, and I agree with you. But here we are, about to launch an H-bomb, and there isn't a thing that either of us can do about it. Let's just do our jobs and pray that we live through this experience."

"T-minus-thirty minutes and holding," the launch director announced. "The warhead will be armed at this time. We anticipate resuming the countdown in one hour."

Within five minutes, Pappy and his crew were at the pad and had delivered the sealed container to the warhead level of the gantry. They ran a total reverification of the Sandia system and were ready to transfer the plutonium core.

The procedure was deceptively simple, considering the potential of the bomb. The operation consisted of rolling the transport box up to the warhead access door, mating the carrier with the warhead receptor, and then using a hydraulic arm to insert the plutonium core into the chamber. The entire operation took less than twenty minutes and was a well-rehearsed routine with Pappy and his crew.

This time Dr. Kile stood by to verify the procedure. Everything went smoothly, and the CORE LOADED indicator on the control room console verified that the warhead was indeed armed. The core would not be inserted into the actual firing chamber until the THOR was airborne, but knowing that it was hot was enough to lift the anxiety level for everyone on the complex.

"This is the warhead arming leader," Pappy reported. "The core is installed and we're ready to clear the pad for system verification."

"We copy," Deitz responded from his console. "You are clear to return to the control room."

Once back at the blockhouse, Pappy and his team began the system verification required after installation of the plutonium core. The huge doors to the control room were sealed, as they would be throughout the remainder of the launch countdown. Even reinforced concrete and steel would be a puny defense against the destructive force of the machine now sitting on the launch pad. But, to the men inside it, it at least represented psychological security.

The verification of the warhead progressed to the point at which the arming circuits were to be cycled on and off. The actual firing circuits were still disabled by a grounding plug inserted in the line.

When the console operator initiated the arming sequence, the entire Sandia console lit up red. "Control, this is Sandia. We show a fault on the system arming monitors."

"Affirmative," the range safety officer said in coordination. "I show a system malfunction on my console also."

Pappy chimed in, "Launch control, this is ordnance leader. I request a hold to investigate the malfunction."

"Affirmative," came the reply from Deitz. "All personnel, we have a Sandia-initiated hold to investigate a malfunction indication in the arming system."

The Sandia console was a beehive of activity as they huddled to discuss the problem. "Listen team," Pappy said calmly. "This is why we rehearse these percedures a dozen times; we need ta isolate the problem quick. That's a loaded rocket out there, and we're on the line. Now, let's git it done! We'll recheck the console diagnostics first."

The engineer loaded the console paper tape reader with the program that would cycle every circuit external to the rocket's airborne package. Within ten minutes the test was completed and the console's green light flashed.

"Flight director," Pappy said as he called Deitz's console, "the system console checks out fine. The malfunction must be in the airborne unit."

"Understood," replied Deitz. "I'll have security escort one of your men to the spares area to secure another unit."

Pappy already had instructed one of his team to go with the security guard to the spare depot while he and another member of the team, along with Wells, headed to the launch site to open the access panel again and unhook the airborne unit. As they were undoing the fasteners holding the access panel in place, a startling thought struck Wells. He shouted, "Pappy!"

Pappy, halfway in the access panel, jumped back from his position, striking his head on the steel ridge around the panel. "What is it, colonel?" he asked as he rubbed his head. "You could get a fella killed shoutin' at him like that. I thought the rocket was on fire or somethin'."

"Sorry, Pap, but the thought just struck me that we're about to use a backup unit that missed all the ground tests you guys have run. Right?"

"That's right," Pappy answered. "But we've verified the ready spares a dozen or more times. It'll fly."

"Are you sure this unit is just as reliable as the old one?"

"Colonel, I'm going to check it out three ways from Sunday. Besides, we really don't have any choice, do we?"

Wells knew they didn't. They had a fully loaded rocket and an armed warhead. Outside of an irreparable system failure, nothing would stop this launch.

Within thirty minutes, the technician was back with the spare unit. In the meantime, Pappy had removed the old unit and reverified the wiring to the control room. When the spare module arrived, Pappy connected the interface plugs before bolting the unit in the rocket. "Just want to be sure it's okay before I install it," Pappy told Wells.

It took the console operator a few seconds to cycle the test tape through the tape reader. Then he called Pappy. "Ordnance leader, this is Sandia control."

"Sandia, this is ordnance leader. Go ahead."

"Pappy, the unit checks out fine, and the system error is cleared."

"Roger," Pappy replied. "We'll button up out here and be back at the control room in about fifteen minutes."

"Launch control, this is ordnance leader, we have tested the spare arming system unit and everything checks out okay. Estimate that we will have the warhead buttoned up in approximately ten minutes."

"Affirmative," replied Deitz. "Congratulations on the quick work, ordnance."

Even as he was speaking to Deitz, Pappy was directing the technician to permanently install the spare unit. In a little less than ten minutes, the unit was bolted in and the access door was being refastened. With the replacement finished and verified, the ordnance team and Wells headed for the blockhouse.

Inside his head, Pappy had the same sensation he had experienced many times during the war: *Something's wrong. But what?*

31

△

Liftoff

Once back inside the control room, Pappy took over the console and began the complete reverification of the airborne arming system. The entire procedure took about twenty minutes, and the unit checked out perfectly—or nearly so.

During one of the arming tests, Pappy thought he saw the altimeter light wink red and back to green. But three subsequent tests failed to repeat the error.

"Well, what do you think, Pappy?" asked Wells when he saw the test-complete light come on.

"It looks good, colonel, but I sure would like to run a system verification and reverify the altimeters too. I had a glitch earlier. Coulda been one of the barometric sensors."

"How long would a systems test take?" Wells asked, knowing that the general would never agree to the additional delay without hard proof of an error.

"A coupla hours to do it right," Pappy replied. "'Bout an hour if I can do it by myself though."

"Not a chance, Pappy!" Wells replied smiling. "Do you have hard data to justify the retest at this point?"

"Not really, 'cept for one little glitch. I just don't like unknowns, and those sensors are an unknown unless I can recalibrate. But I know Reed won't let us do it unless we have a hard failure, which we don't."

"Tell you what, Pappy, I'll request an additional hold to

reverify the altimeters. I trust your instincts, and it would be better to be safe than sorry."

"Good luck, colonel," Pappy replied. "I ain't exactly on the general's favorite person list. But remind him we got a hydrogen bomb out there, and the last thing 'tween us and a mighty big bang are those sensors."

The next ten minutes were spent in a heated debate between Wells and Reed. The outcome was preordained. It ended with Reed bellowing, "If he has a hard failure, let me see it. Otherwise, this countdown will restart in ten minutes. If Moss can't handle the job, I'll get somebody over there who can!"

"Idiot!" Pappy muttered under his breath as Wells grabbed his test data and returned.

"No luck, Pap," Wells said disgustedly.

"I heard, colonel. The world is being run by nitwits. I'm gonna do what I can to reverify the new package; and by the way, you better stay over at the range-safety console for the next few minutes. You might not wanta see what we do at our console."

"I suspect you're right," Wells replied. He unplugged his headset and made his way back to where Lisa was sitting.

"Is everything okay?" she asked, having seen his heated discussion with General Reed.

"Probably," Wells replied honestly. "It's just that Pappy's intuition and my nerves are acting up."

"Exactly what does that mean?" she asked, trying to decide if he was joking or being serious.

"Nothing really. Pappy would like to recalibrate the whole warhead arming system since we had to replace one of the airborne units. But it would cause a delay of at least an hour, and General Reed won't agree because there's no verifiable problem."

"Does the countdown procedure call for a system reverification if the unit is replaced?" Lisa asked.

"Hey, you're getting pretty good at this rocket business, Lisa. No, it's not in the countdown procedure. We just want to be sure that there are no surprises when the THOR is launched."

"Do you know something I don't?" Lisa asked, looking him straight in the eye. "Or, more importantly, do you know something that I should know?"

"Not really. It's just that I have this sense of dread—probably just nerves."

Lisa instinctively touched his hand as she asked, "As security officer, can't you just demand the reverification?"

"Nope, not without some hard data, so we'll just have to do the best we can," he replied. He was tempted to take her hand in his, but remembering her reaction to his kiss, he thought better of it. Regardless, he was glad she was there.

Lisa sensed his apprehension, but not wanting to add to his problems, she simply smiled at him as he got up to return to the Sandia console.

Just then Deitz announced, "The countdown will resume at T-minus-one hour on my mark: Three . . . two . . . one . . . mark. T-minus-one hour and counting to launch."

With the one hour to launch announcement, a whole series of events began. The two B-47s assigned to observe the hydrogen bomb detonation detoured to a course that would provide a wide sweeping arc of the target area. They carried precision electronic equipment to test the effects of the energy pulse released by the explosion.

Further downrange, the Navy sent two destroyers racing through the cleared zone around the targeted area. Along the corridor, two Russian trawlers were also nudging the limits of the forbidden zone. Their dual radar antennae were sweeping the skies for any approaching U.S. aircraft that might be heading in their direction.

At the NASA tracking stations, the technicians were throwing switches and prechecking the equipment that would be locked on the THOR during its short but historic flight. The NASA telescope operator was adjusting his optical tracking viewer in anticipation of the launch.

In the control room, each team was reverifying that their systems were fully operational and ready for the launch. The last critical phase would come at T-minus-thirty minutes, when the ordnance would be connected to the remote destruct system. Then at T-minus-thirty seconds the rocket would be cycled onto internal power from its own batteries, and one last verification would be run.

In the meantime, Pappy had been running his own verification of the warhead system. *I'm convinced there's somethin' wrong with the altimeter arming system,* he thought. *But it passes every test I throw at it. So what makes you think somethin's wrong, you old horse thief?* Pappy asked himself as he stared down at the console with all green lights. *The system test passed, the console says everything's workin' right, and you don't have one shred of evidence that anything's out of the ordinary, except that momentary altimeter warning light that flashed during one of your unauthorized tests.*

Pappy sat staring at the console, trying to relieve that nagging feeling in his mind, but he just couldn't do it. Something was wrong. He could just feel it. But he had nothing but feelings to go on, and feelings won't stop launches. *Besides,* he muttered, *what would I say to Reed? "General, I think I found an intermittent problem while runnin' an illegal system retest." I don't think he'd appreciate that one bit.*

"T-minus-thirty minutes and holding," the launch director announced. "Final ordnance arming will commence immediately."

Pappy was already up and moving toward the blockhouse doors with his static voltage test kit in hand. As he approached the huge doors he heard the hydraulic valves cycling to allow him access to the outside world.

As the doors slid back into their wall recesses, Pappy saw the erector team heading toward the pad area as well. Once he had the ordnance connected and taped so that no violent motions would shake the connectors loose, the erector would be lowered for the launch.

He started at the bottom and worked his way quickly up the levels of the rocket, first testing the firing circuits for stray voltage and then removing all grounding connectors and snapping the mating connectors together. During this time all radio transmissions were halted, lest some stray signal set off the destruct system.

Pappy completed his last ordnance test and was buttoning up the lower bay access panel even as he heard the erector work platform being folded and stored above him. By the time he climbed down the gantry ladder, the erector was being lowered.

He made his way back to the blockhouse and looked back to see the THOR, with its brilliant white nose cone standing naked in the gleaming Pacific sun. The final countdown would commence as soon as the last of the pad crews were safely inside the blockhouse.

The countdown was resumed at T-minus-thirty minutes and continued without incident to T-minus-thirty seconds, at which time both the THOR rocket and its warhead were cycled onto internal batteries. From this point on, all external controls would be limited to either the launch or abort command.

Since no human brain could assimilate all the data necessary to make this decision, the launch director's computer did it. The only telltale indicator was either a green or red light on Deitz' console.

"T-minus-ten seconds and counting," announced Deitz. "Minus nine . . . eight . . . seven . . . six . . . five . . . four . . ."

Bob Wells knew the countdown procedure by heart now. At T-minus-three seconds the safety seals to the engines ruptured, allowing fuel and oxidizer to reach the main engine valves.

"T-minus-two seconds . . ."

The main fuel valve opened, allowing the hydrazine fuel to flow through the cooling tubes that surrounded the engine bell housing. A fine mist of fuel also filled the combustion chamber.

"T-minus-one second . . ."

The main oxidizer valve cycled opened, allowing the nitric acid to rush into the mixing chamber, where the flow from one thousand pounds of fuel per second was spinning the combustion chamber turbines and thoroughly mixing both fuel and oxidizer as they sprayed into the combustion chamber.

Instantaneously, the effect was a controlled explosion generating more than 200,000 pounds of thrust. The sound at the pad area was deafening. Concrete pillars shattered from the intense vibration and sound waves striking the flame bucket.

Thousands of gallons of water were vaporized as the flames from the rocket exhaust roared through the flame deflector. Even with two six-inch water mains spraying cooling water on the test stand, the metals exposed to the rocket's exhaust began to glow and soften.

Lisa was startled by the vibration that shook the reinforced concrete bunker. She let out a slight gasp as the whole complex began to resonate under the strain of the rocket trying to escape its restraints.

Wells put his arm around her shoulder and felt her press against his side. The sensation from the awakened giant at the pad was awesome. No matter how many rocket launches he witnessed, the feeling of anxiety was always the same; only with the THOR it was amplified.

The rocket was straining to free itself from the massive bolts holding it to the launch pad. The raw power pulling against the hold-down bolts caused the rocket's frame to actually stretch nearly three inches. The whole metal structure of the launch pad was creaking and groaning under the enormous stresses being generated.

Guidance sent a signal to gimbal the engines; first to one side and then to the other. With each movement, the launch area issued vibrant protests as welds snapped and concrete exploded into pulverized dust.

"T-minus-zero," the launch director shouted into the headset. With a simple flip of the safety cover and a push on the small button on the launch director's console, the angry giant that had been so rudely awakened was released. An electrical pulse surged through the cordite core of the massive hold-down bolts. The side casings evaporated and, simultaneously, the four bolts restraining the rocket released their hold.

The rocket rose a mere six inches from the platform and seemed to settle there. For a moment, the forces straining to break free appeared to have changed their minds. Then, slowly, the THOR began to rise, balanced on the twin plumes of raw fire erupting from the rocket engines.

"Liftoff," the director declared as calmly as his pent-up energy would allow.

Wells knew, *the die is cast*. The thrust of the twin rocket engines were pushing the vehicle up, up, up into the sky. As the rocket climbed, critical events were taking place inside the nuclear warhead.

The arming system was initiating its launch sequence to prepare the bomb for detonation. Each step of the sequence would be displayed on the Sandia console in the launch center. Nothing except a destruct command could stop the process once it was started.

"Tracking reports that the THOR is on course and accelerating," the range safety officer reported. "Altitude is one thousand feet and climbing."

A noticeable air of relief went through the entire control room as the rocket passed through the critical first one thousand feet after liftoff. From this point, it would accelerate rapidly and the stress loads on the fragile frame would begin to lessen.

The brilliant white plumes of the twin engines were clearly visible to the two periscope observers watching the ascent of the rocket. Only the white vapor trails it left, as it passed through layers of moisture, marked its passing.

"The THOR has reached six kilometers," Deitz announced. "At forty kilometers the rocket will reach its maximum programmed altitude and will initiate targeting sequence."

Once THOR passed through the atmosphere at a height of approximately forty kilometers, it would pitch over and hurdle downrange to the target area. At its assigned reentry altitude of twelve kilometers, safely below the protective ozone layer, the bomb would detonate.

"THOR is twelve kilometers and climbing," Deitz announced.

A shout went up from the entire launch crew when the announcement was made. They were safe from any rocket mishaps. Even total engine failure would still put the rocket miles from the island now. The strain of the last few weeks had worn everyone's nerves pretty thin, but now they could relax.

32

△

Disaster

Sitting at his console, Pappy knew the warhead arming sequences by heart. To ensure that no inadvertent signals could trigger the bomb, the arming system was cycling through its fail-safes. The next phase would be initiated by engine cutoff. Inside the nose cone, the arming sequence had begun. The firing circuits were fully charged, and the plutonium core was inserted into the chamber.

"Tracking radar signals go," said the range safety officer, verifying that the rocket was still climbing and on target. In the control room, the launch director informed range safety that he was inserting his bomb detonation key as prescribed in the launch procedure manual.

"That's affirmative," range safety responded, and Deitz inserted the key. The bomb's manual fail-safe was satisfied.

The only fail-safe not yet satisfied was the barometric sensor verifying that an altitude of twelve kilometers during descent had been reached. All remote control over the rocket and its cargo were now removed. The bird was on its own, and all the men and equipment could do was watch their consoles as data was fed back to the island control room.

Wells had his eyes riveted on the Sandia console as the bomb's arming system fed a steady stream of data back, verifying skin temperatures, barometric pressures, and battery status. Then his mouth gaped wide as the last arming sequence light winked on.

"It's too soon!" he shouted to no one in particular. "The THOR is still climbing."

At twenty-two kilometers above the island, the faulty barometric sensor sent its "go" signal to the firing circuit's relays.

At the speed of light, a powerful electrical strobe surged through the high explosives surrounding the uranium core and a low-yield nuclear fission took place: an atomic bomb.

That reaction started a plutonium implosion, setting off a fusion reaction within the center core of the device: a hydrogen bomb.

For one thousandth of a second, a small sun was created twenty-two kilometers above the earth. All matter within the implosion radius of five hundred yards was smashed into a cubicle so dense that a one-inch diameter ball made up of the stuff would have weighed more than the entire planet Earth. Only in deepest space can such forces be contained and controlled to birth a new star.

So near the mass of the Earth, the particles were hurled outward again with the force of an eruption on the sun. Any living matter in the path of those billions of atomic particles, accelerated to near the speed of light, would be shot through with microscopic buckshot.

Mere chance would decide what happened next. Those unlucky enough to be found in the path of a dense stream of gamma rays would die quickly. Many of the less fortunate would die of radiation exposure from the atomized plutonium core.

It's difficult to say how long it took for the launch crew to realize that the bomb had detonated prematurely and directly above their island. A hydrogen bomb exploding at any altitude will disrupt the operation of electronic equipment. This one, exploding at exactly twenty-two kilometers, within the ozone layer, caused chaos.

Long before the shock wave occurred, there was an enormous pulse of electromagnetic energy that destroyed virtually all of the electronic equipment monitoring the rocket. Several of the nearest ground stations tracking the flight of the THOR saw their cathode-ray scopes explode in a shower of sparks.

These highly sophisticated tracking stations were rendered as useless as glasses would be to a blind man. Inside their steel reinforced bunkers the scientists and technicians could only stumble around in the artificial darkness and wait for backup generators to kick in.

In the THOR control room, all communications with the outside world were cut off. Even after the backup generators came on, they could only look and stare at each other and ask, "What happened?"

Then the sound of the blast descended upon them. Even within twelve feet of reinforced concrete walls, it sounded like the end of the world had come. The walls began to rumble and then the equipment began to rattle. The only way to describe it was pure sound at about one thousand decibels inside the control room.

Outside, those unfortunate creatures who were unlucky enough to be caught in the energy pulse caused by the premature blast faced an even greater devastation when the shock wave hit.

The two B-47 observation crews circling the island to film the launch suddenly found themselves in planes with no power and headed for the Pacific Ocean at three hundred miles an hour. But long before their glide pattern would have ended in the ocean, the shock wave hit, and their planes crumpled like flies hit by a giant flyswatter.

A telescope observer fifty miles from the launch site had just glanced at his stopwatch. Carefully noting that it was nearly six minutes until detonation, he thought, *In four minutes I'll need to flip my sun filter down to avoid retinal damage from the flare of the hydrogen bomb blast.*

The last image his eyes ever recorded was the initial explosion of the atomic bomb trigger. In that split second before the realization of what was happening sunk in, he thought, *You know, looking at an atomic explosion through a high-powered telescope is like peeking right into the heart of the sun.*

When the shock wave reached the blockhouse, it was Pappy who first realized what had happened and shouted, "The bomb's gone off way too soon!"

The members of the launch team sat in stunned silence long after the rumble had ceased. They tried to sort out what it meant that the bomb had exploded prematurely. They were all alive, but beyond that they had little to go on.

"Launch director, this is project safety," said Wells in a somewhat subdued tone. "I would like to have the blast doors opened so that an observation team can go outside."

"Colonel," replied Deitz, "we have no idea what the effects of this explosion will be. I cannot risk members of my team to be observers."

"I don't expect you to," Wells replied, a little less subdued now that the initial shock of the situation had begun to wear off. "I'll go myself, with another volunteer from the American launch team."

"Colonel, this is Pappy. I'll go with you. This may be my only chance to see the results of a hydrogen bomb up real close."

"Thanks, Pappy. I thought you would. How about it, doctor?"

"I have no objection, colonel. But the doors will be sealed behind you. Is that understood?"

"Understood."

Working the huge spinner controlling the locking bars, Wells and Pappy began the process of opening the blast doors.

When the last locking bar receded into its retracted position, the hydraulic pumps came on, and the steel doors began to retract into the walls.

Colonel Wells and Pappy stepped into the air lock between the inner and outer doors just as the outer doors swung open, with a swirl of slightly stale air rushing out.

The two men stepped out into the tropical day that was rapidly approaching dusk in the Pacific. They looked into the sky expecting to see the great mushroom cloud that usually accompanies a nuclear explosion.

But there was no mushroom cloud. There was only what appeared to be a reddish glow, as if the sun were setting in the east, except that the sun was setting in the west, as always.

"What do you make of that, Pappy? Why no mushroom cloud?"

"Best I can figger, since the bomb went off above most of the atmosphere, there wouldn't be a cloud 'cause there's not enough air."

"Of course, you're right, but I'll bet everything below the blast area caught a good dose of radiation. If that bomb went off above the denser atmosphere, it should have made a bright flash but little else. What do you make of that glow on the horizon?"

"Don't have the slightest idea, colonel. But I can tell ya this. I don't like it. Like you said, that bomb shoulda looked like a giant flashbulb."

The two men spent the next few minutes verifying the dosimeters and Geiger counters around the perimeter of the launch complex.

The dosimeters showed that massive doses of radiation had passed through the complex. But the Geiger counters verified that there was no residual radiation.

Minutes later Pappy said, "Colonel, have you been noticin' that sky?"

Wells had been so engrossed in checking the radiation indicators, he had not bothered to notice that the sunset was lingering a lot longer this particular evening.

"My God, Pappy! What is that?" Wells exclaimed when he looked where Pappy was pointing to the sky.

"I don't know, but I'd suggest you call some of our hotshot scientists and have them come out and take a look."

Wells located the closest intercom jack and connected his headset.

"Doctor Deitz, this is Colonel Wells. Come in please."

"Colonel, this is Deitz. Can you give us a report on the conditions out there?"

"The radiation levels are zero out here, but the dosimeters show we got a good shot of gamma. We should all be okay under twelve feet of concrete, but we've got something you need to see right away. It would appear we've set the sky on fire."

"What do you mean, we've set the sky on fire?"

"You just need to get out here as quickly as you can," Wells said abruptly, switching off the intercom.

Two minutes later Wells heard the outside doors to the blockhouse wheeze as the pressurized air from inside rushed out. Deitz stepped outside, followed closely by a red-faced General Reed and other members of the launch team.

"What's all this nonsense about the sky, Wells?" boomed Reed even before he reached the outside doors.

"Shut up, and look up at that sky!" Pappy said contemptuously.

General Reed looked ready to throttle Pappy, and might have, except that he did look up. Like a chameleon, his color changed from a flushed red to an ashen gray almost instantly. So sudden was his change in blood pressure, he almost collapsed.

"My God," shouted Deitz as he looked at the ever-increasing glow in the sky. "How long has this been happening, colonel?"

"We have to assume it was started by the bomb," exclaimed Wells, who sensed the alarm of the normally stoic German scientist. "It's been getting brighter by the minute. Any ideas about what's happening, doctor?"

"I would hesitate to guess," replied Deitz, recovering his composure.

"Listen, doctor! I'm not looking for a scientific analysis, but I would like to know if you have any idea what's happening. Give me a guess."

"Perhaps I can help, colonel," said Dr. Kile, who had just reached the group. "When we were working on the details of a rocket-launched bomb, we had to take into account the various strata that could be affected by the blast. One of the most critical is a layer of dense oxygen molecules called the ozone layer, because it consists primarily of O_3, ozone. Its exact function is not known, although it is thought to block much of the sun's ultraviolet radiation.

"The ozone is a layer of potentially combustible molecules at about the height where our bomb must have exploded. Somehow the fusion reaction ignited these molecules. The chain reaction seems to be widening the combustion. It would seem that we have indeed set the sky on fire!"

"Do you think . . . it will go out?" General Reed asked, his slow wits trying to sort out the impact of the situation.

"I have no idea," Kile answered honestly, his shoulders sagging under the unseen weight of a sudden new revelation.

"What now, doctor?" Lisa asked, sensing his change in attitude.

Kile hesitated before answering, carefully choosing his words. "You must all realize that what I'm about to say is only a theory based on totally inadequate information, but it is quite possible that this combustion could continue to grow until it consumes the entire ozone layer. If so, life as we know it on this planet will cease to exist."

Deitz spoke up: "Doctor, surely that can't be. The ozone is too thin to support continuous combustion."

"I would have assumed so also," Kile replied, "except that the combustion cycle continues even now, nearly half an hour after the explosion. Without a doubt, the process has extended beyond the initial phase. If what we see continues to expand throughout the next few hours, it's possible the combustion could expand indefinitely."

Wells interrupted. "Listen, Doctor Kile, worst case: What happens if this ozone layer is burned off?"

"It is only an educated guess, but I would say most of the Earth's vegetation would be destroyed by exposure to too much ultraviolet radiation. Probably we would have massive weather changes also. Effectively, the Earth could become a dead planet in a few years."

"We have to do something!" shouted Reed almost hysterically. "Do you realize what this could do to my career? It could ruin me if the project I'm in charge of destroys the whole world. I want you to do something about it right now."

The rest of the assembled launch crew looked at the general as if he were an imbecile, recently escaped from an asylum.

Wells moved to where he and Reed were face to face. "What would you have us do, general? Grab a fire extinguisher and put it out? Wake up! That fire is beyond the reach of man now. It's totally up to God. You wouldn't let Pappy reverify the barometric sensors because it might have delayed your countdown another hour. Well, the THOR *was* launched on time. Be sure to put that in your report!"

"Don't you try to put that off on me," shouted Reed. "If your man Moss had done his job right, that bomb would have gone off when it should!"

Pappy spoke up: "You just can't argue with an idiot, colonel. We set the world on fire, and he's worried about how it'll look on his record!"

"There's no question it's expanding," Lisa said. "It's grown just since we've been here."

"I fear you're correct," said Kile despondently. "I believe we have finally succeeded in destroying the world. It didn't take a war after all. A single bomb has done the job."

Looking up at the sky that was glowing brighter as the evening sun set, Wells wondered, *Can this be the end of the world? Is this what God meant when He said we would have a new heaven and a new earth?* He looked over at Lisa and thought, *I'm glad I met you, Lisa Feldstein.*

Lisa felt his eyes on her and looked up. She was frightened and not ashamed to show it. Wells, sensing her emotions, walked over and slipped her hand in his.

Wells whispered, "Don't worry, Lisa. This world is hard to destroy. I'm sure she'll survive this too." But inside, the conviction wasn't nearly as certain as his words.

Lisa lowered her head onto his shoulder, tears streaming down her face. *I think I love you, Bob Wells*, she said silently. *I just hope I have a chance to find out.* Had she looked up just then, she would have seen the tears in his eyes also.

33

△

Fire
in the
Sky

The ring of fire seemed to grow wider by the minute. The entire THOR launch crew stood and watched for the better part of an hour as artificial light dispelled what should have been a dimly lit sky.

"I reckon we've done it this time," Pappy said matter-of-factly. "If that ring o' fire continues to expand at the same rate for about three days, they should be able to turn the lights off in Hawaii. Come to think of it, general, you may go down in history after all. Edison invented the *first* light bulb; but you invented the *biggest* one."

The general was far too morose to do much more than throw a contemptuous glare in Pappy's direction; but Dr. Deitz responded, "I'm afraid the general won't share that distinction alone. We're all going to have to accept the blame for this disaster. I just hope all of humanity doesn't have to pay the price for our foolishness."

"I have to call the president," Lisa said. "He needs to know what's going on out here. Is there any way to make contact with the States?"

"None of our communications equipment is working since the bomb detonated," one of Pappy's crew explained. "I rather doubt there is any working radio equipment within a 300-mile area."

"What about the telephone?" Congressman Hines asked.

"Negative, congressman," replied Major Holmes, the communications officer. "The entire communications system outside of the intercom is totally dead. It looks like we're on our own for a while."

"It really don't matter a whole lot," Pappy remarked. "Washington ain't gonna to pass a law to stop this fire. It's about time we all faced up to this. If that fire don't go out, we're gonna have a worldwide panic—bigger'n anybody ever imagined before."

"I agree with Pappy, to a degree," Dr. Kile said. "What we're witnessing may be just the beginning of a very long cycle of events. The disruption of the ozone layer will likely initiate a series of thermodynamic alterations to our atmosphere."

"Tell me what that means in English," Pappy quipped.

"In short, it means that we have started a cycle that may result in either another ice age or a greenhouse effect."

"What is a greenhouse effect, doctor?" Congressman Hines muttered, fighting to control the panic that gripped him.

"It's a condition in which the Earth's atmosphere is heated until a vapor layer forms around most of the planet. This vapor layer acts like a blanket, trapping more of the sun's radiated energy, and a gradual warming takes place worldwide. This would melt the polar caps and flood most of the populated land masses of the world."

"How long would this take?" Hines asked, his voice trembling.

"No one really knows. I would estimate the present hole in the ozone layer to be at least fifty miles across already. By itself, that may be enough to start the cycle in one direction or the other. The bigger it grows, the greater the land mass that will be exposed to the radiation and the faster the cycle will be accelerated."

"Well, you gotta admit one thing," Pappy said. "It's about the best fireworks display anyone ever saw. Look at that!"

Lisa let out an unexpected gasp as she looked into the sky. The sun had totally set, leaving only the burning ring of fire in the sky to light up the moonless night. "Incredible!" she exclaimed.

Great plumes of iridescent sparks seemed to shoot out from the ever-increasing circle. They looked like giant sparklers filling the sky with their bursts of flame.

In the Hawaiian Islands, thousands of people lined the beaches to look at the greatest fireworks display they had ever seen. Viewed from the distance of several hundred miles, the flaming ozone looked like the solar eruptions seen during a total eclipse of the sun, except that the sun had long since set in the west. Frightened citizens flooded the local radio station with excited calls, trying to find out what was happening.

The transoceanic telephone lines were dead, and virtually all communications were cut off to and from the Pacific Islands.

The fire on the horizon seemed to intensify with the darkness, and the plumes of fire reaching out from the flaming ozone looked like miniature sunspots. Panic was beginning to set in on the Hawaiian Islands. Church services were hastily scheduled as rumors went out that it was the Second Coming of Jesus Christ. A great many confessions of past sins were made that evening, and the aisles were filled with instant converts who thought they could smell the brimstone of Hell's fires.

Natives in the Bikini Island chain watched in terror as the ring of fire seemed to engulf their entire sky. Sacrifices of food and gifts were offered to appease the angry gods. Witch doctors cut and gashed themselves in a futile attempt to make atonement for their people.

At the Pentagon, things were happening fast and furious. The secretary of defense ordered that all information concerning the THOR be classified most secret, by order of the president. A program was initiated to feed only screened information to the press about the phenomenon taking place in the Pacific.

The official explanation coming out of Washington was that showers of meteors were striking the atmosphere above the Pacific Islands, causing an effect similar to the northern lights often seen in the polar regions. A whole legend of government-funded scientific groups, including several major universities, came out in support of this explanation.

Under the guise of avoiding potential hazards from the unusual meteor showers, all commercial sea and air traffic was diverted from the region. The public was assured that, although the phenomenon was rare, there was no danger.

The very lack of information available on the matter served to disarm the rumors surrounding it. With the thoroughness of an entire political system determined to hide the truth, the THOR project was cloaked in total secrecy.

Observation planes were barreling toward the Pacific test range, while Navy ships in the Pacific basin were instructed to establish a one-thousand-mile "safe" corridor around the entire region. On board the USS Alabama, a destroyer on picket duty within the corridor, the scene was not nearly as calm as the press was led to believe.

"Captain, what do you make of that fire in the sky?" First Officer Commander John Allgood asked with understandable alarm.

"I haven't got the slightest idea, but it has something to do with the test of that bomb; that's for certain. Have you been able to reestablish radio contact with any of the ground bases involved in the test yet?"

"No, sir, our equipment is operational, but it's like the other ships and the ground stations have dropped off the Earth."

"I tried calling Honolulu, but the traffic coordinator said that no transmissions are being routed into the base, by order of the head of Naval Security."

"In other words, it's 'Don't call us, we'll call you,'" the captain said.

"That's about it, sir. The men are getting kind of edgy too, and I can't blame them. That's about the scariest sight I've ever seen. It's like the whole sky is burning, and it seems to be growing. I don't think anyone buys the official story that it's just a meteor shower. I've seen plenty of meteor showers while at sea, and none ever looked like this."

"I suspect this meteor shower was started by a hydrogen bomb, commander," the captain said with an air of sobriety. "But we're all paid to do our duty, and right now that means we keep a lookout for strays in the area."

By morning, the ring of fire had expanded to nearly double the size of the previous evening. Even more alarming, it appeared to be growing at an ever-increasing pace. The initial panic that the launch crew felt when they first viewed the burning sky was now almost an acceptance. The lack of sleep was rapidly taking its toll, and sharp minds became dull under the weight of stress and fatigue. Dr. Deitz ordered the launch team to go to their quarters and get some sleep.

"We'll post a watch and call you if anything changes," Deitz promised. "In the meantime, there is absolutely nothing we can do about this situation; and we may need you to be sharp later."

Wells knew the doctor was correct, as usual. His mind was dull and his head ached from the stress of the last several days. He suggested to Lisa that she try to get some rest too.

"Bob, you've probably faced dangers like this before, but I haven't. I'm not really scared; I just feel a dread inside . . . like when my mother died. And I feel a need to do something, but there's nothing to do."

"I know the feeling," Wells replied hoarsely. "I felt the same way many times during the war. It happens when you know someone or something has control of your life and you can't do anything about it. But I can honestly say, I haven't ever faced anything like this either. Right now, though, I've got to sleep."

Wells slept for nearly ten hours and was awakened only then by the pounding outside his Quonset hut. He got up and made his way to the door where one of his security guards was still pounding when he opened it.

"What's the problem?" Wells mumbled as he stepped outside.

The guard appeared to be on the verge of panic. "Colonel, Doctor Deitz has requested that all launch team members meet him in the control room. I think it has something to do with that, sir," he said, pointing to the ring of fire that had encircled them.

Even with the sun still providing plenty of daylight, the ring was totally visible and now encompassed an area well beyond the island. The shock of being surrounded by that great ring of fire, even though it was almost fifteen miles high, roused Wells out of his drowsiness.

"Pretty impressive, isn't it, corporal?" Wells commented, almost-matter-of-factly.

"I'd say that was the understatement of the century, sir. I would use the term terrifying."

"Are the other team members already there?"

"Yes, sir. Actually only you and Pappy were able to sleep more than a couple of hours. Most of the others have been at the control room for several hours."

I guess we've been close enough to death to know that it's best to rest when you can, Wells thought to himself. *But no sense in stirring up the troops any more than they are already.* "Tell the director I'll be there as soon as I've had a shower," Wells said.

The corporal looked as if he was sure Wells had gone mad, but he replied, "Yes sir, I'll tell him."

Wells showered and dressed as quickly as he could. He thought about stopping by the mess hall for coffee, but he assumed there would be no cooks on duty. *Can't blame them,* he thought. *I guess I'd be worried too if I had left anything or anyone behind. But with the possible exception of Lisa, I wouldn't miss anyone or be missed by anyone.* He knew the same was not true for Pappy. Pappy rarely talked about his sister, Anna, but he knew they were very close.

He was ready to leave when Pappy drove up in an Army-issue Jeep. Climbing in, Wells asked, "What do you think about that hole in the sky, Pap?"

"I think we've bought the farm, colonel. It's been nearly twenty-four hours now, and that thing keeps on gettin' bigger. Seems to be gettin' brighter too. I guess I'm ready to die. I knew the risks when I signed on, but sure would like to say good-bye to my sis."

Wells didn't say anything because he knew there was nothing to say.

"By the way, colonel," Pappy added, "my guys got one of the old vacuum tube receivers workin' and picked up a broadcast from Hawaii. The official explanation for what we're seeing is 'a meteor shower's ignitin' the upper atmosphere.'"

"I guess I would have expected something like that," Wells replied.

"Well, accordin' to a Navy alert signal we picked up, all military personnel have been instructed to avoid all outside contact, by order of the president. And my guess is, we're inside a gov'ment-ordered isolation. They're not gonna allow any information on the THOR to leak out."

"I suspect you're right, Pappy. They're probably shopping for a scapegoat right now."

As Wells entered the blockhouse, Lisa came over and put her arm around his waist. The seriousness of the situation had broken down her normal inhibitions. She was frightened and needed support. Wells responded by draping his arm around her shoulder and giving her a squeeze. He knew she had to be terrified. He had known the same feeling himself many times during the war, and he told himself not to read more into her actions than that.

Deitz had been waiting for them, and after Wells and Pappy entered the control room he began, "I don't have to tell you the situation is grave. Doctor Kile estimates the circle of fire is now more than 200 miles in diameter. There seems to be an intensification in the outer ring, indicating that spontaneous combustion may continue indefinitely."

"What about us, doctor?" said one of the engineers. "When will we be evacuated from this island?"

"We received a single telex from Washington informing us that, as of right now, no THOR related personnel will be evacuated until further notice. We have been assured that there is no immediate danger to any personnel if you remain in the control center."

"What about the rest of the world, doctor? Can they stay inside a concrete building for the rest of their lives?" Lisa said more harshly than she intended. Inwardly she blamed Deitz, even though rationally she knew it wasn't his fault.

"I don't know the answer to that any more than you do," Deitz said straightforwardly. "We can receive communiqués, but we can't respond. All I know is that the order about THOR personnel comes from the highest level of government."

"What about calling our families, doctor?" one of the engineers asked. "We at least need to let them know we're alive."

"That's impossible also, I'm afraid. Even if we had stateside communications, the government has put a total blackout on this project, including us. However, I'm sure that all of your families will be notified that you're safe here as soon as possible."

"Yeah, notified by the same people that are tellin' the rest of the world that we're havin' a meteor shower," Pappy growled. "Doctor, does anyone outside the gov'ment know that we're alive?"

"What do you mean?" asked Deitz.

"I mean, if we didn't ever show up again, would anybody outside Washington know we're alive? It might be more convenient for the government to have people think we died in a rocket accident than for the rest of the world to know that the THOR project set the world on fire."

"I'm sure that would never happen," Deitz said without any real conviction in his words. The look on his face told everyone that he realized what Pappy said had some merit. "Let's don't start any wild rumors. This is just a normal precaution until the extent of the danger is evaluated."

Shaken, Deitz stepped down from the platform. He knew he didn't have anyone who would investigate his disappearance; nor did most of the others in the room.

34

△

The
Cover-Up

I don't care what the admiral says. What I see is not caused by any meteor shower," Abraham Flom, managing editor of the *Honolulu Sun,* yelled at the young reporter. "It's somehow related to the tests the government was doing out in the islands. Get me General Marshall at the Pentagon."

"I'm sorry, sir," the reporter said, wincing, "we can't get through to the States; all the lines are jammed. The operator says it's caused by the atmospheric interference."

"Nonsense!" shouted Flom. "The only interference around here is caused by politicians trying to cover their backsides. Go get Dr. Lawrence at the university. Tell him I need to see him right away, and he's not to say anything to anyone else."

"Yes, sir," the junior reporter replied as he scurried away, glad to be out of Flom's sight. He was scared, as were many of the others he had talked to on the paper. There was a total blackout of information to and from the mainland. It was as if they didn't exist as far as the rest of the world was concerned. Whatever was happening out there in the Pacific, he didn't believe it was a meteor shower either.

He reached the University of Hawaii in less than twenty minutes and made his way up the stairs to the office of Dr. Morgan Lawrence, the head of the physics department. He found Lawrence sitting at his desk.

"Sir, I'm from the *Sun.* Mr. Flom would like to see you immediately if possible," the young reporter said.

"Is it about the problem in the sky?" asked the distinguished physicist. Morgan Lawrence had worked for the government throughout World War II, doing research on the atomic bomb project under the supervision of Robert Oppenheimer. He had already guessed the origin of the growing glow in the sky, though not the details. The reports he had heard about the loud rumble just prior to the fire appearing was a tip-off. He assumed the government was testing some new weapon and it had gotten away from them.

Rumors about some new weapon had been circulating among his colleagues in Washington for some time. If the military had detonated a large thermonuclear device at the wrong altitude, it might have caused simultaneous combustion in the upper atmosphere—much as they originally had feared at Los Alamos with the first atomic bomb.

He assumed no one would be stupid enough to attempt such a potentially dangerous experiment. But he often had been amazed by the stupidity of men in government, tinkering with their new toys.

Lawrence knew his theory was close to the truth when FBI agents had come to his office earlier that morning and instructed him that he could not speculate on the nature of the "lights in the sky" and that his information on nuclear energy was still classified as top secret. They had left no doubt in his mind as to the government's position on this subject: Officially, this was the work of meteors and had nothing to do with any government program. After they left, he was reminded of a lesson from *Othello:* "Me thinks thou dost protest too much."

After the reporter's questioning, he had immediately gone to the university's observatory to talk with his friend and colleague, Dr. Tuiassao, head of the astronomy department. He found him sitting in his office staring out the window.

"How are you, old friend?" asked Dr. Lawrence.

"Ah, Morgan . . . glad to see you. I need to talk with someone. I fear this is a dark day."

"Old friend, we have seen some dark days together, you and I." Lawrence knew that Tuiassao had indeed spent some dark days during the war, interned in a refugee camp with his Japanese wife, Misha. Being half Hawaiian and half Japanese, he looked totally Oriental. The hysteria after the bombing of Pearl Harbor had left thousands of loyal Asian Americans, including Dr. Tuiassao, imprisoned for the duration of the war.

"Two men from the government were here earlier. They directed me not to comment on anything I might have observed about the recent fire in the sky. They explained the government's position that it is a meteor shower of unusual proportions and nothing else. They also hinted that my security status was still under review since the government was considering a large grant to the university for research. Now the administration has decided to close the observatory for modifications to the telescope—also being funded by the government."

"Tell me, my friend," said Lawrence, "what *did* you see?"

"Morgan, it is terrifying. The glow is caused by a ring of fire in the ozone that has been expanding steadily. When I first reaimed the telescope to look at the faint glow on the horizon, the ring extended out perhaps ten miles. The last time I was able to study it, the ring was continuing to expand. I would estimate that the perimeter now extends at least 100 miles."

"A hundred miles!" exclaimed Dr. Lawrence. "What will that do to the Earth?"

"I wish I knew, my friend, but I don't. I would need a lot more information, and even then it would only be a guess. Even if the combustion stopped now, it is possible that the damage to the ozone is irreparable. We know so little about how the ozone layer was formed and how it functions. Without an ozone shield, I suspect life as we know it would cease to exist. It is possible that a rift such as we now see will alter the ecological system for generations to come. Do you think it was a nuclear explosion that started the reaction?" asked the weary Tuiassao.

"I don't see how it could have been anything else. I suspect they launched a rocket with an atomic or hydrogen bomb aboard and either it detonated prematurely or they were testing the feasibility of a high altitude detonation."

"Surely the government wouldn't be so foolish," said the astronomer.

"I have seen many foolish things from our government, doctor, as you have also."

"Yes, I saw my wife wither away and die of a broken heart because her country didn't trust us. And now this university, dedicated to teaching the truth, capitulates to keep the government's money flowing."

"You said the ecological system will be altered. What do you mean?" asked Lawrence.

"As I said, nobody really knows. If the combustion is sustained, it will likely engulf the entire world over the next several weeks. I wish I could get back to my telescope and make some careful measurements. This is the opportunity of a lifetime to study the ozone and how it is constructed."

"What will happen to the area below the hole, doctor?" Lawrence asked nervously. He knew, just as the astronomer did, that the hole could expand to cover the Hawaiian Islands in the next few days.

"The ozone is our ultraviolet filter," Tuiassao explained as he drew a diagram of the Earth's atmosphere on the blackboard. "What other functions it serves are not well known at this time. We also believe that the ozone tends to dissolve excess carbon dioxide in the upper atmosphere and thus lessen the potential of the so-called greenhouse effect.

"Below the hole that has developed, the ultraviolet radiation will be increased. Perhaps the life-chain cycle will be disrupted and the plants and animals that can handle large doses of ultraviolet radiation will become dominant. Then the others will slowly die off.

"Skin cancers may become far more common in the future, due to the increased radiation. But much more subtle and potentially devastating will be the changes to our climate caused by the temperature increase."

"But why would the Earth's temperature increase? Ultraviolet radiation doesn't necessarily heat the atmosphere, does it?"

"Not directly. However, if the plankton and algae at the ocean's surface are affected, it is possible for sunlight to penetrate farther into the ocean's depths, causing a gradual warming. We can all be grateful that this disaster did not occur over the Earth's poles. The effect of the Antarctic warming, for instance, could drastically alter the world's climate."

35

△

Tell Them
We're
Alive

Things were beginning to heat up. "What do you mean, Dr. Lawrence won't come," roared Flom. "Didn't you tell him it was urgent?"

"Yes, sir," the reporter replied as he tried to shrink away from the verbal blast he knew was coming. He had dreaded returning to face the editor without Dr. Lawrence.

"Get Lawrence on the phone immediately," Flom shouted.

"He said he was unable to talk with you at all, sir," the reporter squeaked. "It has something to do with the Secrecy Act. He said to tell you he's been gagged and you would know what he meant."

Flom stopped where he was, with the phone in his hand. He put it back in its cradle and sat down at his desk. *So this thing is part of the government. And they've clamped down on the whole island to keep it under wraps. The biggest story since Pearl Harbor and I can't get any facts!*

"Call the airport and get me a ticket to the mainland," Flom said. "If they won't tell me the truth, I'll go to Washington and stir up the waters a little."

Within fifteen minutes the reporter was back again. "I'm sorry, sir, but all flights out of Honolulu have been canceled for the next few days. It has something to do with the meteor shower in the area and potential danger to commercial flights."

"I can't believe it! We're virtual prisoners on this island. This can't be happening in the twentieth century—not in America. Call publications and see if they have the photos of the 'meteor shower' ready for the morning edition. We'll go with a headline that will shake up whoever's behind this whole thing."

"Yes, sir," the reporter said as he rushed to do his boss's bidding. He felt fortunate to escape the wrath that he apparently was saving for the powers behind his inconvenience.

▲

At Anawetok, life had resumed some semblance of normalcy, or at least as much normalcy as was possible within the ever-increasing circle of fire.

"Colonel, I have an idea," Pappy said as they sat in the mess hall drinking coffee. "I think there may be a way to make contact with someone outside the government."

"I'm open to any suggestion, Pappy. Our phone lines are down and all courier service is incoming only. Unless you can swim a couple hundred miles in the open sea, I don't see any way to contact anyone."

"The single-side-band transmitter used on the THOR for guidance communications is very similar to the system used by a lot of ham operators. I believe it could be retuned to their frequencies and a message sent in Morse code."

"But the entire transmission system was knocked out by the blast. How are you going to get it working again?"

"The ready spares depot. It's got solid concrete walls. With your approval, colonel, we'll check out one of the airborne transmitters and start to work on it."

"It's a long shot, but it's worth a try. I may get court-martialed for this, but at least they'll have to bring me back to the States to do it."

"There won't be any court-martials over this fiasco, colonel; then the truth would come out. No sir, they're gonna to try to leave us out here to rot until this whole thing blows over and they can find something or somebody to hang this on."

"That's about the way I see it too, Pappy. So, get to work, or we may be staring at sand for the next thirty years."

Two hours later, Pappy was back. He and his crew had been using all their skills to get a message to anyone outside.

"Colonel, I think we've got a workin' transmitter. It may not be right on frequency, but with the power it's got, it'll bore right through anyone else's signal between here and Australia. All we need now is a good, high antenna. The boys in meteorology loaned us a weather balloon to hoist it."

"I'll just bet they did," chuckled Wells. "Give it a try, Pappy. The most it can get me is thirty years in Leavenworth."

Lisa was sitting next to Wells with his arm resting lightly across her shoulders. Pappy frowned a little as he glanced protectively toward her. After he walked away, Lisa commented, "Bob, I really do believe your friend Pappy thinks I'm sixteen years old and being molested by a lecherous old man."

"Pappy's a great guy, but nothing could be further from the truth, unfortunately," Wells said as he took her hand.

"Why, you *are* a lecherous old man! He might be right after all," Lisa jested. She felt giddy when she looked into his eyes. Wells bent over and kissed her lightly. He knew he wouldn't be going home alone this time. Now all they had to do was find a way to get home.

The rest of the day passed uneventfully, but events were about to ratchet up one notch.

"Doctor, you'd better come outside and see what's happening," one of the guards called to the launch director over the intercom. Deitz awoke from the nap he was taking in the control center. He felt like he had been asleep only a few minutes. But when he looked at his watch, he was amazed to discover it had been nearly four hours.

When he opened the outer doors to what should have been a moonless Pacific night, the light flooded in. As he stepped out into the clearing he saw a sight that made him release an involuntary gasp. The whole sky was ablaze in a circle of fire that seemed to extend beyond the horizon. Particles like bits of sparkling fireflies were being thrown off to be consumed in the denser atmosphere below.

The sight was both frightening and incredibly beautiful at the same time. Dr. Kile was busily taking photographs as fast as he could load and shoot the film in his ancient box camera.

"Here I am in the middle of the most sophisticated equipment in the world," Kile complained, "and the best equipment available to take Pulitzer prize winning photographs is a twenty-year-old camera I kept as a souvenir."

"Don't worry about it, doctor," Wells responded. "The only person who will ever see your pictures will be the custodian at the Library of Congress in about the year 2010, when they release this episode from the secrecy vaults. That is, unless the whole world dies, in which case they will release them earlier."

"I 'spect you're right, colonel," Pappy said. "I understand that the bow and arrow are still considered classified weapons systems in the Pentagon. This fiasco should be good for about 300 years."

"Dr. Kile, do you have any ideas about what's happening?" Wells asked. "What do you make of that smell?"

"The smell is actually ozone being formed," the scientist explained. It is apparently a by-product of some of the denser atmosphere burning. It's kind of ironic actually. Ozone is being created by the very process that is destroying the ozone layer. Unfortunately, the loss-to-gain ratio is probably a million to one." Then he added, "But that's just a guess, colonel."

"If you want my opinion, colonel, it smells like the fires of hell to me," said Pappy.

"You could be more right than you think, Pappy," Wells agreed. "This may be the beginning of Hell on Earth."

"Look at that!" Lisa cried out, as a luminous bolt of sparkling fire reached out across the sky. Thousands of tiny fire droplets cascaded down from the sky around them.

"It's like being caught in a rainstorm, only without gettin' wet," Pappy said as the droplets disappeared above them. "The fire never reaches the ground."

"That's because those are merely electrically charged particles, much like static electricity," Dr. Kile offered. "We are literally seeing the upper atmosphere melt, Mr. Moss."

Pappy snorted at the use of his formal name. Then he decided it wasn't worth the argument and said, "Why the change in the ring of fire, doctor?"

"I would say the fire is expanding at an exponential rate now. By my measurements, it has grown over five hundred square miles in the last five hours. At this rate, it will ring the entire Earth in less than a month."

"The best kept secret in the world won't be a secret by this time tomorrow," Wells said, as he squeezed Lisa's hand. "It will be over the Hawaiian Islands by then, and we'll have a chance to see how the average citizen reacts to seeing the sky on fire."

Several hours passed during which Pappy and his crew hoisted their makeshift antenna on their "loaned" weather balloon. They had retuned the THOR transmitter and were about to turn the power on.

"Colonel, we're 'bout ready to try to make contact with someone from down under," Pappy said. "My guys tell me it won't be simple because of the upper atmosphere disturbance caused by the fire."

"How are you planning to beam a signal all the way to Australia with a transmitter designed only to send a few hundred miles at best?" Wells asked.

"In theory it's pretty simple. We aim at the sky and bounce a signal off the ionosphere. If we guess the angles right, some guy in the great outback will hear us and contact his friendly local newspaper with the story of the century."

"Wait a minute, Pappy," Wells said. "You can't say anything about the THOR, and especially about the bomb. We're still under the Secrecy Act and bound to obey the orders we were given."

"Just kiddin'," Pappy said with a broad grin. "Besides, you forgit that our little secret won't be a secret when the whole world sees the sky burnin'."

"We'll leave it to the politicians to explain how the sky caught on fire. Our job is just to let someone in the real world know we're here and waiting for rescue. That will be sufficient incentive for the government to bring us home. Keep it simple and to the point: We've been marooned by the phenomenon in the sky, and we want our families and friends to know we're alive and kicking."

"Will do," Pappy quipped. "You know I always play by the rules."

"Yeah, Pappy," Wells replied, wrinkling his brow, "but the difficulty is that they're usually rules you make up."

In Washington the atmosphere was only slightly less charged than the sky above the Pacific Islands.

"Mr. President, I believe you need to look at this report from our observation aircraft in the Pacific," said Arnold Grey, the assistant secretary of state.

"Unbelievable, Arnold! Is this for real?" the president asked as he looked at the photos taken from the B-47s.

"I'm afraid so, sir," the secretary replied. "And it has grown since those photos were transmitted, nearly twelve hours ago. It seems to be increasing its rate of growth as it expands. By the estimates of the boys at NASA, it will reach Hawaii in about thirty hours."

"Have communications been contained on the islands?" the president asked as he slumped down into his rocking chair behind the Jefferson desk.

"Yes, sir, but the press got wind of it, and now they're hot on our tails. We won't be able to keep this thing bottled up much longer."

"Well, keep it contained as long as you can, Arnold. Do you realize what a panic this will cause around the world? It looks like the end of the world in those pictures."

"It's not really as bad as all that, Mr. President. Dr. Van Pell, head of the National Oceanic and Atmospheric Agency (NOAH), says that his figures show that even if the entire ozone layer is destroyed we will only feel a gradual change as the climates adapt and the Earth begins to warm. As far as the cancer thing is concerned, our scientists think a good sunscreen lotion will avoid most of it."

"So we'll hand out suntan lotion to the millions who will starve when their food supply dries up? Don't you realize this is the biggest potential disaster to face the human race since the flood?"

"Mr. President, I suggest that we do everything possible to distance this administration from the responsibility of this act," the assistant secretary said.

"Just how do we do that when it was our rocket that launched the bomb? And what do we do with the 300 people assigned to the THOR project—not to mention the several dozens of others attached to the observation teams. Would you suggest we gas them and bury the bodies?"

"Of course not, sir, but I would suggest leaving them in isolation until this fire has run its course and the hysteria has died down. We have dozens of eminent scientists ready to attest to the fact that it was a freak meteor shower that ignited the ozone."

"Arnold, I never cease to be amazed at the ingenuity of your people. I guarantee you I'll never believe one word I hear once I leave this office. But do what you have to do. Just be sure this thing doesn't come back to bite us where we're most vulnerable."

"Yes, sir, Mr. President," the secretary said. He knew exactly what had to be done.

36

△

Find a Scapegoat

In Washington, the political maneuvering was accelerating.

"What's the latest word on the hole in the ozone, doctor?" the vice president asked Dr. Van Pell.

"I'm sorry, sir, but that information has been classified most secret, and I can't discuss it with anyone except the president."

The vice president's temper flared, but he fought to get control. He wasn't used to anyone challenging his right to know anything he wanted to know. He knew more about running the government than that arrogant rich kid who'd gotten elected on his daddy's money ever would.

Well, he'll be gone soon. Then I'll be running the country. But if word of this disaster gets out, he'll drag me down with him. There won't be another Democrat elected for two decades. Why couldn't this have happened under a Republican? This whole rocket thing was Eisenhower's idea anyway.

He had attempted to get in contact with his man on the project, but all communications were still cut off to the Pacific region. *Well then, I'll just wait and see how this thing goes. If it really starts to unravel, I'll get Hoover to leak information to the press that I opposed the idea from the beginning. Yeah, this may work out after all,* the vice president decided.

▲

On the island, Pappy and his team had been trying, unsuccessfully, to reach Australia when Wells walked into their hut.

"No luck, colonel," Pappy said in a downcast tone. "That fire is creatin' so much radio interference, I couldn't even reach the other side of the island. It's like we're in a big hole and the only radio beams that can escape are those that go straight up. We'll just have to wait this thing out until it either dies or gets big enough to take in some inhabited areas so we can broadcast inside the hole." Pappy took the headsets off and laid them in the chair next to his desk.

"It's been nearly seventy hours since the explosion, Pappy, and I would estimate that hole covers a good six- to seven-hundred miles now. At this rate, we'll be able to call Hawaii tomorrow . . . if we live that long."

"Colonel Wells, come outside quick!" shouted the sergeant, who was standing outside the hut. "Somethin's happenin'! I think we're gonna die!"

Both Wells and Pappy sprinted for the door and rushed outside, where most of the other team members were already gathered. It was nearly dusk, and the sun was just dipping beneath the ocean horizon. The sky was ablaze with flashes of sparks from the ring of fire. They were getting brighter as charged particles raced first in one direction and then the other while the hole expanded at an ever-increasing rate.

"What's happening, doctor?" Wells shouted to Dr. Kile as he approached the group. Lisa immediately moved over to be beside him.

"I wish I knew, colonel, but this is my first time to see the sky on fire too," Kile said nervously. "Either the combustion is expanding to the atmosphere, or it has reached a new stage in the process that we haven't seen before."

"Think we're about to die, doc?" Pappy asked without any apparent concern in his manner.

"Well, Pappy," the normally formal scientist replied, using his nickname for the first time, "if indeed the fire has jumped over to the atmosphere, we'll all die of asphyxiation in just a few minutes. If we don't, we'll know that's not what happened."

"Can't we just get some of the emergency oxygen bottles from the control room?" one of the engineers asked.

"What for?" Pappy quipped. "So that three or four of us can survive another couple of hours? No thanks. I'll take my lumps. If the Big Man wants me now, I don't want to put Him on hold another minute."

Suddenly the evening sky lit up with a blaze of fire as it literally exploded with sparks that seemed to reach all the way down to the Earth. The smell of the air being ionized permeated their senses. In spite of himself, Wells let out a gasp, as did Lisa. Pappy let out a whoop that startled the entire team as he prepared to finally meet his Maker.

Then as suddenly as it had started, the fire blinked one last time and went out. The sky looked totally black through their constricted pupils. The darkness was so intense for those few seconds that none of them could see the others.

"Are we dead?" Pappy asked in such a serious tone that the others began to laugh.

"No, I don't think so, Pappy," Wells replied in his most serious voice.

"Good," said Pappy, " 'cause my corns still hurt, and I couldn't stand the thought of goin' through eternity with hurtin' feet." The rest of the crew broke up at his comment.

"What happened?" Wells asked of nobody in particular.

"I would say the fire snuffed, colonel," replied Dr. Kile.

"What do you mean snuffed?" Wells asked, his eyes beginning to adjust to the lesser light of the setting sun.

"Apparently, the rate of expansion exceeded the supply of fuel and the fire simply went out. I would say this crisis is over—except that we now have a very large hole in the ozone layer. The effects of that problem will not be known for many decades."

"But not this year?" Pappy said, as he stuck a second piece of gum in his mouth.

"No, not this year, and maybe not in our lifetimes. But someone will pay the price for our foolishness in this place."

"And I can gar-ahn-tee you that our Uncle Sam will want to keep this under wraps like nothin' you've ever seen," Pappy said, as if confirming what the others were thinking too. "I believe I'll try to reach one of our Aussie friends to let 'em know we'd like to go home this year."

▲

In Washington the president was asking the assistant secretary of state, "Have you made arrangements for the launch team and the other members of the support units?"

"Yes, sir. We'll hold them at Holliman for debriefing and lectures on security procedures. The only problems I anticipate are Congressman Hines, Dr. Kile, Dr. Feldstein, Dr. Deitz, Colonel Wells, and a maverick ordnance engineer by the name of Moss."

"The congressman I'll manage," said the president. "The secretary of defense has assured me that his name is all over the authorizations for the THOR system. If word of this leaks out, he couldn't get elected as dogcatcher. Besides, we'll assure him a cabinet post. He'll keep his mouth shut."

"I know Kile well," Dr. Van Pell offered. "He and Edward Teller started some nuclear opposition group after the H-bomb was developed. We'll need to keep him isolated for awhile. And Dr. Deitz is a problem. He has demonstrated a tendency to reject authority. I recommend that he be held in isolation for awhile too."

"Do whatever you have to do," the president ordered, "but nothing illegal . . . you hear?" The president stared directly at the vice president and the FBI director when he made the last comment.

"And I don't think Dr. Feldstein will be a problem," said Van Pell, trying to avoid the vice president's glare. "She needs her top secret clearance to work at any university in the country. She swore to the Secrecy Act on the THOR before you sent her, sir, and she won't violate her oath. She will keep silent."

"Colonel Wells and Mr. Moss are problems, though," the secretary said, dropping the debriefing reports on the desk. "Both have been very vocal in the debriefings. We've had to separate them from the other team members. I would suggest that we keep them both confined indefinitely, Mr. President."

"On what grounds? These men haven't done anything wrong yet, and until they do I won't have them arrested or falsely imprisoned. I just won't have things like that happening while I'm president."

What an idiot, the vice president thought to himself as the others left the briefing. *That fool could sink us all. When I'm president, I'll solve that problem—permanently!*

"What about this story you have in mind?" the president said, addressing the vice president in a barely civil tone. "It sounds far-fetched to me."

It would, the vice president thought darkly, but he held his temper. "It's a long-term solution to the whole issue, sir. We won't be able to keep the hole-in-the-ozone secret forever, and some of our brain-trust guys at the institute have come up with a logical explanation.

"The environmental weirdos are always looking for a cause to champion. We'll give them one: a hole in the ozone caused by industrial chemicals."

"How in the world are you ever going to convince anyone that chemicals burned a hole in the sky?" the president asked without trying to cover his irritation.

"I'll let Dr. Van Pell explain that to you," the vice president replied in a barely civil manner.

"Mr. President, what we propose is not altogether fabricated. Dr. Barnes from MIT has opposed using fluorocarbon-based compounds in any sizable quantities since the first refrigerators began using Freon, back in the early thirties. It has long been his contention that fluorocarbons will erode the ozone layer. Many prominent scientists agree with his conclusions that prolonged use of these compounds may seriously erode the ozone."

"And you think that will explain away a 500-mile hole in the ozone, doctor? Give me a break! The public's not altogether stupid."

"It may be years before anyone has proof of this hole, Mr. President. And almost certainly it won't remain where it is. The Earth's rotation will relocate it—probably to somewhere above the South Pole, we believe."

"But isn't that worse? I thought your people said Antarctica was very vulnerable."

"It doesn't matter," the vice president said, interrupting. "We can't fix the hole; all we can do is keep the blame off our backs."

"Just give me the bottom line," the president said sharply. He was thoroughly irritated by being trapped into any further deception.

Van Pell was feeling sick from nervousness, but he continued. "We'll stick to our original story—that what the public saw was an unusually large meteor shower. We have several eminent astronomers who will back us up. The ozone hole may never be discovered. Some of our people think it may even heal itself. But if and when it is discovered, we will already have convinced the public that fluorocarbons did it."

"Think of it like playing a game in which the score is already decided," the vice president added. "Pretty hard to lose that one. By the time the hole is discovered, the whole world will blame the fluorocarbons."

"Shouldn't we warn the people living under that hole?" the president asked.

"We can't do that, Mr. President," the vice president drawled. "If we tell anyone, the word'll get out and the Pacific will be swarming with Commies carrying radiation equipment, trying to make the U.S. pay for this whole thing."

The president looked up with a scowl on his face. He was about to say something when Van Pell continued.

"We *really* don't know the long-term effects of the ozone hole. Maybe we can turn this into some good. It may become the rallying point for reducing our chemical pollution."

"Look at it this way, Mr. President. As long as we're selling the public something that's really in their best interests anyway, I don't see the problem," the vice president said with a loud horselaugh.

"Just be certain this THOR debacle is buried forever," the president ordered the vice president.

"You can count on it, Mr. President. You *can* count on it."

Part Three

The Conspiracy Exposed

37

△

The
Last
Message

Bob Wells stopped the recorder to gather his thoughts before continuing. Since the THOR incident in the Pacific, not one word had been leaked to the public about the real cause of the disaster. Once the fire went out the public lost interest, and outside of a few scientific journals that had reported on the unusual meteor showers, nothing further was forthcoming.

After the fire snuffed, Pappy was able to make contact with some ham operators in Australia who had passed word to the press about a research team stranded on Anawetok. Within a few days, the crews had been sent back to the States for debriefing in scattered locations. After Wells and Pappy had insisted during the debriefings that the public should be told the truth, they had been isolated from any other THOR team members.

Wells had heard rumors of some defections among other members of the launch team regarding THOR secrecy. He also had heard some disturbing rumors of several deaths among THOR crew members. There was nothing specific that he could verify since all word of the THOR and the launch team had been clamped tight.

Through friends at the Pentagon, he learned that Deitz had died of a massive stroke, and coincidentally, Dr. Kile had died of a heart attack shortly thereafter. General Reed had received his third star and was promoted to the head of the Ballistic Missile System Command.

Wells and Pappy had been sent to the Alamogordo, New Mexico test range and held in limited isolation. It was only because of Lisa's contacts at the White House that she had been able to join Wells there.

He thought back over the months that he and Lisa had been married. They were the best months of his life. He had decided to retire from the military and return to his family's ranch in Wyoming when his current commitment expired in six months. But before he did, he and Pappy knew they had to document the truth about THOR. After discussing it, they decided that the real facts about the THOR needed to be preserved for posterity.

Wells had kept many of his own documents intact, and Pappy had enough records to make Wells conclude that he had rifled some files before departing the island. How Pappy had succeeded in getting his records through security, Wells didn't know and didn't ask.

"Pappy," Wells said soberly, "I don't intend to violate my security oath. I want to be sure this tape and those records don't become public knowledge as long as project THOR is still classified as top secret."

"Agreed, colonel. But there's been too many deaths among the THOR team for me. I've heard a lotta rumors 'bout several of the launch team dyin' accidental like."

"Murder is a pretty drastic step, even for politicians," Wells replied. "But who knows what some people will do to stay in power?"

Wells flipped the tape recorder back on and began to speak again.

▲

"Perhaps by the time anyone hears this tape the truth will already be known about project THOR; but, if not, I trust that those who hear our recorded message will make it public. Pappy and I are still under close scrutiny. We both have spotted what appears to be government agents tailing us virtually everywhere we go. I'm absolutely certain that my quarters are monitored, much to Lisa's displeasure. But such is the life of a security officer in the military.

"Perhaps it is coincidental that both Pappy and I are assigned to a new project again after nearly a year of virtual isolation. Perhaps not. If either or both of us are killed or missing under mysterious circumstances, it should be assumed that it was more than merely a coincidence.

"If we're still alive and growing old with our grandchildren, you will know that we simply had overactive imaginations. Thanks for hearing me out, whoever you are."

▲

The tape was flapping as it spun off the spool. Jeff reached over and turned the machine off. He sat for several seconds just staring at the recorder before he moved.

He had been listening to the tape so intently that he had not heard Karen enter the room. She had been listening for several minutes. Jeff looked up when she asked, "Was that . . . ?"

"Yes," he replied, without waiting for the rest of her question. "It was my father." In an audible whisper Jeff continued, "Karen, my father was murdered by our government to keep him quiet . . . and maybe my mother too."

It hurt Karen to see her husband so upset. "What are you going to do?"

"I'm going to Thomas Galt and ask him to help me get the truth out. Do you realize that a great deal of the environmental movement is built on a phony premise? The hole in the ozone wasn't caused by any chlorofluorocarbon emissions. It was put there by our own government. And the ERTS program shows there's no real evidence of global warming or massive industrial pollution. The government's whole environmental program is built on one fraud after another."

"But why?" Karen exclaimed. "What do they have to gain?"

"Control, my dear," Thomas Galt said as he entered the room. "Control. We're talking about trillions of dollars to spend and billions of people to control. But this movement has grown beyond just greed now. It's a religion: a religion of people who believe they should be God and decide who lives and who doesn't. They believe the world is too crowded, and therefore, some people need to be 'thinned out.'"

"Surely not," Karen answered. "But how would that be possible?"

"Simple really," Galt answered. "Global in scope, but simple in concept. I should know. I was a part of it. First, they need to deindustrialize countries like the U.S., which can feed billions of people. Second, they need to force the productive countries to ban most pesticides. That would, and has, further diminished the food supplies and promoted disease as the insect population exploded.

"Third, they need to eliminate refrigeration so that poor countries can't store food or medical supplies. That was accomplished by the worldwide ban on Freon—a chlorofluorocarbon product which was supposed to have caused the hole in the ozone that started this environmental craze. And last, it would be useful to create a disease that cannot be cured and introduce it into the most populated countries."

"Surely you don't mean AIDS!" Jeff said.

"Think about it, Jeff. There's always been a question about AIDS being a germ warfare virus that got out of control. And it certainly has depopulated the African continent."

"I guess I'd believe about anything at this point. The question is, What are we going to do about letting the public know?"

38

△

The
Plan

L et's review our options," Galt said, "starting with the information purchased from Shoer. We have a great deal of data on the original THOR project. And it's almost certain we also have murder, to cover up the disaster. It's pretty clear, there were too many deaths among launch team members to be coincidence. Someone at the highest levels of government in the sixties authorized the cover-up, including the deaths of your father and Moss, and it's still going on."

Jeff was still stunned by what he had heard on the tapes. It was like living in a time warp. For the first time in his life he was confused. His mind was superbly equipped to deal with facts and figures but not with emotions. He felt cheated. He had been denied the right to know his own father.

"But why?" Jeff asked, more as a comment than a question. "My father made it clear he would not have exposed the THOR project."

"Apparently someone wanted to be absolutely certain. The FBI reports show that your father and Moss had been inquiring about several of the crew members. I think they had too much information to trust them with it.

"Apparently the FBI knew about the missing documents that we now have, but they weren't able to locate them. The false bottom in the old trunk was never discovered. How Moss was able to get the tapes and documents out of Alamogordo without anyone knowing it, we'll probably never know. Anyway, he hid them away in his sister's trunk, apparently without her knowledge.

"That old trunk was hauled a dozen places after Moss died. It was actually in storage at the time of his sister's death. The government actually paid to have it shipped to a relative, Jimmy Moss, who along with his wife was also killed later. He had a brother, Andy Moss, who was the EPA intern who gave the THOR documents to Crawford; which brings us back full circle—almost."

"Andy Moss . . . I saw that name on the authorizations for some death certificates." Jeff was caught between his grief over his father's murder and concern for his own family. It was painfully clear that the cover-up extended through several administrations. He had no illusions that the Rand administration would stop the cycle. They were already involved up to and including murder.

"What about Crawford?" Jeff asked. "What's his involvement?"

"Crawford told me the whole story about how he got the THOR documents and started running," Galt replied. "It's like he pulled a thread that unraveled the sweater. But so far, all we have is a fifty-year-old rocket mishap, some stolen documents, and the word of an accused spy. We need more hard evidence—something that links Rand and his administration directly to murder and treason.

"I know how you must be feeling, Jeff, but we have to think through our options very carefully. For now, it's a standoff between us and the administration, but as soon as we make any overt moves to disclose what we know, I have no doubts they'll take positive steps to silence us, just like they tried in L.A. They'll kill us all and burn this place to the ground if it becomes necessary."

"Surely they couldn't get away with such a thing, could they?" Karen exclaimed. "Not even the president could order that!"

"Maybe not," Galt lied. "But you need to understand, my dear, that those involved with this cover-up have nothing to lose. If the truth gets out they will all stand trial for treason—provided we can prove our case."

"Mr. Galt is right," Jeff said. "We can't do anything to tip them off until we have a plan. So far, they think they have us totally isolated from the outside world; and that's our biggest asset. It buys us some time."

"In the materials Shoer stole from the CIO files there are some amazing photos of the fire in the sky. I'm sure you can recover those, Jeff. If you can get all the information we need together, including the tapes your father made, we can broadcast it through the WNN network."

"That's still not good enough," Jeff replied. "Like you say, we need proof of President Rand's involvement, as well as everyone else who had a part in this cover-up. This time we're going right to the core of this corruption: The Society. I need to talk to this Dr. Shoer. I have to have access to the CIO's computer files."

"That's going to be a little hard to do," Galt said, shaking his head. "You can bet Shoer is long gone. The CIO doesn't look lightly on one of their top computer analysts defecting. With my twenty-five million dollars he can do a lot of hiding in some very nice places."

"We can trace him through the money," Jeff said matter-of-factly.

"Not possible," Galt replied. "It was deposited in a Swiss account. I'm sure it's already been shifted again, and the Swiss won't reveal any transactions. Since the government started confiscating assets for environmental violations, a lot of wealthy people have shifted money into the Swiss banking system—just in case."

"If you can get me the original account number I can probably find out where the money has gone. The banks may not reveal their secrets but their computers will. Remember, I had total access to the world banking system records when I was developing the Data-Net program."

"I'll get you the account number where I sent the money, but if you really can trace that money through the best guarded banking system in the world, I'm going to convert my money to gold and bury it," Galt said, only half in jest.

▲

At the White House the atmosphere was extremely tense. President Rand had called a hurried meeting in the Oval Office.

Henry Watts was shocked to see the physical condition of the president. He seemed ten years older, and his normally impeccable appearance was crumpled; he had obviously slept in his clothes. But what really shocked Watts was his maniacal ranting.

"I want a plan of attack drawn up now!" Rand screamed at Watts. "I want those THOR papers! Do you hear?"

"Mr. President, I don't think it would be wise to . . ."

"I don't care what you think," Rand railed. "I listened to you imbeciles before, and that's why we're in this mess now. I want those THOR documents destroyed, and I want Wells gone once and for all! He escaped us in L.A. He won't escape again!"

Watts decided that reasoning with Rand was out of the question. *I sure wish I knew where Houseman is,* he thought to himself.

Roger was always able to keep Rand under control. Since he disappeared, Rand is falling apart.

Watts decided to make one more attempt to convince Rand. "Mr. President, Thomas Galt is the world's wealthiest man. We can't just go attack his ranch. Every paper in the world would carry the story. We'd have reporters by the thousands here."

"I want it done!" Rand shouted in a rage. "Find some way to make it look like one of the radical groups is behind it." Almost as soon as he said it, Rand's demeanor changed. *Yes,* he thought to himself, *blame it on the Earth pillagers.*

"Look," Rand said more in control now, "Galt is clearly identified with the environmental movement. It is entirely logical that one of the radical opposition groups would want him dead. Right? What about that group in Wyoming that's been giving us so much trouble? The one headed by that Baptist preacher?"

As Watts thought about it, what Rand said made sense. Since the incident in Oregon the latest polls showed that nearly sixty percent of the public considered the anti-environmentalists dangerous and would support the use of military force to control them if necessary. The group in Wyoming, under the leadership of the Baptist preacher, John Elder, was by far the most visible. They had virtually taken control of the state and even had elected their own congressional representative and senator.

Watts suddenly had a brilliant idea of his own. "Mr. President, suppose we were able to make the attack on Wells' Wyoming ranch look like it was done by Elder's group? If the ranch were burned, we could say that Wells and his family were killed by the radicals. As long as we keep Galt's Montana ranch secure until we deal with them, no one would be the wiser."

"Great idea, Henry," the president said much more calmly. Suddenly it was as if a weight had been lifted from his shoulders. His meeting with Cho had not gone well. Cho had made it clear that The Society would not tolerate another failure.

"Get a plan together, Henry, and have it ready as soon as possible," the president ordered.

"It will be ready," Watts said confidently, "but we have one additional problem we need to discuss."

"Is it that CIO thing?" Rand growled.

"Yes, sir. Apparently Dr. Shoer has disappeared."

"Any idea what he took from the files?"

"Not yet, sir. The auditors have been combing the records looking for anything. So far they have found nothing that would indicate a leak. But we know Shoer didn't just take off on an unscheduled vacation. We've found at least three dozen different sets of IDs in his home. There is no telling how many he has with him. He's a very bright guy."

"Well keep on it," Rand snapped. "There's no chance that Shoer is somehow tied in with this THOR thing and Wells, is there?"

"None that we know of," Watts replied, lying. He didn't tell the president about Shoer's connection with the THOR breach. Rand was almost irrational about that topic. He feared for his own safety if Rand went off the deep end.

"Use whatever resources you need to track down Shoer," Rand commanded, "and when you find him, I want to be sure he never surfaces again. Understood?"

"Understood."

The Shoer thing was a real mystery. He never tipped his hand; he just took off. Watts had absolutely no idea what prompted his defection, or what he sold to raise the cash he would certainly need. Inside he had the sinking feeling that it was somehow connected to the THOR and Thomas Galt's unlimited resources. But every audit done on the system showed no unauthorized data entries or transfers. But Shoer sold something to someone—and probably for megabucks.

Watts decided to stop trying to figure out why Shoer had defected and concentrate on where he had gone. He knew where large amounts of money were involved, the Swiss would be too. He would use his contacts at the World Bank to search out any abnormally large transfers in or out of the Swiss banks. The Swiss wouldn't help, but the World Bank would.

▲

At the Galt ranch Jeff was already one step ahead of the CIO search. He had the original Swiss account number into which the money was deposited and was into the bank's computer system looking for answers.

The safety codes built into the numbered accounts proved to be tricky. All of the old codes he had used for Data-Net had been changed. He spent the better part of an hour trying first one random access routine after another—without success. Maggie proved to be invaluable in this process. Working from inside the computer, she created a masking routine that kept the internal security programs from detecting his entry.

Actually it was Maggie who found the right codes. Being a computer entity, she had scanned all of Jeff's original Data-Net codes and found that only one had been overlooked. It was the master code provided for then-president Hunt. After his assassination, his personal code, known only to a few insiders, had never been used again, but neither had the code been purged. When Maggie accessed the internal funds transfer routine using Hunt's code, the computer responded: ACCESS APPROVED.

"Dr. Wells, you now have access to the internal funds transfer records," Maggie said in a cheerful voice.

"Thanks, Maggie, I knew you could do it." He went to work tracing the transfer of Galt's twenty-five million dollars.

Jeff was impressed with Shoer's skill at hiding the transfers. He had set up more than a dozen shell corporations and transferred various amounts to them in the form of payments and fees. Each had the correct international tax IDs, as well as UNEEA approval codes. Tracing the money was a long and arduous job. Even as gifted as Jeff was, he might have lost track of the money except that in the end the trail came together again. More than half of the $25 million was routed to various accounts in Argentine banks.

"Bingo!" Jeff exclaimed. He made a call to Galt's study: "He's in Argentina, Mr. Galt—probably Buenos Aires, since that's where most of the money went."

"Remind me to close out my Swiss accounts, would you, Jeff?" Galt quipped. "If you can find Shoer, eventually the CIO will too. Call up my personnel file and see if you can make contact with Edgar Bonds in Buenos Aires. Ed is my security chief in Argentina. He's as trustworthy as they come. By the way, have you seen the latest news?"

"No, I haven't," Jeff replied. "I've been on this trace for the last several hours."

"Well, the link you provided to our WNN satellite works, and I just watched the latest government spin on us. Apparently the Feds have burned down your ranch and announced that you and your family have been murdered by John Elder and his radicals."

"What? But why?"

"Apparently since Elder moved his religious group into Wyoming and got involved with politics there, they also made Rand's subversive list. This looks bad, Jeff. If the Feds have announced your death, it can only mean that they intend to make it so. They'll move a full-blown army unit in here to hit us and blame it on Elder and his people. Pretty smart, really," Galt said grudgingly.

"What do you want me to do?"

"Just what you're doing now. I'm about to call in every favor owed me."

▲

In Cheyenne, at the headquarters of the Liberty Foundation, Pastor John Elder was meeting with his leadership staff: "I don't know if Jeff and Karen are really dead," General Joe Sharp, commander of the Wyoming National Guard said, "but I doubt it. I provided air support for Galt's security team when the regulators attacked the ranch. We airlifted Jason and most of Galt's team out of there to his Montana ranch. I'm sure Thomas would have told me if Jeff were dead. I can't get a message in or out of the ranch though; the Feds have it totally sealed off."

"Is there anything else we can do?" Elder asked his longtime friend.

When Elder had made the bold move to recruit 200,000 families to move to Wyoming, he had known the risk. They virtually dominated state politics and elected their own senator and representative in Congress. Wyoming had become a maverick state and a thorn in the Rand administration's side.

Newly elected Governor Attwood had directed his Wyoming constituents to withhold paying their federal taxes until the government ceased meddling in state affairs through bureaucratic regulations. With $30 billion in cash reserves from mineral rights sales, Wyoming had a better financial statement than the federal government—by far!

Attwood was heading up a governor's committee to reign in the federal government, and the state was getting ready to mint its own currency, backed by $10 billion in gold stored in the Wyoming state vaults. Governor Attwood was flexing his Tenth Amendment rights and had confiscated all federal lands in his state. Wyoming was quickly becoming the leader in a small but growing state's rights movement. Already the American stock exchange had agreed to bid the Wyoming currency against the ever-inflating U.S. dollar. The exchange rate was currently 1,000 to 1—dollars for Wyoming's "liberty" currency.

Now that Wyoming had taken the step toward holding a constitutional convention, twelve other states had made preparations to join in. With all of its other troubles, the Rand administration had not been able to mount an effective response. Now it was clear they had a new strategy: military intervention.

The meeting at the governor's mansion was still in progress when the phone rang. It was Galt.

"Thomas, we were just talking about you," Elder said warmly. "How in the world are you able to call? Have you seen the latest news from Washington?"

"It's a long story, John, and yes I have seen the news. That's why I'm calling. We were closed off by the feds—until Jeff figured out a way to make contact . . ."

"Then Jeff and Karen are all right?" Elder interrupted.

"For the time being," Galt gruffed, "but I'll guarantee you this promo piece about Jeff's ranch is a prelude to an all-out assault on my ranch; and your people will get the blame. Have you had any problems yet?"

"No. In fact we're somewhat confused about this whole thing. We thought the administration would use this as an excuse to attack our group here."

"Not until they make their move on us first. Is General Sharp there? I need to talk to him."

"Yes, he is. I'll put him on." Elder handed the phone to the general.

Joe Sharp had been the head of the Air Force's Strategic Air Command until the military phasedown. He had been forced into retirement when Rand became president and began the phaseout of most of the SAC installations. Sharp returned to his native state of Wyoming, and when Attwood was elected governor he promptly appointed Sharp commander of the Wyoming National Guard. Since his appointment, he had been fighting a continual battle with Washington to keep his guard unit free of federal control.

"Hi, Thomas. I'm glad to hear that Dr. Wells' death has been greatly exaggerated. What are you up against there?"

"It's hard to tell just yet, Joe, but as you have probably guessed, I think Rand is going to use the trumped-up raid on Jeff's ranch to get rid of two thorns at one time: namely, you and me."

"That's about the way I see it too. I thought they had you boys locked up tight on the ranch. How'd you get out?"

"It would take a lot more smarts than Rand's people have to stump Jeff. He found a way to communicate. We think we can put a plug in Rand's plans, Joe, but I don't know how much time we have. I need your help. Remember that idea we talked about a while back, in case either of us got caught between a rock and a hard place?"

"You think things are that bad, Tom?"

"I do. If we can't stop Rand and his Green movement right now, there won't be enough left of this country to call it the land of the free anymore."

"I'll do what I can, Tom, but if this idea goes sour they'll hang us both."

"They probably will anyway, Joe. Thanks."

As General Sharp put the phone down, he had a scowl on his face.

"Problem, Joe?" Elder asked.

"I think we just decided to declare war on the United States government."

39

△

The
Hunt for
Shoer

In Buenos Aires, Alan Shoer was scared stiff. He knew someone
had him under surveillance and was tracking his every step. He
had already paid out more than $800,000 to the Argentine inter-
nal security chief with a promise of a million more, so he was certain it was not the Argentines tracking him.

At first he thought it was the CIO, but the CIO would have
already moved in. He had no illusions that they could not extract
him from Argentina. He had read too many internal reports where
other defectors, far less important than he, had been "snuffed," as
Henry Watts was fond of saying.

That left only Galt as a possibility. But he had no gripe with Galt.
He had delivered just as promised, and the money was scattered
where Galt could never get to it again. Besides, he doubted that
Thomas Galt would miss a few million out of his billions, or maybe
trillions.

Shoer tucked his automatic under his pillow and took a couple
of sleeping pills. It had been a nerve-racking day, dodging in and out
of taxis and buildings trying to shake his pursuer. He set the intruder
alarm before lying down. It was the most sophisticated alarm system
money could buy. He knew nothing could reach him without trip-
ping the alarm and signaling his paid Argentine security forces
downstairs. Tomorrow he would have to make plans to move again.

To Edgar Bonds, all security systems were little more than a
nuisance. The system that Shoer purchased was about a five on a

scale of ten. It might have stopped a common burglar, but not a trained intelligence agent. Within thirty seconds he was in the room and had the system disabled.

He stood over the bed, pointing Shoer's own pistol in his face while pouring a glass of water on him. Shoer woke up sputtering from the water he had breathed in while snoring loudly.

"Wha . . . ," he started to say when he saw the figure above him holding his own gun.

"Just keep quiet, Dr. Shoer, and you'll live. I'm not CIO. I was hired by Thomas Galt to find you. Let me assure you that the CIO is not far behind. You may have been a great computer jock, but you're a pretty average spy."

"What do you want?" Shoer sputtered, trying to gather his senses.

"Mr. Galt wants you to come with me. If you agree to help us, then I'll help you hide so the CIO will never find you. In fact, if all goes well, there may not even be a CIO when this is all over."

Shoer quickly sorted through his options. He didn't have any. If Galt could find him, so could the CIO. He decided he would rather be found by Galt and his people. "I'll go," he said.

"Wise decision," Bonds quipped, uncocking the semiautomatic.

▲

Three hours later the communicator alarm at the ranch went off. The shrill sound startled Jeff, who was in deep concentration. He punched the voice module on as Galt entered the room rubbing his eyes.

"Hello, Mr. Galt," Bonds hummed into the satellite phone link.

"This is Jeff Wells," the big scientist answered. "Mr. Galt is just coming in."

"Bonds, what do you have?" Galt said.

"I have your man Shoer here. He has seen the light and is ready to chat with you."

Suddenly both Wells and Galt were wide awake. "Put him on," Galt ordered.

"Mr. Galt," Shoer said somewhat defiantly. "I understand you'd like me to help you."

"That depends on whether you would like to stay alive," Galt snapped back irritatedly. He didn't like the man's arrogance.

There was a long silence on the other end, then Shoer replied, "I think that would be of benefit to both of us."

Galt nodded to Jeff, so he took over. "Dr. Shoer, we need to retrieve some more data from the CIO files. Can you help us?"

"Ask Mr. Galt what the information is worth to him," Shoer said glibly.

Galt leaned over the microphone and replied, "You might live long enough to spend some of my twenty-five million dollars if you help. Otherwise, Mr. Bonds will simply deliver you back to your room. I rather suspect our friends in Washington may be there by now."

"What do you need?" Shoer asked more contritely. He knew Galt was probably right. The last place he wanted to be was back in his apartment.

"I need to access the CIO's data files," Jeff said, "and I also need to know what else we might expect to find in your files." Jeff had already guessed how Shoer was able to hide information from the CIO auditors. He either would have made file copies on laser disc, which would have been very risky, or he had installed additional memory in the CIO computers.

"I have some hidden files in the system," Shoer confirmed, "but it's only accessible through my own program, which is a non-resident routine. If you access the computer from outside you'll set off the alarms."

"You must have some means to access the system from outside," Jeff stated matter-of-factly.

"I can't access it," Shoer lied. He knew he might eventually need more information, so he had left himself a way in. If he called in from outside and gave the right code, the computer would access his non-mapped memory, which in turn would allow him to export information. He figured that even if an auditor found the program, which he doubted, he had nothing to lose anymore. But he wasn't about to give all that information away for nothing.

Galt spoke up again. "Bonds, take Dr. Shoer back to his apartment. I'm not in the mood for any more games."

"Wait," Shoer said quickly, "I'll tell you what you need."

"No more games, doctor," Galt warned. "The next time we'll terminate this conversation."

"Will you swear that you'll help me get away?" Shoer asked contritely.

"You have my word."

"Dr. Wells, you need to call in on the Langly data line via Satcom satellite channel four. Send the code 487662 immediately when the connection is made. That will allow you to input my recovery program. I have ten gigabits of unmapped memory filled with details on covert missions of the CIO, FBI, and EPA—including the current administration. I couldn't store all the detailed records, but the references are there, pointing to the active CIO file locations. But if you attempt to access any active CIO data files, the alarms will go off."

"Don't worry about that," Jeff said. "Just give me the codes for your routine."

Jeff spent the next several minutes writing down the details of Shoer's access routine. "Pretty smart," he remarked to Galt. "Dr. Shoer is a good programmer."

During the next hour Jeff made the necessary preparations for accessing the CIO's Satcom satellite. Once that was done, he told Galt, "Well, here goes nothing." He punched in the access code for Satcom via his own link through to the WNN satellite. Immediately the screen showed: ACCESS CONFIRMED, SATCOM.

"Okay, we're on line," Jeff said, exhaling after having held his breath. "Now let's see if we can talk to Langly and the CIO." He typed in the CIO access code. ACCESS CONFIRMED, the terminal responded.

Immediately Wells hit the return key on his computer and the codes provided by Shoer were transmitted. If the codes were wrong, there would be alarms going off all over the CIO building, and the link would be terminated immediately.

ACCESS CONFIRMED, the screen displayed once again. CPU ON LINE.

Wells hit the return key again and transmitted Shoer's recovery routine. If the CIO had not already discovered Shoer's pirated memory, the computer would allow him in.

ACCESS CONFIRMED, the computer responded.

Jeff spent the next few minutes scanning the data base stored by Shoer.

"Incredible," Galt muttered, looking over his shoulder. "He's got names, dates, and places of political assassinations, bribes, and the worst graft imaginable. Can you recover some of that stuff, Jeff?"

"I'll have all of Shoer's files transferred to our location. But we also need more of the detailed documentation. It will show who authorized the assassinations and other illegal acts. I don't know how much time we'll have once I start roaming around in the active CIO files," Jeff warned. "If they're looking for Shoer's secret hoard of information we may spring their trap."

"We'll just have to take that chance," Galt replied. "We need as much verifiable documentation as possible."

"I'll set up a storage area in Shoer's memory to dump as much as possible. Even if the computer shuts down the input and output, I can override this channel. But . . ."

"What?" Galt asked, sensing Jeff's hesitancy.

"If the CIO people are as good as they should be, they'll know it's us in the computer."

"So they'll try to kill us a day sooner. We're on a short fuse now. Let's do it!"

▲

The data was streaming from the CIO computer through the satellite hookup to Montana when the internal alarms went off. Immediately the CIO computer center was a beehive of activity. With practiced precision the security team went to work tracing the illegal entry. Within fifty seconds the entry had been identified and a shutdown initiated.

The control room operator reached over and punched the alarm button off to silence it while they located the exact source of the entry. Immediately the alarm sounded again.

The operator placed a hurried call to Henry Watts' office. "Sir," he said excitedly, "we've had a security breach, just as we expected, but we can't terminate the link. As soon as we initiate a cutoff, the link is reestablished."

"Shut down the whole system, you fool!" Watts screamed into the phone. "Kill that data transfer immediately, and locate the source—now!"

The rattled operator dropped the phone and reached over to punch the system power button, which would initiate an emergency shutdown. He had always assumed this procedure would only be used in the event of an enemy invasion. It would take days to clear the jammed files. The emergency shutdown even bypassed the standby battery system.

He lifted the protective cover and was in the process of pushing the button when the alarm stopped. He knew it signaled the illegal entry had been terminated, but his hand was already in motion. When he pushed the button, the CIO computers quite simply died. It would require two full days to restore them to use.

When Henry Watts heard the details of the security breach, his blood ran cold. The breach had been initiated through the WNN communications satellite. That could mean only one thing: Galt. The operator was certain that the data transmission had been completed before the system shutdown.

"What!" Rand screamed as he heard Watts' explanation. "What data did they get?"

"Names, dates, places . . . we think just about everything we had on covert operations. What do you . . . ?"

Rand had dropped the phone. His face was ashen gray.

"What has happened?" Cho demanded.

"Galt, or Wells, tapped into the CIO computer," the shaken Rand said. "They got enough to hang us all twice."

"Do we know how they were able to break through our communications blockade?" Cho shouted in uncharacteristic fashion.

"No. You know Wells is a genius; he apparently figured out a way."

"Attack the ranch immediately," Cho commanded his puppet president. "That information must not get into the hands of the press. We could not suppress information of this magnitude."

"Yes, you're right. We should attack the ranch. We'll kill them all. Then we'll wipe out that nest of subversives in Wyoming too. We can't sacrifice our environmental agenda."

"I don't care about your stupid environmental nonsense," Cho snapped angrily. "We will not lose the chance to control the world. You will stop this breach now or you will die! The group I represent will not tolerate failure again. We made you president, and we can remove you."

Rand's eyes flared, "You can't talk to me like that! I'm the president of the United States!"

"You deceive yourself, you pompous peacock," Cho spat out. "There is no more United States. You helped to destroy it. If you do not do exactly what you are told the media will be informed of the whereabouts of Roger Houseman—your missing chief of staff, I believe? There is also the issue of some recordings made of your conversations."

Rand stopped as if he had been struck deaf and dumb. He had always assumed he was in charge and Cho was simply helping him. Now he realized that the exact opposite was true. The president of the United States was little more than a puppet. Rand slumped down in his chair behind the grand old desk that had been the workplace of many presidents before him.

▲

At the ranch Jeff had been poring over the data transmitted from the CIO's computers. "Un-believable!" he said for at least the tenth time in thirty minutes. "There are authorizations for political assassinations of supreme court justices, federal judges—even a congressman or two. Each was made to seem like they had died from natural causes. Millions of dollars have been paid to various media people to promote stories beneficial to the environmental groups. There are records of falsified court documents, bribery, extortion, drugs. . . ."

"I have really been an old fool," Galt said, looking over some of the documents Jeff had printed out. "They used me to manipulate the media."

"We have simply allowed our government to take over the role of a mother to us all," Karen added with a note of bitterness. "Now the question is, how do we tell the world about this?"

"And will anyone really care?" Galt added sarcastically. "Do away with big brother, no matter how corrupt, and people will have to start taking care of themselves. I wonder if they'll really want to? The Russians have made Stalin into their national hero again and voted in another dictator. Maybe the American people will react the same way."

"I have to believe there are still enough moral people in this country to make a difference," Jeff said resolutely. "I don't intend to leave my son in the hands of thieves and murderers. We can do it."

"You're right, Jeff. I guess I've gotten to be a cynical old man. Let's address the problems one at a time."

"I remember something that John Elder said in one of his messages," Karen remarked. "The cares of this day are sufficient for today; don't worry yourself so much about tomorrow's problems."

"Good advice, Karen. I built what I have by planning for the future but concentrating on the present. Let's see what we can do presently."

"We have to presume that the powers in Washington know we have this data and will not want it made public," Jeff said.

"To say the least," Galt quipped. "In fact I would say they are probably mounting a considerable assault force right now. Our little band won't be able to hold them off long, unless help arrives.

"Jeff, you need to make contact with our WNN offices in Bangkok, Brussels, Paris, Hong Kong, and Atlanta. I'll draft an order preempting all regular broadcasts at seven o'clock this evening. In the meantime we need to edit this stuff and select the most damaging material. We want to be sure to include some of the documents from the Rand top officials, authorizing political assassinations, especially the Baylor assassination. They had a Supreme Court justice killed because he supported state's rights.

"The sooner we can transmit the data to our offices the better off we'll be here. Rand and his regulators are going to want their pound of flesh, so we'd better be ready."

Jeff spent the next several hours transmitting the data to WNN's Bangkok office, where it would undergo a final edit and then be transmitted to other locations for broadcast. It took several conversations directly with his station managers for Galt to convince them he was still alive and directing the network. Access to the CIO data was limited to a few select people Galt knew he could trust. The last thing he wanted was for news of the broadcast to leak out prematurely.

This time there would be no quiet cover-up of the government's corruption. When he and Jeff had exposed the plot to take over the government ten years earlier, he had been convinced that telling "all" would threaten the stability of the government. Now he knew it was time to let the American people know every dirty detail. He smiled through his anger.

If I were still interested in ratings, this would most certainly be the highest rated program in television history—live and on TV, the plan to destroy America, starting with a project called THOR. "Boy, the Green movement will go berserk," he muttered.

"What did you say?" Jeff asked as he finished his transmissions.

"Oh nothing, but I sure would like to be a fly on the wall in Rand's office when this program airs."

Just then the phone rang. It was General Sharp on the satellite link. "Thomas, I just received word from our contact in Washington that the stops have been pulled. Rand has authorized a government assault on your ranch. He has all the proper court approvals that show you have a known fugitive on the ranch. I have already taken steps to initiate our response to the assault. By the way, I have dubbed it 'project overlord' in honor of our 1944 battle to free Europe. Now we have a chance to free America."

"Joe, I'll need some support to move Crawford off the ranch. Would you be able to transport him to Casper? Governor Attwood has agreed to put him in protective custody until this thing with Rand is settled. And it'll be settled one way or the other pretty shortly."

"You got it, Tom. I'll send one of our fastest planes to the ranch to pick him up. I understand that most of the FBI's senior agents have refused Rand's order to team up with the regulators to storm your ranch. Rand wouldn't dare use any of the regular Army troops, so you'll be facing mostly untested regulators—but a lot of them. They plan to airlift about fifteen hundred troops to your location. I'll keep you informed, but they should reach your location by about 13:00."

"What's that in English, Joe?"

"That's one o'clock in the afternoon—in English."

"We'll be ready. Thanks, Joe."

40

△

The
Assault
on the Ranch

eff had completed the transmission of the CIO data to
WNN/Bangkok. The edited copy would be run as a two-hour
special on all the WNN worldwide outlets that evening at
seven o'clock. Galt had been in almost constant communication
with his documentary chief, Rachel Simmons, during the screening
and editing process. The result was a truly revealing account of rot
and corruption at the highest levels of government.

Simmons asked one last time, "Are you really sure you want to
run this, Thomas? This thing could destroy the government and
spark riots in the streets."

Galt responded, "I guess you haven't visited the U.S. since you
moved to Bangkok, have you? We already have riots in the streets,
and I don't think the honest people of America will destroy their own
country when they know the truth. The Master Teacher once said,
'And you shall know the truth, and the truth shall make you free.' All
we're going to do is tell the truth and set the American people free."

The documentary truly was a work of art, considering the short
amount of time the WNN team had to review and edit all the data.
It would begin with a dramatic account of the THOR project,
including digitized film shots of the launch, explosion, and result-
ing fire in the sky. It would conclude with detailed accounts of
political assassinations by the Rand administration.

"You're the boss," Simmons replied. "I can't wait to see this
thing myself, and I helped to edit it. This stuff is dynamite! But why

wait until seven? We have it ready now; why don't we just put it on and run it all day?"

"No, I want to give Rand and his lackeys a chance to resign first. If we can clean out the whole bunch without airing this, I'm willing to do it. If they agree, which I'm sure they won't, we'll just run the environmental documentary."

"Good luck, boss," Simmons said admiringly. "Keep your powder dry there."

▲

In Washington President Rand had set in motion a full-scale assault on Galt's ranch. He fell back on one of the military's own adages: overwhelming and decisive force. The assault team, under the direction of the EPA, would consist of fifteen hundred regulators supported by light tanks and armored vehicles.

The lessons learned through defeat at Wells' Wyoming ranch were not forgotten. Rand would have used air support except that doing so would have required bringing in the military, which Watts advised against. Intelligence within the military command had consistently shown that the general staff would not support such an assault—certainly not to capture one man. Besides, Rand wanted to be very sure that there would be no survivors at the ranch. The military would never have allowed that.

Rand was still in the Oval Office at 2:00 P.M., awaiting word on the assault teams preparations, when his secretary buzzed him on the intercom. "Mr. President, you have a call from Mr. Galt. Will you take it?"

The president blanched gray as the words sunk in. *Galt? How could he get through, and what could he possibly want?* "Tell him to hold," Rand croaked. He then punched the intercom to the office where Cho had set up. "Dr. Cho, Thomas Galt is calling on my private line. What . . . ?"

"I will be right there," Cho snapped. Within seconds he had entered unseen via the west wing door. "Put him on the speaker phone," Cho instructed.

"Rand here," the young president voiced with all the authority he could muster. His knees felt weak, and his head was pounding. The last thing on Earth he expected was a call from Galt.

"Rand, you and whoever is with you from The Society, as you call it, need to listen carefully because I'm only going to say this once. First, let me say that we have prepared a thoroughly enlightening documentary from the CIO file data."

"You had no authority . . . ," Rand started to say.

"Shut up and listen!" Galt snapped back. "This documentary will be aired at 7:00 P.M. Eastern time tonight on every WNN worldwide affiliate, and there is absolutely nothing you or your would-be world masters can do about it. There are at least twenty copies being distributed to outlets all over the world, even as we speak. You will find one at the WNN center there in Washington.

"I took the precaution of removing all my people from Washington, so just ask one of the security people to give you the disk with your name on it. We have documents, tapes, and signatures from your administration authorizing everything from bribes to murder. You also may want to watch some interesting scenes of a project, code-named THOR."

Rand felt sick as he listened to Galt. *How many documents did I sign personally?* he wondered. He had no idea, but he was sure there were enough to implicate him in at least a dozen assassinations.

"Second, I know you have authorized an illegal assault on my personal property, namely my Montana ranch. If this assault takes place, you can count on stiff opposition from my people."

"You're harboring a dangerous criminal," Rand mumbled into the phone.

"Don't be more of an idiot than you already are," Galt barked, "and don't insult my intelligence. You and I both know that Crawford is not a criminal; nor is he dangerous. Future generations will look on him as a hero. He had the courage to bring the THOR hoax public. Besides that, he's no longer here. He is in the protective custody of Governor Attwood in Wyoming."

Rand blanched again. *The whole plan's falling apart. Now Crawford's gone too—and in the custody of the Wyoming radicals.*

▲

Earlier, when the twin engine jet approached the Galt ranch, two of the EPA regulators had asked their headquarters for instructions. The plane bore the seal of the governor of Wyoming, and the pilot refused all attempts to communicate with the task force surrounding the Galt ranch.

"Shoot it down," Marjorie Franklin instructed the agents who called. Watts' instructions had been piercingly clear: No one was to be allowed in or out of the ranch—no one!

Having heard the instructions, the agent raised the heat-seeking missile to his shoulder. He had to wait until the jet had passed over his position to get a clear shot at its exhaust. He was almost in position when the assault helicopters appeared from behind a hill. He was looking up into a massive array of firepower, all aimed in his direction.

The helicopter pilot called over his address system: "Put the weapon down and put your hands in the air—now!" Even as he spoke he rotated the .50 caliber Gatling gun into position to fire. The effect was immediate and predictable: The would-be terrorist dropped the missile launcher and raised his hands—high.

The chopper pilot held his position while the sleek jet made its landing, took on a passenger, and took off again. Although he hadn't known who the passenger was then, Rand now did.

▲

"What is it you want?" Rand muttered while glancing toward Cho. The president of the United States looked more like a trapped rabbit than a world leader.

"I want you and all of those named in the CIO files to resign, effective immediately," Galt demanded. "I also want you to sign a statement detailing the involvement of The Society in the internal affairs of our government. Then, I want a full disclosure of your involvement in the plot to overthrow the true authority of the United States, namely the American people. And I want all of this in writing no later than three o'clock today.

"I'll hold the documents for safekeeping just in case any of you try to renege on this agreement. Don't worry about dismantling the Green movement you're so proud of. Once the American people see the lies they've been sold, I think the true environmentalists will throw the radicals out."

"You must be crazy," Rand shouted. "I'm the president of the United States. You can't . . ."

"Three o'clock!" Galt growled as he punched the line off.

"Well, that ought to stir up some action," he said to Jeff as he hung up.

"Won't Rand just move the assault up?" Jeff asked his longtime friend. *I trust Galt's instincts, but I'm also concerned about Karen and Jason,* he thought.

"I would certainly think so," Galt said without further elaboration. As he headed out to discuss the looming confrontation with his security chief, he looked back and added, "Trust me, Jeff."

▲

In Washington Rand sat motionless for several moments after

the line went dead. "What can we do?" he asked Cho, sounding like a frightened child.

"We must act swiftly," Cho replied. "Commence the attack on the ranch immediately. The Congress is not in session, and there are few members of either party still at hand. You must declare total military law in the country. We will use the terrorists' activities as justification. Order the regulators to assume command of all existing military installations under your Emergency Powers Act. They will meet little resistance if the commander-in-chief orders all military units to stand down. By the time the opposition is organized we will be in control of the country."

"Yes, that would work," Rand almost blathered. "There are fewer than two hundred thousand regular army forces left, and most of them will obey the president's orders. I can announce the military law executive order over the networks."

"No!" Cho snapped. "We must first take control. There must be no warning."

"Of course, you're right," Rand agreed. His mind was near the breaking point. He had to rely on Cho; he knew what was best.

In less than an hour, Rand had called a meeting of his closest cabinet members, outlining the plan.

"This is a big risk, Mr. President," Watts said. The others just sat in stunned silence.

"There's no other choice. If we wait until that documentary is aired, it'll be too late. It will show names, dates, and places, with documents to back it up. Do you want to stand trial for treason?" Rand screamed.

"Then we'll need to act swiftly," Watts replied. "It's almost three o'clock. We won't be able to suppress the military after that program airs. I'll organize the regulators immediately. If we can secure Washington and shut down the Pentagon, maybe we can bluff our way through the rest of it."

"Do it!" Rand commanded. "Use whatever force is necessary. I don't want one of those generals left alive to rally his troops."

▲

Cho left right after Galt's call and hurried to the Chinese Embassy a few blocks away. Members of The Society's inner council had been gathering in Washington for the past week to discuss the Korean situation. Thus far, none of the missing atomic bombs had surfaced.

Faced with this new crisis, he ordered an emergency meeting of the council. Within one hour, twelve of the most powerful men in the world gathered to determine the fate of the world once the United States was firmly in their grasp. "Brutal power is all these weaklings understand," Cho said through gritted teeth. "We will show them power." The others merely nodded in agreement.

▲

At 5:10 P.M. the sound of rumbling trucks and the thump, thump, thump, of helicopter rotors could be clearly felt, if not heard, along the perimeter defense of the Galt ranch.

Roy Sloan called the ranch. "Mr. Galt, they're coming."

"I know," Galt replied. "I can hear the choppers. Keep your men well concealed. This time the regulators will have some armored support, you can be sure. Don't make any move unless they try to penetrate the ranch or you're fired upon."

"Right," Sloan replied, taking a big breath. *This is it,* he thought. "I'll keep this channel open. Any word from General Sharp?"

"He'll do what he promised. Just play it cool." Inside, Galt was not as sure as he sounded. *I haven't heard a word from Sharp in more than six hours. If word of our plan has leaked out, the general could well be fighting his own little war. If so, we're all in big trouble.*

▲

Even before the trucks totally stopped, hundreds of regulators were pouring out and spreading across the field in front of the Galt ranch. With only one entrance and exit to the ranch, it gave only one front to defend, but it also meant only one way out.

Deputy Attorney General Marjorie Franklin, leader of the aborted assault on the Wells' ranch, stepped forward holding a battery-powered megaphone. She ordered, "Throw down your weapons. I have a legal search-and-arrest warrant for Dale Crawford. I demand that you lower your weapons."

"Crawford's not here," Sloan shouted back through the megaphone he was holding. "He's being held in protective custody by Governor Attwood in Wyoming. I have his written and sworn statement to that effect. You have no authority here."

"I don't care about any falsified statement," Franklin shouted. "Stand aside, or we will be forced to fire."

Sloan saw hundreds more regulators scattering from the helicopters. Behind them at least a dozen armored vehicles armed with machine guns and cannons were moving forward, with platoons of armed regulators following close behind. "It's going to be a 'bad day at Black Rock' unless the general gets here," he muttered.

"Sorry, I can't do that, ma'am," he shouted in response. "Mr. Galt said no uninvited guests, and I reckon that means you too." With that Sloan dropped down behind a huge boulder.

Franklin gave the signal and all twelve of the armored vehicles opened fire with their machine guns. Although the noise was deafening, the defensive positions held by Galt's security made them virtually invulnerable to the gunfire.

The mass of armed regulators surging in behind the assault vehicles looked more like a mob than an organized military unit. It was painfully obvious to Sloan that a great many of them would not live to see another day if he were forced to defend his position. Had he desired to do so, he could have signaled his men to mow down the first wave of regulators. But in compliance with Galt's orders, he was waiting until the advance threatened the security of the ranch. Looking at the mass of armed men approaching, Sloan knew his men would eventually be overwhelmed by sheer numbers.

Marjorie Franklin, on the other hand, interpreted the lack of response as a sign of cowardice in the face of what she perceived to be her overwhelming military power. She signaled the first wave of regulators to rush Sloan's defensive positions, leaving them totally exposed to his better armed and better trained force.

Sloan knew the regulators might be able to bridge his defenses by sheer numbers if he delayed any longer. Just as he pushed the talk button on his communicator to tell his men to open fire, he heard an unbelievable noise.

Roaring in from the east were twenty or more ancient C-130s, dumping parachutists behind the regulators' lines. From the wave of planes rushing in, it was obvious the regulators would soon be in the wrong place at the wrong time. With Sloan's men in front of them and the paratroopers behind, the regulators were trapped. Franklin ordered the armored vehicles to turn about and confront the paratroopers when two additional C-130s, equipped as gunships, came roaring in just over the tree tops. Each plane was armed with dual 20mm Gatling cannons. Both aircraft were spitting fire that rattled Sloan's teeth.

The C-130 gunships were chewing up the ground in back of the armored vehicles, making it impossible for them to turn and face the paratroopers. No sooner had the planes disappeared over the trees than ten Cobra attack helicopters appeared, flying in close formation with guns pointed directly at the government troops on the ground. They paused just short of the front line, and Sloan heard the booming voice of General Joe Sharp over the P.A. "Throw down your arms," he ordered the advancing line. "If you do not we will open fire on your positions."

The National Guard paratroopers had dropped their chutes and were advancing from the rear even as Sloan moved his men into view from the front. The C-130s made a second pass over the line, signaling their readiness to join the fracas if necessary.

The regulators, scared out of their wits, stopped where they were and, in spite of all the cursing and threats by Franklin, began tossing their weapons on the ground. Within minutes the scene had dissolved into a rout with the young regulators running in every direction—except forward. Their assault vehicles were abandoned as the drivers and support personnel piled out and ran.

Sharp headed his chopper toward the ranch and was just landing as Thomas Galt came out.

"Joe, you old war horse, that adage I heard about you is still true: never late, but never too early," Galt shouted over the sound of the rotors winding down.

"I was just over the hill, Tom. Thought I'd wait until they were nice and bunched up. I believe those boys just set a new track record. It's a long hike back to town. I expect they'll be a long time in returning."

"Like never, if our TV special comes off as planned tonight," Galt chuckled.

▲

News of the rout in Montana was just beginning to filter in to the White House as some 60,000 regulators were fanning out across the city to carry out Rand's orders. More than 2,000 were assigned to take the Pentagon building alone. When they reached the building, they were shocked to see it was almost deserted. General Sharp had called the nation's top-level military leaders earlier and advised them to leave the city. Most had followed his advice and had already fled the city for more secure military installations.

When word that the Washington operation had also gone sour and virtually every military base was abandoned, except for the few troops loyal to the administration, Rand was frantic. Watts found him in the Oval Office lying on the floor in a fetal position, virtually incoherent.

At the Chinese embassy, Cho and the other eleven members of the inner council were assessing their position: "When the program airs this evening, we can assume the usefulness of Rand and the environmentalists is ended. I don't have to tell any of you how disappointed the leader will be," Cho said angrily. "However, we all have diplomatic immunity, and no one outside of the president himself has any direct knowledge of our existence. I took the precaution of having one of our operatives on his staff give him a drug that will render him permanently incoherent. We have an aircraft scheduled to fly us to the People's Republic this evening at eleven o'clock. We will remain in the embassy until that time. Remember, my brothers, this is not the end of the war. It is only the loss of one small battle."

The WNN documentary dubbed "The THOR Conspiracy" aired right on time that evening. The response around the world was shock, but in the U.S. it was anger. All telephone lines into Washington were jammed from about 7:30 P.M. on. Later, even the most liberal media commentators would call the documentary, "the single most important newscast in history."

Perhaps every politician in Washington would have been forcefully removed from office, except for another purely coincidental event that had been scheduled for the nation's capital that same evening.

At exactly 9:00 P.M., a city bus pulled up in front of the Chinese Embassy. Its schedule had been pre-arranged, based on the twelve leaders of The Society assembling there at one time. Also, at exactly the same time, a call was made to the WNN headquarters in Atlanta from an unknown party, who announced in an Asian dialect: "In the name of General Hyong and the people of the free nation of Korea, I regret to announce that an atomic device will be detonated in Washington, D.C., in exactly two minutes.

"I trust this will serve as the final warning to all who would enslave a free nation. In deference to the American people, the device we have chosen to use is of minimal size. The additional devices we control will not be used as long as the world community respects the right of the Korean people to be free."

At 9:04 a five-kiloton atomic bomb was detonated outside the Chinese embassy, obliterating most of downtown Washington, D.C.

With the nation in turmoil over the telecast by WNN, and the announcement that an atomic bomb had wiped out the nation's capital, immediate leadership was crucial. With the president and vice president both dead and the speaker of the House and several other members of the Congress identified as traitors, the title of interim president fell to the House minority whip, Paul Newton.

His first official act was to move the capital to its original location in Philadelphia and convene a national advisory board, made up of citizens and politicians, to put the country back on track. Thomas Galt was named chairman and commissioned to help establish sound economic and environmental policies that would lead the nation out of the depression.

Jeff, Karen, and Jason moved to Philadelphia, where Jeff would work with the newly formed Environmental Policy Foundation to document and report on current and future environmental trends. The U.S. withdrew its support of the United Nations Environmental Enforcement Agency (UNEEA), citing conflicts with U.S. sovereignty.

A young ex-federal bureaucrat by the name of Dale Crawford was named by President Newton as director of the restructured Environmental Protection Agency. His first official act as director was to dismantle the EPA regulators and begin a phasedown of EPA personnel.